Europe Restructured

Europe Restructured

The Eurozone Crisis and its Aftermath

David Owen

METHUEN

First published in Great Britain in 2012 by
Methuen & Co.
35 Hospital Fields Road
York
YO10 4DZ

David Owen has asserted his rights under the Copyright, Designs
and Patent Act 1988 to be identified as the author of this work.

A CIP catalogue record for this book is available from the British Library.

ISBN 978-0-413-77744-7 (book)
ISBN 978-0-413-77745-4 (ebook)

Typeset by SX Composing DTP, Rayleigh, Essex
Printed by CPI (UK) Ltd, Croydon, CR0 4YY

Contents

David Owen was Foreign Secretary in James Callaghan's government. Later he co-founded the Social Democratic Party and was its leader for two separate terms. He trained as a medical doctor and has long been interested in the effects of ill health on heads of government and business leaders and two of his recent books, *In Sickness and In Power* and *The Hubris Syndrome* deal authoritatively with this subject.

Owen now sits as a cross-bencher in the House of Lords and has remained active and influential in several spheres. As chairman of *New Europe* he campaigned against Britain adopting the euro. In *Europe Restructured* he shows that with the financial crises in the Eurozone still unresolved, the European Union is in urgent need of change.

Key dates in the history of European integration

1950

9 May

Robert Schuman, the French Minister of Foreign Affairs, puts forward proposals based on the ideas of Jean Monnet, proposing that France and the Federal Republic of Germany pool their coal and steel resources in a new organisation which other European countries can join.

This date is regarded as the birth of the European Union and 9 May is now celebrated annually as Europe Day.

1951

18 April

In Paris, six countries — Belgium, the Federal Republic of Germany, France, Italy, Luxembourg and the Netherlands — sign the treaty establishing the European Coal and Steel Community (ECSC).

1955

1–2 June

At a meeting in Messina, the foreign ministers of the six countries meet.

1957

25 March

In Rome, the six countries sign the treaties establishing the European Economic Community (EEC) and the European Atomic Energy Community (Euratom), coming into force on 1 January 1958.

1960

4 January

At the instigation of the United Kingdom, the Stockholm Convention establishes the European Free Trade Association (EFTA), comprising a number of European countries that are not part of the EEC.

1963

20 July

In Yaoundé, an association agreement is signed between the EEC and eighteen African countries.

1965

8 April

A treaty is signed merging the executive bodies of the three communities (the ECSC, the EEC and Euratom) and creating a single Council and a single Commission, coming into force on 1 July 1967.

1966
29 January
The 'Luxembourg compromise'. Following a political crisis, France agrees to take part in Council meetings once again, in return for an agreement that the unanimity rule be maintained when 'vital national interests' are at stake.

1968
1 July
Customs duties between the member states on industrial goods are completely abolished, eighteen months ahead of schedule, and a common external tariff is introduced.

1972
22 January
In Brussels, treaties of accession to the European Communities are signed with Denmark, Ireland, Norway and the United Kingdom.

1973
1 January
Denmark, Ireland and the United Kingdom join the European Communities, bringing their membership to nine. Norway stays

out, following a referendum in which a majority of people voted against membership.

1974
9–10 December
At a Paris summit, the political leaders of the nine member states decide to meet three times a year as the European Council. They also give the go-ahead for direct elections to the European Parliament, and agree to set up the European Regional Development Fund.

1975
28 February
In Lomé, a convention (Lomé I) is signed between the EEC and forty-six African, Caribbean and Pacific (ACP) countries.

22 July
A treaty is signed giving the European Parliament greater power over the budget and establishing the European Court of Auditors. It comes into force on 1 June 1977.

1979
7–10 June
The first direct elections to the 410-seat European Parliament.

1981

1 January

Greece joins the European Communities, bringing the number of members to ten.

1985

14 June

The Schengen Agreement is signed with the aim of abolishing checks at the borders between some member countries of the European Communities.

1986

1 January

Spain and Portugal join the European Communities, bringing membership to twelve.

17 and 28 February

The Single European Act is signed in Luxembourg and The Hague, coming into force on 1 July 1987.

1989

9 November

The fall of the Berlin Wall.

1990

3 October

German reunification.

1991

9–10 December

The Maastricht European Council adopts the Treaty on European Union, laying the foundation for a common foreign and security policy, closer co-operation on justice and home affairs and the creation of economic and monetary union, including a single currency.

1992

7 February

The Treaty on European Union is signed at Maastricht, coming into force on 1 November 1993.

1993

1 January

The single market is created.

1995

1 January

Austria, Finland and Sweden join the EU, bringing its membership to fifteen. Norway stays out again following a referendum in which a majority of people voted against membership.

27–28 November

The Euro-Mediterranean Conference in Barcelona launches a partnership between the EU and the countries on the southern shore of the Mediterranean.

1997

2 October

The Amsterdam Treaty is signed, coming into force on 1 May 1999.

1999

1 January

Start of the third stage of EMU: eleven EU countries adopt the euro, which is launched on the financial markets, replacing their currencies for non-cash transactions. The European Central Bank takes on responsibility for monetary policy. The eleven countries are joined by Greece in 2001.

2000

23–24 March

The Lisbon European Council draws up a new strategy for boosting employment in the EU, modernising the economy and strengthening social cohesion in a knowledge-based Europe.

7–8 December

In Nice, the European Council reaches agreement on the text of a new treaty, coming into force on 1 February 2003. The presidents of the European Parliament, the European Council and the European Commission solemnly proclaim the Charter of Fundamental Rights of the European Union.

2001

14–15 December

Laeken European Council. A declaration on the future of the EU is agreed. This opens the way for the forthcoming major reform of the EU and for the creation of a convention to draft a European constitution.

2002

1 January

Euro notes and coins are introduced in the twelve euro-area countries.

13 December

The Copenhagen European Council agrees that ten of the candidate countries (Cyprus, the Czech Republic, Estonia, Hungary, Latvia, Lithuania, Malta, Poland, Slovakia and Slovenia) can join the EU on 1 May 2004.

2003

10 July

The Convention on the Future of Europe completes its work on the draft European Constitution.

4 October

Start of the intergovernmental conference responsible for drawing up the constitutional treaty.

2004

29 October

The European Constitution is adopted in Rome (subject to ratification by member states).

2005

29 May and 1 June

Voters in France reject the Constitution in a referendum, followed three days later by voters in the Netherlands.

3 October

Accession negotiations begin with Turkey and Croatia.

2007

1 January

Bulgaria and Romania join the European Union. Slovenia adopts the euro.

2008

1 January

Cyprus and Malta adopt the euro.

12 December

Switzerland joins the Schengen area.

2009

1 January

Slovakia adopts the euro.

1 December

Lisbon Treaty comes into force.

2011

1 January

Estonia adopts the euro.

2012

2 March

Fiscal Compact Treaty signed by all EU member states except the Czech Republic and the United Kingdom. It will enter into force on 1 January 2013 provided twelve members of the euro area ratify.

Dates sourced from
http://europa.eu/abc/12lessons/key_dates/index_en.htm

EU terminology

European Union (EU) abbreviations and jargon are a terminology set that have developed as a form of shorthand, to quickly express a (formal) EU process, an (informal) institutional working practice, or an EU body, function or decision, and which are commonly understood among EU officials or external people who regularly deal with EU institutions.

EU institutions

ACP (African, Caribbean and Pacific countries)
The ACP countries are one of the groups of beneficiaries of the EDF.

Acquis Communautaire
The body of Community law, as well as all acts adopted under the second and third pillars of the EU and the common objectives laid down in the treaties.

COSAC (Conference of Community and European Affairs Committee)

COSAC was proposed by the French National Assembly and has met every six months since 1989. It consists of national parliament bodies specialising in European Community affairs and six MEPs, and is headed by two vice-presidents responsible for relations with the national parliaments. It discusses the major topics of European integration. COSAC is not a decision-making body.

Council of the European Union (Council of Ministers)

The Council of the European Union comprises the representatives of each of the twenty-seven member states at ministerial level, chaired by the President. The work of the council is prepared by the Committee of Permanent Representatives (Coreper II) and the Committee of Deputy Permanent Representatives (Coreper I). Their work is in turn prepared by various working groups, working parties and committees.

ECJ (Court of Justice of the European Union)

The ECJ ensures that EU law is interpreted and applied in the same way in all EU countries, and that the law is equal for everyone. For example, it provides a check that national courts do not give different rulings on the same issue. The court also ensures that EU member states and institutions do what the law requires them to do. The court is located in Luxembourg and has one judge from each member country.

ECOFIN (Economic and Financial Affairs Council)

ECOFIN is composed of the economics and finance ministers of the twenty-seven EU member states, as well as budget ministers when budgetary issues are discussed.

ECSC (European Coal and Steel Community)

The ECSC was founded by the Treaty of Paris (1951). Its members were Belgium, France, Italy, Luxembourg, the Netherlands and West Germany, who pooled their steel and coal resources and created a common market for those products. It was the predecessor of the European Communities.

EDF (European Development Fund)

The EDF is the main instrument for European Community aid for development co-operation in the ACP countries, as well as the OCT lands.

EFC (Economic and Financial Committee)

The EFC was introduced with the Maastricht Treaty as part of EMU (Economic and Monetary Union), and is a committee of senior representatives of member states' finance ministries and central banks, plus representatives of the ECB and the Commission. The EFC prepares the work of ECOFIN, in particular regarding excessive deficit procedures and issues related to the euro.

Élysée Treaty

The Élysée Treaty, also known as the Treaty of Friendship, was concluded by Charles de Gaulle and Konrad Adenauer in 1963, and established a process of reconciliation for ending the rivalry between France and Germany.

European Commission

The European Commission is independent of national governments and its job is to represent and uphold the interests of the EU as a whole. It drafts proposals for new European laws, which it presents to the European Parliament and the Council.

It is also the EU's executive arm, responsible for implementing the decisions of the Parliament and the Council, implementing its policies, running its programmes and spending its funds. Like the Parliament and Council, the European Commission was set up in the 1950s under the EU's founding treaties.

European Ombudsman

The European Ombudsman investigates complaints about maladministration in the institutions and bodies of the EU. The ombudsman is completely independent and impartial. The current ombudsman, Nikiforos Diamandouros, was elected by the European Parliament and has held office since 1 April 2003. The Parliament elected the first European Ombudsman in 1995.

European Parliament

The European Parliament is the only directly elected body of the EU. The present parliament, elected in June 2009, has 785 members from the twenty-seven EU countries. It is elected every five years by the people of Europe to represent their interests and to pass European laws. It shares this responsibility with the Council of the European Union, and the proposals for new laws come from the European Commission. The Parliament and the Council also share joint responsibility for approving the EU's €100 billion annual budget. The Parliament has the power to dismiss the European Commission.

The main meetings of the Parliament are held in Strasbourg, with others held in Brussels. The Parliament elects the European Ombudsman, who investigates citizens' complaints about maladministration by the EU institutions.

Fouchet Plan

The Fouchet Plan was drawn up by Christian Fouchet as Charles de Gaulle's unofficial spokesman for European affairs. The Fouchet Plan was aimed at restructuring the European Community into a voluntary union of member states with a new headquarters in Paris, and by subjecting EU law to national law. The rejection of the Fouchet Plan by the other five member states had far-reaching consequences, such as the vetoing of the UK's entry into the EU, the 'empty chair' crisis and the 'Luxembourg Compromise'.

Luxembourg compromise

The Luxembourg compromise was a compromise (not recognised by the European Commission or the ECJ) that extended the lifespan of the national veto beyond what was foreseen in the Treaty of Rome. It originated from the 'empty chair crisis' instigated by President de Gaulle, and its effect was that qualified majority voting was used far less often and unanimity became the norm.

Merger Treaty

The Merger Treaty, signed in Brussels on 8 April 1965 and in force from 1 July 1967, provided for a single Commission and a single Council of the then three European Communities (the ECSC, the European Economic Community and the European Atomic Energy Community).

Messina Conference

The Messina Conference was held in Messina, Italy, in 1955 and discussed the subject of a customs union. The conference entrusted Paul-Henri Spaak with the preparation of a report that eventually led to the creation of the 1957 Treaty of Rome.

OCT (Overseas Countries and Territories)

Territories that have a special relationship with one of the EU member states. Along with the ACP countries, they are beneficiaries of the EDF.

Rome Treaty

The Treaty of Rome established the European Communities (EC), comprising the European Economic Community (EEC), the European Atomic Energy Community and the ECSC, and was signed in Rome on 25 March 1957 by the six founding members: Belgium, France, Italy, Luxembourg, the Netherlands and West Germany. It came into force on 1 January 1958.

Safeguard clause

A rapid reaction measure which can be invoked by a member state whenever a new member state fails to live up to its obligations in the areas of the internal market or justice and home affairs.

Schengen Agreement

The Schengen Agreement, dealing with cross-border legal arrangements and the abolition of systematic border controls among the participating countries, was created independently of the EU. However, the Treaty of Amsterdam incorporated the developments brought about by the agreement into the EU framework, effectively making the agreement part of the EU.

SEA (Single European Act)

The first major revision of the Treaty of Rome, aimed at creating the single European market by 31 December 1992.

Financial bodies

ECB (European Central Bank)

The ECB is the EU institution that administers the monetary policy of the seventeen eurozone member states. It is thus one of the world's most important central banks. The bank was established by the Treaty of Amsterdam in 1998, and is headquartered in Frankfurt. The primary objective of the ECB is to maintain price stability within the eurozone, in other words to keep inflation low. On 9 May 2010, the twenty-seven member states of the EU agreed to incorporate the European Financial Stability Facility, whose mandate is to safeguard financial stability in Europe by providing financial assistance to eurozone member states.

EMS (European Monetary System)

The EMS was an arrangement established in 1979 where most nations in the European Economic Community linked their currencies to prevent large fluctuations relative to one another.

Werner Plan

At the European summit in The Hague in 1969, the heads of state and government of the European Communities agreed to prepare a plan for the creation of an economic and monetary union. In October 1970 the Werner Report was presented, drawn up by a working group chaired by Luxembourg's President and Minister for the Treasury, Pierre Werner.

Common Foreign and Security Policy

CSDP (Common Security and Defence Policy)

The CSDP, formerly the European Security and Defence Policy, is a major element of the Common Foreign and Security Policy pillar of the EU. The CSDP is the successor to the European Security and Defence Identity under NATO, but differs in that it falls under the jurisdiction of the EU itself, including countries with no ties to NATO.

EDC (European Defence Community)

The EDC was a plan proposed in 1950 by René Pleven, the French Prime Minister, in response to the American call for the rearmament of West Germany. The intention was to form a pan-European defence force as an alternative to Germany's proposed accession to NATO, meant to harness its military potential in case of conflict with the Soviet bloc. The EDC was to include West Germany, France, Italy and the Benelux countries. A treaty was signed on 27 May 1952, but the plan never went into effect.

EUMC (European Union Military Committee)

The EUMC is a department of military officials under the High Representative for the Common Foreign and Security Policy and the PSC. The EUMC gives military advice to the PSC and the High Representative. It also oversees the EUMS. (Not to be confused with the former racism monitoring centre, also EUMC, now subsumed into the Fundamental Rights Agency.)

EUMS (European Union Military Staff)
The EUMS is responsible for supervising operations within the realm of the CSDP. It is directly attached to the private office of the High Representative for the Common Foreign and Security Policy.

GAERC (General Affairs and External Relations Council)
The GAERC is composed of one representative at ministerial level from each member state, and the council members are politically accountable to their national parliaments.

Pleven Plan
The Pleven Plan was a plan proposed in 1950 by the French premier at the time, René Pleven, to create a supranational European army as part of a European Defence Community.

PSC (Political and Security Committee)
The PSC monitors the international situation in the areas covered by the Common Foreign and Security Policy and contributes by delivering opinions to the Council of the European Union, either at its request or its own initiative, and also monitors the implementation of agreed policies.

Police and judicial co-operation in criminal matters
Eurojust
Eurojust is an EU agency dealing with judicial co-operation in criminal matters. The seat of Eurojust is in The Hague. Eurojust

has no powers to investigate or prosecute crimes on its own. Its task is to improve the co-ordination of investigations and prosecutions among the competent judicial authorities of the EU member states when they deal with serious cross-border and organised crime, in particular by facilitating the execution of international mutual legal assistance and the implementation of extradition requests. Eurojust was set up in 2002 by the Council of the European Union and went through a significant revision in 2009. Eurojust is composed of twenty-seven national members, one from each EU member state, who form the College of Eurojust. The Treaty on the Functioning of the European Union foresees that in order to combat crimes affecting the financial interests of the Union, the Council may establish a European Public Prosecutor's Office from Eurojust.

Europol (European Police Office)
Europol is the EU's criminal intelligence agency. It became fully operational on 1 July 1999. The establishment of Europol was agreed to in the Maastricht Treaty, which came into effect in November 1993. The agency started limited operations on 3 January 1994, as the Europol Drugs Unit. In 1998 the Europol Convention was ratified by all the member states and Europol commenced its full activities on 1 July 1999. Europol allocates its resources from its headquarters in The Hague. The size of Europol belies the fact that it is in constant liaison with hundreds of different law enforcement organisations, each with its own individual or group seconded to assist Europol's

activities. As of 2007, Europol covers all twenty-seven member states of the EU and co-operates with a number of third world countries and organisations. Europol was reformed as a full EU agency on 1 January 2010. This gave it increased powers to collect criminal information and allowed the European Parliament more control over its activities and budget.

International relations

Council of Europe

The Council of Europe (CoE) is not related to the EU. The CoE is the oldest international organisation working towards European integration, being founded in 1949. It has a particular emphasis on legal standards, human rights, democratic development, the rule of law and cultural co-operation.

EEA (European Economic Area)

The EEA was established on 1 January 1994 following an agreement between the member states of EFTA and the European Community. Specifically, it allows Iceland, Liechtenstein and Norway to participate in the EU's internal market without a conventional EU membership. In exchange, they are obliged to adopt all EU legislation related to the single market, except laws on agriculture and fisheries. One EFTA member, Switzerland, has not joined the EEA.

EFTA (European Free Trade Association)

EFTA is a European trade bloc which was established on 3 May

1960 as an alternative for European states who were either unable to, or chose not to, join the then-European Economic Community (now the EU). Today only Iceland, Norway, Switzerland, and Liechtenstein remain members of EFTA (of which only Norway and Switzerland are founding members).

The Nordic Council

An advisory body to the Nordic parliaments and governments, established in 1953, dealing with economic, legislative, social, cultural, environmental and communication policies.

OSCE (Organization for Security and Co-operation in Europe)

The OCSE is the world's largest security-oriented intergovernmental organisation. Its mandate includes issues such as arms control, human rights, freedom of the press and fair elections. The OSCE is an ad hoc organisation under the United Nations Charter. The EU is not strictly speaking a member of the OCSE, although the then Commission President, Jacques Delors, signed the Charter of Paris for a New Europe (1990), which is the origin of the OCSE.

*Much of the information above was retrieved from the Wikipedia page 'European Union acronyms, jargon and working practices' but with further material added.

Introduction

'There is, however, a limit at which forbearance ceases to be a virtue.'

Edmund Burke

This book concentrates on what has become the single most important aspect of the European Union, following the crisis in the eurozone from 2009, namely what are the limits to integration which will have to be maintained if an EU member state wishes to remain a self-governing nation. As I write no one can even be certain that the eurozone will survive, let alone continue with seventeen member states, but everyone accepts that, in order to survive, the eurozone states need to become ever more integrated.

Hitherto, there have been only two basic models for Europe as it moves through the second decade of the twenty-first century. The first is to keep to the present union of self-governing states with a separation of powers between the supranational – those passed from the nation state to a multinational body – and the intergovernmental – those remaining within the nation state.

This division is an arrangement long favoured by the UK but is also an acceptable compromise to many other member states. The European Commission is expected to lead on the supranational areas of policy with a substantial role for the European Parliament. The European Central Bank controls monetary policy much as the Bundesbank used to do and other national banks still do outside the eurozone. The European Council, comprising the Heads of Government, has a structured leadership role on all aspects of intergovernmental decision-making involving foreign and defence policies and global economic policy, and it is the forum for democratic debate, with its democratic legitimacy a reflection of the democracy in the nations that make up a unique union.

The second model is to develop a fiscal union within the eurozone, more and more explicitly championed as the desirable long-term development by Germany, the EU's largest and most powerful state. This model offers a bicameral legislature in which the European Parliament would embody the lower legislative chamber and the EU Council of Ministers the upper.* The President of the European Commission and the President of the Council would be elected, and the Commission would be an executive and virtually a European government, with federal authority within the EU for trade, economic, industrial, social, justice, environmental, agricultural, fishing, foreign and defence

---

* The Council of Ministers is now officially called the Council of the European Union but its previous title is retained in this book to avoid confusion with the European Council (of heads of government).

policies. The European Central Bank would be given more authority within the eurozone and replace the need for national banks; they might remain as symbols but not as independent decision makers. There would be an ending to the separation of powers between the supranational and the intergovernmental, the so-called pillar approach which emerged out of the Maastricht Treaty but which has been progressively eroded particularly since the most recent Lisbon Treaty. Under a fiscal union the explicit expectation would be that all EU member states would eventually join the eurozone.

The EU is reaching the point, because of the eurozone crisis, when it cannot continue to be ambivalent about these two models. In the UK, but also in some other countries, there are growing public demands for a principled and consistent position to resist any further merging of the two models, because the people in these countries want to remain self-governing, in that they are determined to retain their own currency and remain in control of foreign, defence and fiscal policies. Yet these same countries see the argument for greater integration within the eurozone to help resolve its continued crisis. The way these issues can be resolved Europe-wide is to enable those countries within the eurozone who wish to integrate further to do so and to allow those countries who do not envisage ever becoming part of the eurozone to remain in a restructured single market.

For this to happen without long and tortured arguments and challenges to the legal interpretation of the treaties and allegations of bad faith, all EU countries must be involved as equals in an agreed restructuring of the EU. All should remain full members of a single market based on the EU's existing *acquis communautaire* but it should become a larger, separate organisation. It should continue to operate under qualified majority voting based on a revitalised single market and customs union, and would hopefully include Turkey as a full participating member as well as other members of the European Economic Area (EEA).* Such a grouping of thirty-two states or more with Turkey could be called the European Community, funded and controlled by all its member states. It would have common international environmental policies and could use the old Political Co-operation mechanism for co-ordination of foreign and security policies, in addition to the NATO membership enjoyed by most of its constituents. It would have its own secretary general and it might be best for whoever is the EU external trade commissioner to be at least initially the single negotiator worldwide on behalf of the group. It is important to recognise that the European Parliament is greatly involved with single market legislation now that most of it is adopted under ordinary legislative procedure, that is by co-decision between the Council of Ministers and the Parliament. This means that the EU will inevitably be the lead element in devising the legislation for the wider single market but not the ultimate authority.

Progressively what will also emerge as part of this restructuring is a eurozone whose economic, fiscal and monetary

*The EEA comprises the twenty-seven current members of the EU (twenty-eight when Croatia joins in 2013) plus Iceland, Liechtenstein and Norway.

policies, taken with the Lisbon Treaty arrangements for foreign and security policy, will develop in ways that involve, to all intents and purposes, though not in name, a single government. This will probably be acceptable for most but not all of the existing eurozone countries and potentially for many other countries who intend to become members of the eurozone. Such a grouping would continue to be called the European Union.

In 2012, in order to make the eurozone work more effectively, twenty-five countries, comprising all those in the zone and others aspiring to join, created new financial and economic disciplines with a Fiscal Compact Treaty outside the EU treaties. This is now in the process of being ratified in some countries and being negotiated over in others. It represents a limited move towards a single economic government. The UK and the Czech Republic did not sign. Some of the countries, particularly Germany, want further economic integration beyond the Fiscal Compact. The German Chancellor, Angela Merkel, made it clear to her party, the Christian Democratic Union (CDU), early in 2012 that she saw Europe as a 'community of destiny' and she will ask for a mandate to achieve that from German voters in their federal election in the autumn of 2013. The present opposition party, the Social Democratic Party (SPD), shares much of her vision. Some have likened this new situation in Europe to the point in the creation of the USA where the 1787 Constitution was adopted. Since the German people will provide the money for any fiscal union, they will have to agree it first through a federal election as there is no place in their constitution for referendums. But there is a past precedent for grand coalitions in Germany between the two largest parties, the CDU and the SPD. There will be resistance to the German design of a fiscal union from France under President François Hollande but he is likely to choose, as did his only Socialist predecessor and role model, François Mitterrand, to continue the Franco-German route making a success of their single European currency. But Mitterrand only narrowly won the referendum to do this in 1992. With a reinvigorated political right, following the defeat of President Sarkozy, Hollande might have difficulty in winning another referendum in France. But even if he did lose, Germany would not let the euro fall and return to the deutschmark. It will assemble a small group to keep the euro intact and expect, at some later date, that the number of countries within the eurozone will increase.

Other countries, such as Greece, Portugal, Ireland, Italy and Spain, inside the eurozone but with mounting economic difficulties, may find public criticism of the austerity bias, which many claim is too dominant within the design of even the Fiscal Compact, too strong to withstand. Public opinion may demand more and more measures aimed at greater economic growth and in the process become resigned to leaving the eurozone. What is not clear is whether, if they leave, these countries will be able to stay in the EU hoping to rejoin the eurozone; if they are not welcome they will be fully entitled to be members of the single market and European Community.

The UK government divorced itself initially in 2011 from the debate over the Fiscal Compact design. This was wrong. Distancing the country from the European debate did not work and the UK re-engaged in the debate to try to ensure that the rules and obligations of any such arrangement that would apply to the eurozone would not impact in any damaging way on the continuation of the single market legislation applying to EU member states outside the eurozone. In the referendum debate in Ireland over the Fiscal Compact Treaty considerable criticisms were voiced and it will be necessary to take account of the views of President Hollande before full ratification and prior to the further debate on the design of the fiscal union that Germany envisages restarting towards the end of 2013. The focus will in the short term be on economic growth, perhaps by making more money available to the European Investment Bank to stimulate such growth.

In the UK, by the general election of 2015, unless the Conservative Party and the Labour Party change the situation over Europe, the UK Independence Party (UKIP) may grow in strength as it develops a wider agenda to include public anger against crime, immigration and plays on feelings that the British are being pushed around by eurozone integration. At the very least UKIP will be the lever for forcing a Conservative government to concede a referendum on Europe as James Goldsmith's Referendum Party did in 1997. Labour will be forced to concede as well. But a referendum will be lost in the UK and perhaps in some other countries if the only option is ever greater integration within the EU. It will only be won if the present Europe is restructured and the choices in a referendum are different and more attractive.

In all logic saving the eurozone, whether it continues with the existing number of countries or fewer, demands the restructuring of Europe as a whole. The degree of integration needed within the eurozone must become predominantly an issue for those countries who intend to be part of it. The UK and some other European countries outside the eurozone must assert their rights as well. A country like Turkey, for example, cannot be left on the sidelines of any European restructuring. We owe it to such a country to ensure it is involved in a restructuring with all the existing EU member states and the countries of the existing EEA. Any redesign of the EU must seek to accommodate the interests of those EU countries outside as well as inside the eurozone, those countries who wish eventually to become part of the eurozone and those who do not.

No-one, however, can sensibly contribute to restructuring the EU without studying relevant aspects of its history and development. I have tried in this book to draw on my fifty years of personal involvement with Europe's development since 1962, to trace a path which might be able to resolve the present crisis. It is bound to suffer from being only one UK politician's perspective, but at least it comes from someone who still has a full-hearted commitment to achieving greater European unity such that it led me to spend nearly three years as the EU peace envoy in the former Yugoslavia from 1992 to 1995, but also one who has for over two decades argued consistently that the eurozone design is fatally flawed. I have long believed too that in the UK there must be limits set to the process of European integration. The EU generally needs to take full account of the views of those Europeans who want to live in a self-governing country with which they fully identify.

In writing about this restructuring of Europe, I have eschewed the hostile language of anti-Europeanism and also the institutional language of 'variable geometry', a 'two-speed EU' or an '*Europe à deux vitesses*', or even a 'two-tier Europe'. Who knows whether in a wider Europe of more nations, built around the single market and including Turkey, those outside the eurozone will grow faster or more slowly than those inside? Who knows whether an inner, more integrated European Union built around a single European currency will grow faster than the countries who decide not to be part of such a union but prefer a model based on the less integrated European Community? We need instead to resolve to live and let live in a wider Europe restructured by agreement with goodwill and good relations between each of its elements, a European Community and a European Union.

A referendum on the future of Europe I believe is inevitable at some point between 2013 and 2016 at the latest. I would hope in such a referendum we would be able to vote on a restructured Europe of the sort I advocate in this book and pose something like the following choice.

Do you want the UK to be part of the single market in a wider European Community?   Yes/No

Do you want the UK to remain in the
European Union, keeping open the option
of joining the more integrated eurozone?   Yes/No

The first question would most probably be answered by the British public with a 'Yes', and any British government would urge them to do so. The second question would be harder to predict, but it would be a genuine choice, and the government might be in effect neutral on the outcome, ready to follow rather than lead public opinion. If both questions were answered 'No', a response that might be championed by UKIP, this would in effect mean a total withdrawal.

Most existing EU member states will probably choose to keep their options open on future eurozone membership. The temptation to hedge one's bets is very strong in the culture of politics. However, one or two countries, including the UK, may assess that it is preferable to opt out of trying to be part of the new more integrated eurozone entirely.

Whether these two questions can be narrowed down to one depends on the shape of the negotiations. It may be that the concept of restructuring the Single Market in the way I have suggested is accepted and becomes so uncontroversial in the UK that it does not need to be a single question. It is an all-too-human characteristic of the British electorate that whilst its intuitive judgement is pretty good, its readiness to grapple with complexity and subtlety is perhaps not as great as one would want. This is one reason why it has always been argued that referendum questions should be as simple and unambiguous as possible. The Electoral Commission has now established the position that it is consulted on these issues relating to the wording of referendum questions and that is wise. My objective is to get the Prime Minister to mobilise Chancellor Merkel's enthusiastic support for keeping the UK as allies in a Single Market based on a small number of adjustments to the present treaty language on the *acquis communataire* on the Single Market, recognising that the separation from the overall EU *acquis* has already been done in the EEA agreement.

That secured, the referendum question could be single and clear cut. Should the UK continue to be part of the Single Market as developed from within the European Community EC or should the UK join the new eurozone EU?

The UK timetable can be related to eurozone changes. If they delay we can delay. What the UK has the right to ask for is a fair and generous design for a restructured Europe. The present model of the EU is not working for all its member states. There is broad agreement that EMU and the eurozone will fail unless this important part is substantially changed. All European political leaders should try to find solutions in a climate of goodwill and generosity. The British must be ready to listen to good arguments for general restructuring and eurozone restructuring. Those who advocated joining the eurozone must also listen a little more than hitherto to those who predicted its flaws. A mood of exasperation is also growing within the peoples of Europe against a single prescription of unrelenting austerity, and against the refusal of the Commission and the European Parliament to take on the budgetary restraints that they prescribe for the rest of us in Europe. The best way to proceed is through the unanimity provision in the treaties for amendment. The UK government would give its support for a restructured eurozone, provided other member states give their support to a restructured single market. All of this should be done with a minimum of change to the language in EU Treaties.

I have previously kept open a possible future entry into the eurozone from its inception – I have never said never, although I did campaign against entry between 1999 and 2005 through the New Europe organisation. New Europe was wound up when it became very clear that eurozone membership was off the agenda in the UK for a decade or more. In 2012 I feel it would be in the best interests of the UK to decide that in a restructured Europe we will never join a new integrated eurozone. It would therefore be wisest for the UK to relinquish a more integrated EU and to take advantage of the freedoms and opportunities of a new model European Community. This would mean we would regain the running of our own agricultural, fishing, industrial, social and foreign and security policies. In taking that position we would be able to reinvest the substantial sums of money we contribute to the EU budget, less the cost of the single market, and we would no longer have any need to be part of the European Parliament.

We would lose some advantages. Few choices are ever so one-sided that it is all gain. We could even surprise ourselves that, just as when we left the Exchange Rate Mechanism in 1992, we might be able to embark on a period of sustained economic growth and rediscover the freedom of the European Community which we joined in 1973 rather take on more of the shackles of the European Union, which since the creation of the eurozone has increasingly threatened to constrain us.

On 23 June 2012, having sent a copy of the ebook version of this book to George Osborne, Chancellor of the Exchequer, he replied that it was a timely publication which he was sure would contribute to the lively and very important debate about the UK's place in the EU and its approach to closer integration in the euro area.

He went on to say, "I have said for some time now that the euro area needs to follow the remorseless logic of monetary union that leads to closer fiscal integration, for example through more pooling of resources whether through Eurobonds or some other mechanism. The euro area needs a share backstop for the banking system and closer collective oversight of fiscal and financial policy. And all Member States must comprehensively address Europe's growth challenge."

"Of course there are profound implications of these moves toward closer integration for the euro area itself and the UK. The UK intends to, and must, remain a full and active member of the EU single market which has huge benefits for the UK economy. Indeed we want to deepen and enhance the single market. We therefore need to ensure that there are the right safeguards in place for the single market and those outside the euro area. Without the right safeguards, political integration within the euro area could significantly alter the structures and dynamics of the European Union.'

The German position has also become clearer with the hint by their Finance Minister, Wolfgang Schäuble, in Der Spiegel, ahead of the late June Summit of EU Heads of Government, that Germany could hold a referendum to bring the country's postwar Basic Law into line with the greater integration within the eurozone that most influential Germans, whether in politics or business, want. It will be as Marcus Kerber, the Chief Executive of the Federation of German Industries, describes where "like-minded nations form a closely integrated eurozone, with political sovereignty shared along relative weights before national wealth is shared. It will be one in which those who bail out banks will in exchange own those banks to run them properly. It will be a eurozone with a European Fiscal Fund (EFF) based on the European Stability Mechanism statutes, with powers to restructure ailing economies and to co-determine and, if needed, sanction national fiscal and economic policies."

It is a major departure for Germany to have a referendum indicative of the immense importance these issues are for its citizens. It is noteworthy from Kerber's article that he states "the coming days and weeks will demand big steps forward into a political union of eurozone members" and he invokes the words of Schumpeter "nothing shows as clearly what kind of wood a people is cut from, that what it does in monetary policy".*

*_Financial Times_, "and don't despair of my fellow stubborn Nein-sayers", 4 July 2012

The British are clear about what wood they are cut from. They do not wish to surrender so much national sovereignty as will be involved in such a eurozone. Yet for the most part we understand why Germany, which has been for centuries cut from a different wood, want these disciplines before they fund the indiscipline of their fellow eurozone members. Whether Greece, Portugal, Spain, Italy and Ireland can live within such a disciplined framework is an open question. There will be other more important eurozone countries too which will have to face fundamental political questions and may be quite speedily, if the world markets decide to test the cohesion of the eurozone. The French President, François Hollande, will face resistance from some French socialists as well as those on the Right on transferring such significant national economic powers to the eurozone and in particular the ECB. The National Auditor report published on 2 July 2012 by the Cour des Comptes spelt out the huge challenge facing the new French administration to meet their commitment to reduce the budget deficit to 3% of GDP next year and eliminate the deficit by 2017 and they estimate that France could see its public debt hit 90% of GDP in 2012. The other major country that will face political questions and is due to have a General Election in September is the Netherlands where the steady rise of public feeling against ever greater integration will be difficult to manage.

No one can be sure how fast the eurozone will have to make these fundamental decisions, but the pace of change is quickening and as yet it does not appear that the British

Government, let alone the British Parliament, has determined its position. It is inconceivable that the UK can let these changes through without establishing beforehand, and as part of a deal, what the UK needs over the single market. To seek safeguards *after* eurozone integration has been waived through would be a folly. That is why the British Prime Minister must be enabled to negotiate Treaty amendments over a weekend, while the financial markets are closed, ensuring that the transfers of power to the eurozone under the 2011 Referendum Act are not significant for us. At the same time the UK must be satisfied that our position within the single market is safeguarded with specific changes. In these circumstances, and not withstanding that the referendum requirement in the 2011 Act is not triggered, the Government could and should still decide to introduce legislative provisions calling for a UK referendum on its changed relationship with the EU.

To show how a restructured Europe could look, on the following pages are two tables. The first, titled 'Existing Europe', lists the members of NATO, the European Economic Area, the EU and the eurozone as currently configured. The second, titled 'Restructured Europe', again gives the members of NATO, along with those of the new single market called the European Community and the changed EU increasingly shaped by a more disciplined and integrated eurozone, as proposed in this book.

Existing Europe

NATO	EEA	EEC/EU	Eurozone
1949	*1994*	*1957*	*As of June 2012*
Belgium	Austria	Belgium	Austria
Canada	Belgium	France	Belgium
Denmark	Denmark	Italy	Cyprus
France	Finland	Luxembourg	Estonia
Iceland	France	Netherlands	Finland
Italy	Germany	West Germany	France
Luxembourg	Greece	*1973*	Germany
Netherlands	Iceland	Denmark	Greece
Norway	Ireland	Ireland	Ireland
Portugal	Italy	United Kingdom	Italy
United Kingdom	Liechtenstein	*1981*	Luxembourg
United States	Luxembourg	Greece	Malta
1952	Netherlands	*1986*	Netherlands
Greece	Norway	Portugal	Portugal
Turkey	Portugal	Spain	Slovakia
1955	Spain	*1990*	Slovenia
West Germany	Sweden	(East Germany	
		following	
1982	United Kingdom	reunification)	
Spain	*2004*	*1995*	*Microstates using the*
			euro

1990
(East Germany following Reunification)
1999
Czech Republic
Hungary

Poland
2004
Bulgaria
Estonia
Latvia
Lithuania
Romania
Slovakia
Slovenia
2009
Albania
Croatia

Aspirant countries
Participating in Membership Action Plan
Bosnia & Herzegovina
Macedonia
Montenegro

Cyprus
Czech Republic
Estonia
Hungary
Latvia
Lithuania

Malta
Poland
Slovakia
Slovenia
2007
Bulgaria
Romania

Austria
Finland
Sweden
2004
Cyprus
Czech Republic
Estonia
Hungary
Latvia
Lithuania
Malta
Poland
Slovakia
Slovenia
2007
Bulgaria
Romania

Joining in 2013
Croatia

Candidate countries
Turkey
Iceland
Macedonia
Montenegro
Serbia

Potential candidates
Albania
Bosnia & Herzegovina

Andorra
Monaco
San Marino
Vatican City

Adopted euro unilaterally (with no representation in Euro Group)
Kosovo
Montenegro

Restructured Europe

NATO	Single market European Community	EU/eurozone
1949	Austria	Austria
Belgium	Belgium	Belgium
Canada	Bulgaria	Bulgaria
Denmark	Croatia	Croatia
France	Cyprus	Cyprus
Iceland	Czech Republic	Estonia
Italy	Denmark	Finland
Luxembourg	Estonia	France
Netherlands	Finland	Germany
Norway	France	Hungary
Portugal	Germany	Latvia
United Kingdom	Greece	Lithuania
United States	Hungary	Luxembourg
1952	Ireland	Malta
Greece	Italy	Poland
Turkey	Latvia	Slovakia
1955	Lithuania	Slovenia
West Germany	Luxembourg	

1982

Spain

1990

(East Germany

following reunification

1999

Czech Republic

Hungary

Poland

2004

Bulgaria

Estonia

Latvia

Lithuania

Romania

Slovakia

Slovenia

2009

Albania

Croatia

Aspirant countries
participating in
Membership Action
Plan
Bosnia & Herzegovina
Macedonia
Montenegro

Malta

Netherlands

Poland

Portugal

Romania

Slovakia

Slovenia

Spain

Sweden

United Kingdom

Iceland

Liechtenstein

Norway

Turkey

Potential candidates

Albania

Bosnia &
Herzegovina

Macedonia

Moldova

Montenegro

Serbia

Ukraine

The following countries will or may need a referendum on whether to stay in the EU/eurozone

Czech Republic

Denmark

Netherlands

Sweden

United Kingdom

The following countries may not wish to stay under the new EU/eurozone financial disciplines

Bulgaria

Hungary

Romania

The following countries may not comply economically with EU/eurozone requirements

Greece

Ireland

Italy

Portugal

Spain

Chapter 1

The nature of post-war European unity

Before we go about restructuring Europe in the twenty-first century it is worth understanding the nature of the debate that was held on the way to pursuing the ideal of European unity in the late 1940s, 1950s and 1960s. Those who argue that signing the Treaty of Rome in 1957 by the original six nations* meant only one thing – an eventual European state – show little knowledge of how the present EU evolved over time, and of how its very nature changed with the decision in 1990 to have a European currency, the euro.

General Charles de Gaulle returned to power in France in 1959, two years after the Treaty of Rome was signed. When he had dealt with Algerian independence de Gaulle directed his attention to Europe. He never showed the slightest inhibition that France's signature to the Treaty of Rome constrained him from pursuing his own ideas on the future of Europe. Not for

*Belgium, France, Italy, Luxembourg, the Netherlands and West Germany.

nothing did Harold Macmillan remark of de Gaulle, 'He talks of Europe and means France.' As de Gaulle's biographer, Jean Lacouture, makes clear, while de Gaulle saw the Treaty of Rome as an ideal framework for the economic development of his country, he would never have agreed to a supranational framework for a political union. European leaders like Konrad Adenauer, the West German Chancellor, and Jean Monnet, the influential French architect of institutional Europe, were under no illusions at the time that de Gaulle was ever going to take the supranational route to a United States of Europe. They also accepted that there was nothing in the Treaty of Rome to bind him to do so. This is worth emphasising since in 2003, in the run-up to the Intergovernmental Conference on the Future of the Union, political integrationists argued that those who sought to establish defined limits to prevent a United States of Europe emerging were defying the meaning of the treaties which their countries had signed (in the case of the UK only in 1972). It was the Netherlands and France, original signatory countries, who voted against that Constitutional Treaty in the 2005 referendums. It is also a reminder to those who despair of making changes in the nature of the EU and who simply want the UK to leave that there is a French precedent for the UK to reject becoming part of a full federal integrationist model, and if necessary to exercise our veto power to block it.

Interestingly, Adenauer and Monnet saw de Gaulle in the early 1960s as an ally in the immediate task of building up the Common Market even while he was expressing his vision of a

Europe with no supranationality in its political governance. They knew only too well that there was an undefined ambiguity as to the destination of Europe and they were prepared to wait, believing that moods change and that all they had to do was foster a mood that integration was inevitable. Jean Monnet was quite open that he could only have ever persuaded the Six to sign up for the Treaty of Rome if that ambiguity existed. In his memoirs he wrote that 'political Europe will be created by men, when the moment comes, based on realities'.*

On 10 February 1961, just over three years after the Treaty of Rome came into effect, de Gaulle called the other five heads of government together in Paris to try to delimit integration by building a European political identity and demonstrating that Europeanism and integrationism were not one and the same thing. He asked Christian Fouchet, a trusted aide, to define an '*Europe des états*'. Many people forget that Adenauer gave his approval to the essentially intergovernmental preparatory committee chaired by Fouchet because he saw it as a way for de Gaulle to come around to at least a confederation for Europe. In those negotiations, which started on 31 October 1961, Adenauer supported the French concept because he wanted above all else to strengthen Franco-German co-operation. Opposition to a 'Europe of states' came initially only from the Dutch, later to be joined by the Belgians, while the Italians were mistrustful of French ideas but wanted to be part of the 'Big

*Jean Monnet, *Mémoires* (Paris: Fayard, 1976), pp. 505–6.

Three' countries. Fouchet was the head of the French delegation and also chairman of the body set up by heads of government of the Six to lay the foundations of a new structure which they saw as adding a political dimension. He and his colleagues were later asked to draw up statutes for a political union characterised as a 'Union of Peoples' in an attempt to overcome the clash exposed during the preliminary talks between those who wanted more supranationalism and those who wanted less. The word 'peoples' as distinct from 'states' in the present European treaties has a long history within the debate about European integration, which started even before the Messina Conference of 1955. There was initially no wording, as in the American Constitution, which asserted the existence of 'one people' because such a commitment was too far for public opinion even in the original six states.

For the UK, joining the Common Market of the Six was not conceived of as an option by any substantial grouping in the House of Commons and there were formidable groups against in the two main parties. Even the Liberal Party then had a small element opposing entry. The reasons for this were multiple and complex. The simplest was a reflection of human nature. That post-war generation of ministers in government – first Attlee, Bevin and Morrison, then Churchill, Eden and Butler – had seen the growth of fascism in the 1930s, anxiously watching the virtually unopposed rise of Hitler and Mussolini. These were popular regimes at the time, not just violent and manipulative dictatorships. Britain's defiance despite the military collapse of

Belgium, Holland and then France in the 1940s and the miraculous escape of the British Expeditionary Force at Dunkirk had been a triumph of national will. These leaders had expected and waited for Britain to be invaded. They knew how few planes and pilots we had to win the Battle of Britain in the air and how close a shave that victory was. They knew how delicate in US domestic politics had been President Roosevelt's almost clandestine support until Japan struck at Pearl Harbor, how critical had been the outcome of the Battle of the Atlantic as our Merchant Navy had to avoid being sunk by German submarines if it was to bring sufficient food into Britain. They had held their breath before and during the Battle of El Alamein in north Africa and then as British troops, with the Americans, fought up through Italy. They had weighed the risks together with the US of the Allied D-Day invasion across the Channel.

They found themselves unable to relax militarily even after the war. While Britain was by then a greatly weakened world power, it emerged with the pre-war Empire still intact but, in a very different world, ready to accept independence for India. Three powers were present at Potsdam: the United States, the Soviet Union and Britain. But appearances were very deceptive. The UK had massive external debts and much-reduced gold and dollar reserves. In retrospect it may seem obvious that in the late 1940s and early 1950s, a fundamental reappraisal of Britain's role in the world should have taken place to take account of the changes in the international system triggered by World War II. But relief at having emerged victorious was apparent in those

British leaders' minds, coupled with a belief that the Commonwealth offered a way forward distinct from the two superpowers and the eclipse of Europe. The process of decolonisation had hesitatingly begun and, very slowly, Britain began to adapt to the role of a medium-sized European power. This transition was accepted as part of a period of painful and profound adjustment. But the existence of garrisons in Hong Kong, Singapore, Aden, Egypt and the Gulf, Cyprus and Malta, together with the large British Army of the Rhine, encouraged the assumption that Britain could continue to play a world role. British leaders felt they had no choice but to assume with the US the burden of maintaining forces in Germany as the Cold War developed. There was no-one else to whom the American government could turn to help stand against Soviet communism. Germany and Japan were then, by definition, excluded. France was weak and divided. It seemed only right and natural that Britain should play a leading role in the creation of a new Atlanticist international order for the post-war world.

The UK made a major contribution to the setting up of the United Nations during and immediately after the Second World War. We helped shape the International Monetary Fund (IMF), the World Bank and the North Atlantic Treaty Organization (NATO). The purpose of these international institutions and mechanisms was to make impossible a return to the Great Slump of the 1930s. The Foreign Secretary, Ernest Bevin, was largely responsible for Europe's enthusiastic response to the European Recovery Programme, better known as the Marshall Plan, and for setting up the mechanism for administering it in the form of the Organisation for European Economic Co-operation. Similarly, Britain's role was central in the running of NATO after 1949, seeing that if western Europe failed to respond promptly either to the American offer of Marshall aid or to the urgent need to build a system of collective security based on the North Atlantic, the United States might withdraw from the region and the European–American relationship revert to the distanced one of the 1920s and 1930s. Built into Britain's firm support for the Marshall Plan and the North Atlantic Treaty was the recognition that without America's assistance western Europe was unable either to rebuild its economy quickly enough or to guarantee its security.

This enormous co-operative endeavour, first of all during the Second World War following Pearl Harbor in December 1941 and then in the reconstruction of western Europe into the 1950s, was the cement of the relationship between Britain and the United States. To the old ties of language and culture something more substantial was added: a perceived common interest in, and shared responsibility for, the preservation in European countries occupied by the Nazis of a free, democratic way of life in conditions of international peace and prosperity. The more they got together, the better for everyone, but it was felt they had to build that unity as part of the continent of Europe, they had to make the bricks and cement them together.

Clement Attlee and Ernest Bevin were ready to ask the Cabinet to face the difficulties and the dangers of sustaining and defending Berlin against the Soviet Union. They accepted that the UK had to contribute forces, nominally under the UN but in reality under US command, to defend South Korea. But over and above those commitments, to expect that generation of Labour and Conservative leaders, still governing a Britain that was paying a heavy economic price and still carrying a disproportionate defence burden draining its resources, to join and lead a supranational European organisation was more than human flesh and blood could deliver. Entry to the European Coal and Steel Community (ECSC) was rejected by Attlee and Bevin in government and Churchill and Eden in opposition. Joining the EEC was rejected initially by Churchill and then Eden as Prime Minister, and by Hugh Gaitskell and Aneurin Bevan in opposition. There was never any significant political counter-pressure to these leaders' judgement in the House of Commons at the time. Messina was twenty years too soon for the British people, as was demonstrated by Britain needing to wait until the referendum in 1975 for the full-hearted consent of the electorate to being part of the European Community.

Those who wish to misinterpret Winston Churchill's Europeanism sometimes recall his somewhat quixotic suggestion, to a France in 1940 at the point of suing for peace with Germany, of a union between France and Britain. In truth this was an emotional response to a particular and dire crisis. It cannot be invoked to disguise the fact that everything that Churchill stood for in British politics indicates that he was wedded to Britain remaining a self-governing nation. No myth has been more assiduously peddled by the European integrationists in the UK than that Winston Churchill in a series of speeches after the end of the war, particularly in Zurich in 1947, was in favour of Britain joining a 'United States of Europe'. It is true he used that expression but he did so while making it crystal clear that such a 'United States' was for continental Europe. Europe would form one of his three circles of power and influence outside the Soviet empire – the other two circles being the United States of America and Britain with its Commonwealth. That the board of governors of the BBC should in 2000 have had to be forced, publicly to contradict its programme makers for implying Churchill was in favour of a United States of Europe to include Britain shows how hard it had become to counter such propaganda. Then some wished to distort Churchill's true record and pray him in aid not just for European integration but to support their wish for Britain to join the single currency. By an historic standard of objectivity it is highly improbable that Churchill, who as Chancellor of the Exchequer disastrously returned Britain to the gold standard and was then subjected to a withering attack by Maynard Keynes in a best-selling pamphlet, *The Economic Consequences of Mr Churchill*, would have supported British membership of the eurozone. He would have been more than usually wary of repeating anything like that mistake again. It is all too easy to rerun the 'ifs of history' without investigating how people thought at the time and setting their judgements against their immediate experience.

The commitment in the preamble to the 1957 Treaty of Rome

to 'lay the foundations for an ever closer union among the peoples of Europe' has never been a commitment to a United States of Europe. The Rome treaty contained a formal indication that belonging to the union, in the words of an eminent European lawyer,* 'in no way casts doubt on Members' continued existence as States, in the fullest acceptation of that slippery notion'. It is seen today in Article 6(3) of the Treaty on European Union, which says that the 'Union shall respect the national identities of its Member States'. That treaty provides a further oblique indication that members' survival as states in the full sense is a basic assumption of the constitutional order since the unification aimed at is one of *peoples* and not of states;† and, while there is a process, that process is viewed as of an indefinite nature. What we have in the treaties is a formulation that European unity is cultural, social, economic and political, but the treaties carry within them no preconception as to the allocation of governmental powers, except that decisions must be taken as close as possible to the people. A consequence of the present unique design of the EU, still with intergovernmental and supra-national decision-making, is that there is no commitment to the European Parliament being the only democratic safeguard. Democratic power has to be shared with the national parliaments. Where a nation retains control of its internal security, foreign and defence policies and, if it desires, economic policy

---

*Alan Dashwood, 'States in the European Union', *European Law Review*, vol. 23, no. 3 (1998), p. 203.
†Ibid.

outside the eurozone, the national parliament, therefore, remains both the dominant and the ultimate democratic safeguard.

In the preamble to the Fouchet plan and its eighteen articles it was specifically stated that it concerned a 'union of states'. No attempt, however, was made to disown existing commitments. So the then European Coal and Steel Community (ECSC), European Economic Community (EEC) and European Confederation of Agriculture were accepted as continuing 'in their respective domains'. In Article 1 it talked about the proposed union as respecting the 'personality' of the 'peoples and member states'. Article 2 defined the scope of co-operation: namely diplomacy, defence and culture. Articles 5, 6 and 7 described the Council, the Assembly and the Political Commission. The Council, which was to be made up of heads of government or foreign ministers, was normally to meet three times a year and its decisions were to be made by unanimity. The Assembly was to be made up of delegates from the existing national parliaments with largely consultative powers. The European Political Commission was to be composed of civil servants and to be based in Paris. As discussions went on into the winter of 1961 Harold Macmillan, then the British Prime Minister, made it clear that the UK wished to be involved in the Fouchet discussions and that he viewed the concept favourably. The Dutch tried to get the UK involved, which only incited General de Gaulle to question, not unreasonably, how the Dutch could both be in favour of more supranationalism and British entry into the Common Market.

In early 1962 de Gaulle, annoyed that French diplomats had been too compromising, added in his own hand what a French diplomat – in a magnificent understatement – called 'two or three touches' to the draft Fouchet plan. These 'touches' were designed to be a considerable hardening of the French position and had the effect of blowing the plan completely out of the political water. De Gaulle made the Political Commission's decisions non-binding, he removed any obligation of trust and put a line straight through the cleverly crafted words covering defence which talked about 'strengthening the Atlantic Alliance'. He also added that the new Council would have economic powers, which in effect would have given any member government the power to override the EEC.

By April 1962 the five other countries tabled counter-proposals to the French which for the first time used the expression 'European Union'. Though never taken up then, the word 'Union' re-emerged years later in the 1990 negotiations and became part of the Treaty of Maastricht. The Dutch demand that defence be developed 'within the NATO frame-work' was another form of words that was to return to future treaty drafting sessions, particularly those surrounding the Treaty of Lisbon. The Dutch and Belgians were adamant that a precondition to any Fouchet plan was the admission of Britain to the Common Market. De Gaulle conceded references to the Atlantic Alliance but the new chairman of the ministerial committee, who had replaced Fouchet, could obtain no substantive agreement and the meeting held in April 1962 was the last. The negotiations had by then completely run out of political steam. Paul-Henri Spaak, the Belgian Foreign Minister, was not convinced that the plan represented a European advance, while Joseph Luns, his Dutch counterpart, thought the time was not ripe for a political union of the Six; Luns wanted the UK to join, having all along argued that a Europe of only six was not really Europe.

This breakdown in negotiations some in Britain saw as helping our application because everything had been left loose and indeterminate on political union and the UK did not have to accept an already defined confederal structure. Others, by contrast, felt that by failing to establish definite limits to the supranational areas of European activity and also not making clear the key political areas that were to be reserved for inter-governmentalism, an historic opportunity was lost to halt creeping integration in the future. Had de Gaulle been less stubborn and had something like the Fouchet plan been established it would have helped settle a major recurring UK fear over the years of Community membership: namely, that by adopting sensible measures of integration we only created a rod for our own back when, as was inevitable, we felt we had to resist those measures of integration that threatened taking the UK across a threshold for remaining a self-governing nation. Any British government would have found a specifically confederal model much easier to sell to public opinion from 1962 onwards than the one on offer, which left us with this potentially momentous issue open on whether or not the eventual destination was a single state. It was always going to be, however, very difficult to agree wording that would effectively close that issue down. We were saddled with constructive or destructive ambiguity depending on how one looked at the issue.

European integration after the Second World War did not begin with France and Germany or the Common Market of the Six, but with a customs union between Belgium, the Netherlands and Luxembourg (Benelux) which started in January 1948. The foundations for this union were laid during the war with a monetary agreement in 1943 and a customs union treaty signed by the three governments in exile in London in 1944. The French, after the war, wanted to link with Benelux but not at that stage with Germany. However, in 1949 the Dutch declared their refusal to countenance a wider customs union unless it involved the new state of West Germany.

The building of post-war Europe and today's EU started with the European Coal and Steel Community (ECSC), whose obvious purpose was to bind together the belt of coal and steel production that ran across the Franco-German frontier so that never again could the two countries fight each other by rearming to destroy each other. The French were very concerned by German reindustrialisation and felt threatened by excess German steel capacity and having to pay higher prices for German coal. French planners believed that if a supranational organisation could control German industry it could also be used to control German rearmaments. The plan, which was revealed publicly on 9 May 1950, was deliberately prepared without consulting or informing the British. The process had been given a significant push, however, in November 1949 by Dean Acheson, the US Secretary of State, when meeting his French and British counterparts, Robert Schuman and Ernest Bevin, in Paris. He argued that unless Germany could become part of western Europe it would inevitably develop along nationalistic lines.* Bevin wanted the continent to unite but like Winston Churchill saw it as a European project from which Britain would stand aside and he was not at all keen on British membership of the ECSC. Public opinion in Britain was also not ready for membership; neither the coal and steel industrial leaders nor their trade union leaders wanted membership. To pretend that there was a real choice over the ECSC which our then political leaders failed is abstract theory and a distorted reading of the realities of the post-war political decision-making environment.

The ECSC had been designed by Jean Monnet's staff in the French Planning Commission and came into effect in July 1952. It was controlled by the High Authority, a supranational body with far more sovereign authority than the European Commission has ever been able to acquire. The ECSC Treaty also explicitly laid down a federal aim, something not included later in the Treaty of Rome. Following major retrenchments in both the steel and coal industries it has had less and less to do and its few residual activities were taken into the European

* Alan Bullock, *Ernest Bevin: Foreign Secretary* (London: Heinemann, 1983), p. 739.

Community in 2002.

The ECSC has, however, undoubtedly been the most important single factor in building the Franco-German alliance as the motor of European unity. It has bedded the two countries' civil servants into a habit of working together at every level of government and it can fairly claim along with the creation of NATO in 1949 to have had the major responsibility for making war again between these two countries virtually inconceivable.

Somewhat surprisingly, it was the invasion of South Korea on 25 June 1950 which proved to be the most important single factor in promoting the cause of European unity because it created the political climate which overcame resistance to the full involvement of Germany with the countries it had occupied. President Truman began to openly advocate in September 1950 that Europe should increase its land forces and suggested ten West German divisions. The French Prime Minister, René Pleven, said in October 1950 that France would only accept German rearmament in the context of a European army under the control of a single minister of defence. He also made ratification of the ECSC a precondition for rearmament. All this followed a motion passed in the Council of Europe on 11 August formally proposed by Winston Churchill, then leader of the opposition in Britain, calling for a continental European army under a European minister of defence. But as with all Churchill's post-war European initiatives his calls for European unity specifically excluded British participation.

What was initially called the Pleven Plan was approved by the

French National Assembly by 348 votes to 224. However, the difficulties inherent in creating a European Defence Community (EDC) soon became obvious. First, it was necessary to establish some common ground between the newly established American-dominated NATO and the proposed EDC. Second, a defence community faced the problem of West Germany's relationship to the occupying powers. Fundamental changes in the Occupation Statute would have been necessary in order for West Germany to be able to participate. It is interesting that America was still an occupying power following Roosevelt's statement in Yalta that the 'United States would take all reasonable steps to preserve peace, but not at the expense of keeping a large army indefinitely in Europe, 3,000 miles away from home'. Initially the American occupation after the Second World War was limited to two years. It was Churchill who championed France being given an occupation zone and being a full member of the Allied Control Commission.* It was these three – the US, UK and France – which had to respond to the Soviet blockade of the western sectors of Berlin on 24 June 1948. Bevin was in favour of firm action from the start. He led the Western response and demanded an airlift from the military. He welcomed the US sending to Europe B-29s capable of dropping atomic bombs and agreed that some might be stationed in Britain.

Berlin was my first real memory of an international crisis. At the age of ten I watched the airlift begin on the Pathé news at our

*Martin Gilbert, *Winston S. Churchill, vol. 8: Never Despair, 1945–1965* (London: Heinemann, 1988), p. 1180.

local cinema. It was a very formative experience. We were helping the Germans; our enemy was now Soviet communism.

Before the EDC could be established, the all-important question had to be answered of how to develop financial and political control mechanisms which would effectively integrate a grouping of national armies. The early 1950s was a time when the idealism lying behind the concept of a united continental Europe was openly and frankly stated. European integration was not subjected to the critical scrutiny and scepticism developed later in France under General de Gaulle. At the EDC conference held in Paris on 15 February, 1951, the climate was such that Robert Schuman reminded the delegates that nations once deeply divided were meeting round the same table, forgetting their past struggles in an 'attempt to substitute for the very instrument of these struggles – national armies – a common army that will be able to act only in defence of their common civilisation'.* These were fine sentiments, particularly coming from the French, who still had bitter memories of two world wars fought on their territory. They were, however, the language of a political elite that was becoming increasingly out of touch with French opinion. The EDC did not initially arouse profound resentment, but slowly the critics gained in strength. In France, there were genuine fears of German rearmament and the opposition became particularly bitter. Some prominent French Europeans opposed the EDC on the grounds that military

*F. Roy Willis, *France, Germany and the New Europe, 1945–1967* (London: Oxford University Press, 1968), p. 134.

integration should not precede political integration, and there was also disappointment that the EDC did not embrace the whole of Europe and particularly Britain.

On 5 June 1954, General de Gaulle, out of office since 1947 and waiting in his home at Colombey-les-Deux-Églises to rescue his country once again, gave one of his rare but influential press conferences. He bitterly attacked the EDC concept. De Gaulle was still a crucial influence on the party he had formed, and on a significant wider section of French opinion. Michel Debré, speaking in the National Assembly in 1953, voiced the Gaullist arguments against the EDC Treaty, which were to become the dominant theme of French foreign policy throughout the 1960s. 'It is necessary to tell all the theologians of little Europe point blank: Europe is not a nation; it is an aggregate of nations. Europe is not a state; it is a grouping of states. To create Europe, this reality must be taken into account.'* It was the French National Assembly which in effect rejected the EDC Treaty when it eventually came up for ratification on 30 August 1954. The rejection was of fundamental importance for it challenged both the assumption that institution-building was the only way to build European unity and, even more important, that there is no inherent difference between economics and defence policy-making.

After 1954 the advocates of European integration put foreign and defence policy to one side and concentrated on building the

*France, Conseils de la République, *Débats parlementaires*, 27 October 1953, pp. 1640–47.

institutional framework for trade within a common market. This they did with great single-mindedness but the dream of the institution builders like Jean Monnet remained. Monnet wrote in the winter of 1962–3: 'European unity is the most important event in the West since the war, not because it is a new great power, but because the institutional method it introduces is permanently modifying relations between nations and men.'[*] This institutional method, by then called the 'community method', was still being invoked by the Commission in 2001 as the only way to proceed into the future.[†]

Mistakes were made in the 1950s and 1960s but they were not mainly over Europe. France and the UK made a clandestine agreement with the Israelis in October 1956 whereby Israel would attack Egypt in Sinai, then British and French forces would come in posing as an independent intervention force to safeguard the Suez Canal. This was international deceit on a grand scale and denounced by the then US President, Dwight Eisenhower. Many of my generation felt ashamed that Britain and France broke the UN Charter so irresponsibly and let the Soviet Union days later escape world censure over its invasion of Hungary. The consequences of the Franco-British military debacle over the Suez Canal intervention and the lessons of military overstretch were only fully learnt when the UK

[*]Jean Monnet, 'A Ferment of Change', *Journal of Common Market Studies*, vol. 1, no. 3 (1963), pp. 204, 211.
[†]Commission of the European Communities, *European Governance: A White Paper*, COM(2001) 428 Final, 25 July 2001.

withdrew from military bases east of Suez following the devaluation of 1967.

In the aftermath of the failed Suez invasion there were choices to be made. The French from their point of view chose wisely to put their weight behind the newly established European Community. The British, from the point of view of a Europe still facing Soviet communism, wisely chose to repair their relationship with the United States of America. The French saw the European Community as the means of challenging what they called the hegemonic powers of America. The British strove to balance the commitment to the Anglo-American relationship epitomised by NATO with their application for membership of the European Community. The brick wall was not just de Gaulle but the relationship between France and Britain. Stacked with history and full of ambivalence it continues to this day to reflect different European and world perceptions and priorities. Germany was bent on securing its partnership with France. Britain, by 1973, was focused on the European Community and on strengthening Europe–US relations. The policy has had its ups and its downs. Its biggest up was the first Iraq War of 1991. Its greatest down was the second Iraq War of 2003 to 2010.

Chapter 2

The UK and the Common Market

The Treaty of Rome, which established the Common Market, was signed in 1957 and became operative for the six original countries on 1 January 1958. Britain watched its early years of development with growing interest and some concern that our manufacturers were going to face increasing difficulty in jumping the Common Market's trade barriers for our goods. The main arguments, by 1961, for joining the Common Market were increasingly presented in the UK in trading and economic terms. The Europe of the Six was slowly becoming our natural trading partner, whereas neither the Commonwealth nor the European Free Trade Association (EFTA),* in which we were trading partners, seemed to offer a sufficiently large market.

In 1956, as a young natural scientist at Cambridge University, immersed in the anatomy of the body, I was becoming fascinated by reading the history of science and much struck by how much

*The original EFTA countries were Austria, Denmark, Norway, Portugal, Sweden, Switzerland and the United Kingdom.

time William Harvey, our greatest anatomist, spent studying and lecturing at Padua University in Italy at the start of the seventeenth century. It was not just science but art, architecture, poetry, literature, music and philosophy which began to show me their deep roots in European culture. I travelled extensively around Europe as a student, particularly to Greece, France, West and East Germany and Czechoslovakia. I loved the diversity and depth of the different cultures. I was enchanted by the identification of individuals in Europe with their village, town or city, and in most cases, their nation too. All of this seemed to come together under the term 'European'. Living in the West Country and sailing in and out of little French ports in Brittany, I was well aware that the fishermen had had centuries of special fishing arrangements in each other's territorial waters. Rivalries and jealousies existed of course, but even though we had been fighting each other in ships of war for centuries, there were shared bonds of seamanship, deepened by sheltering in each other's harbours and from time to time rescuing each other in bad weather.

I was then, and still am today, proud to call myself a European. I am not a Eurosceptic in the way this term has been used for people hostile to Europe. But mine is a cultural identification. I never felt in the 1960s or now, that Europe was or would ever become my country. Europeans are friends and neighbours with whom I feel we have much in common, but they are not, for me at least, my fellow citizens. The British, as an island race, were never going to find it easy to join what was then called continental Europe.

In late 1959, the Prime Minister, Harold Macmillan, was becoming convinced that it would be essential to join the Common Market if Britain was to prosper economically. How desperate Macmillan, whose trademark was his *sang-froid*, became was revealed by a diary entry on 23 December 1960 contemplating the start of the new year: 'The problems which now confront Britain, internally and externally, are really terrifying. No-one seems to realise their complexity.' By 1961 Macmillan was persuaded that our best financial hope lay in membership of the Common Market and he was ready to signify his intention to join. The overall mood of the country was then more resigned than hostile. It was to his credit that he was also able to persuade his own Conservative Party of the case for entry and that he allowed the European enthusiasm of some of his younger ministers, such as Edward Heath, to flourish. Yet I did not feel that Macmillan was the man to persuade Britain into the Common Market. In the middle of July 1962, in what the press called the 'Night of the Long Knives', he sacked his Chancellor of the Exchequer, over differences on economic policy, and many other prominent members of the Cabinet too. This prompted the Liberal MP Jeremy Thorpe to make the often quoted witticism 'Greater love hath no man than this, that he lay down his friends for his life'.

The mood of my generation in the early 1960s was anti-'establishment', a term made famous by a journalist, Henry Fairlie. We had earlier laughed at the depiction of Macmillan when cartooned by Vicky as 'Supermac' in the late 1950s. But by 1961, in the satirical show 'Beyond the Fringe', Supermac had become a figure of the past and, more seriously for the Conservatives, a symbol of Britain's economic decline. The politically aware, left or right, fumed or enjoyed the political satire in the TV programme *That Was the Week That Was*. They started to read *Private Eye*. A fashionable paperback, *The Stagnant Society* by Michael Shanks, sold 60,000 copies. A feeling that the country was in relative economic decline with a decaying infrastructure became fashionable, heightened on the left by an image of a decrepit Tory leadership, out of touch, related more to shooting on the grouse moors. Youthful imagination was more often gripped by the young American President John F. Kennedy, who, despite the debacle over invading Cuba at the Bay of Pigs early in his presidency, appeared energetic and forward looking. Kennedy then demonstrated considerable leadership skills over the thirteen days of the Cuban Missile Crisis in October 1962, when in the evocative phrase of Nikita Khrushchev, leader of the Soviet Union, 'the smell of burning hung in the air'. We now know there were Soviet nuclear warheads placed on missiles poised to fire into the US military base of Guantánamo in Cuba if the American air force, under General Curtis Le May, launched a pre-emptive strike, which initially Kennedy assumed he would authorise. We felt the world was unsafe.

It is impossible to overestimate, looking back over the last fifty or sixty years, how haunted my generation were, firstly by the events in Hungary in 1956 and the utter feeling of helplessness that, despite having NATO, our governments felt unable to do anything but watch the brutal suppression of this revolutionary flowering of freedom in eastern Europe, and secondly by the Cuban Missile Crisis, followed by the suppression in 1968 of Czechoslovakia by Soviet tanks. Freedom eventually triumphed in 1989 with the fall of the Berlin Wall. But it was a long Cold War.

Many of my generation across the political divide in Britain were, by the early 1960s, starting to look with favour on the ideal of greater European unity and saw that as involving the United Kingdom joining the Common Market. The Common Market was not seen by our generation as a way of ending Franco-German enmity, for that had been achieved through the European Coal and Steel Community and NATO. We saw the Common Market primarily as providing the means of giving Britain and Europe greater economic strength to confront the Soviet Union and prosper in the wider world. Also, we saw political cohesion in Europe as helping the United States through NATO to stretch and counter the Warsaw Pact's military might while eroding through détente the ideological basis of Soviet communism. That all this might lead to the break-up of the Soviet empire was a hoped-for, but not widely envisaged, outcome.

The British application to join the Common Market would never have been contemplated by the then Conservative Party, let alone steered through the Cabinet, had it not been for Harold Macmillan. After much wringing of hands and political hesitation, he put the full weight of his leadership behind joining. Interestingly, it was the young, intelligent and somewhat laid-back President of the Board of Trade, Reginald Maudling, later an expansionist Chancellor of the Exchequer, who was the only Cabinet minister to oppose entry into the Common Market. He strongly preferred that Britain should remain one of the seven EFTA countries and even publicly was warning: 'We should apply to accede only on the basis that we want some amendments of the basic principles and objectives to meet our special requirements.' Meanwhile Macmillan, not just one of our best actor Prime Ministers, but also a successful publisher, on 9 July 1961 was again writing pure gloom in his diary, clearly not as confident of his choice as his general demeanour pretended: 'Shall we be caught between a hostile (or at least less and less friendly) America and a boastful, powerful "Empire of Charlemagne" – now under French but later bound to come under German control? Is this the real reason for joining the Common Market (if we are acceptable) and for abandoning (a) the [EFTA] Seven (b) British agriculture (c) the Commonwealth? It's a grim choice.'*

On 27 July 1961, the Cabinet formally applied to accede to the Treaty of Rome as a prelude to detailed negotiations. On 16 September, Macmillan minuted his private secretary: 'I do not think Sir Frank Roberts [then our permanent representative to NATO] realises that we are a country to whom nothing else

*Harold Macmillan, *The Macmillan Diaries, vol. 2: Prime Minister and After*, ed. Peter Catterall (London: Macmillan, 2011), p. 256.

matters except our export trade.' Most of the Cabinet believed that exclusion from the customs union of the Common Market would place British industry under a progressive disadvantage and it was the trade argument which was so crucial for their decision to apply to join. That argument remains one of the main motives of Conservative-leaning business people's commitment to the EU.

It is hard to recapture the economic gloom present in the early 1960s within Britain. The economy was suffering that combination of inflation and stagnation soon to become known as 'stagflation'. It was the British disease and the abiding feeling was that the failure of the economy for many years past was the key factor in dragging us down. It was in this mood, almost of defeatism, that Macmillan's official biographer concluded that beyond all pragmatic considerations, 'Macmillan felt that full entry into Europe would provide a great psychological boost to the British people, and would have an energising impulse – impossible to quantify – on the economy which was already once again looking sickly.'*

The summer of 1962 was the first time that I, and indeed most people in Britain, felt the need to decide as to whether we should join the Common Market. I had just qualified as a doctor of medicine and had no serious intention of becoming a politician. I accepted an invitation to be nominated for selection as the prospective Labour parliamentary candidate for the

*Alistair Horne, *Macmillan, vol. II: 1957–1986* (London: Macmillan, 1989), p. 256.

Torrington constituency in north Devon but was very surprised to be adopted for this unwinnable seat. In August at the age of twenty-four, I found myself pitched into the increasingly passionate political debate about Europe which was opening up prior to the annual party conferences. I welcomed that debate and it has continued throughout my political career.

My knowledge of politics at the time was minimal. I just managed to find time at St Thomas' Hospital to read the *Guardian*, the *Observer* on Sundays and the weekly *New Statesman*. On Europe, the biggest issue facing the country, I was totally unaware of all the complexity of the trade issues which would be central to the negotiations on joining the Common Market. The Prime Minister, speaking in the House of Commons in 1961 about the political fears that were being expressed if we joined the Common Market, had clearly stated his preference for a confederalist rather than a federalist Europe, and that seemed sensible to me, though I had little knowledge then of the powerful federalist passions of the founding fathers of the Common Market and I was not really sure what a confederation meant.

It was against this background that I began to visit and campaign in the Torrington constituency. It was in Torrington that I discovered why Hugh Gaitskell, the Labour leader, had felt able to talk openly of his love for the Labour Party.* It is hard

*Opposing the resolution on unilateral nuclear disarmament at the 1960 Labour Party conference in Scarborough, Gaitskell said: 'There are some of us, Mr Chairman, who will fight and fight and fight again to save the party we love.' The resolution was passed but was defeated in 1961.

today with so many people taking a cynical view of politics and the role of political parties to understand such an emotional attachment. Yet I found that most party workers were trying to create a more generous, fair and just society. There was little envy or malice in their aspirations; they knew that the more equitable society they wanted would evolve not out of confiscation but from persuasion. Many were Methodists and saw their political activity as an extension of their chapelgoing, but they were also interested in the wider world, giving generously to overseas poverty projects and often travelling to the cheaper holiday resorts in Spain and Portugal.

At that time, in 1962, I was more than content to follow Hugh Gaitskell's lead on Europe. I had joined the Labour Party to support him as a student after voting for the first time for Labour in the general election of 1959. I admired his brave, though some thought foolhardy, attempt after defeat to rid the Labour Party of Clause IV: a part of its constitution by which it was committed to the nationalisation of private industry. Gaitskell wanted in 1960 to make it clear to the country that Labour did not aim to nationalise every private firm or to create an endless series of state monopolies. The clause was eventually rewritten, to Tony Blair's credit and the Labour Party's electoral advantage, in 1995. I also supported Gaitskell's courageous resistance to unilateral nuclear disarmament. So when I heard his cautious approach to the Common Market on TV in May 1962 it seemed fair enough to me. 'To go in on good terms would, I believe, be the best solution,' he said. But could we obtain good terms? The terms of entry began to be for Labour, then and again in the early 1970s under Harold Wilson, the defining issue, at least in opposition. At the time the public did not know that when Harold Macmillan had met President de Gaulle in the Château de Champs in June 1962, de Gaulle had very explicitly repeated his preference for a Six without Britain. But there were warning signs of a lack of enthusiasm coming in the political air and I sensed we were not going to join before the next general election.

In my first public speech as a prospective candidate in the summer of 1962 I said the Common Market would be irrevocable and not something one joined and got out of, nor was it just economic, but fundamentally political with its motives including some form of federation or supranational authority. Much to my regret I never met Hugh Gaitskell and I had no idea at the time of his inner thinking. His official biographer, Philip Williams,* believes Gaitskell finally decided on his course of opposing European federalism and linking this to joining the Common Market between mid-July and mid-September 1962, heavily influenced by clashes with the powerful Dutch socialist and federalist Paul Henri Spaak, and reflecting the content of another earlier meeting in April with Jean Monnet. Both had a strong federalist vision and disliked Gaitskell stressing that nobody in Britain was advocating moves to early federation and his refusal to go further than the exact wording of the Treaty of Rome.

*Philip M. Williams, *Hugh Gaitskell: A Political Biography* (London: Jonathan Cape, 1979), Chapter 25: 'The Common Market'.

I watched the evening TV on 21 September when Gaitskell replied to Harold Macmillan's broadcast the previous day. Asking rhetorically if Macmillan wanted to enter a European federation he warned that if so, 'it means the end of Britain as an independent nation; we become no more than "Texas" or "California" in the United States of Europe. It means the end of a thousand years of history; it means the end of the Commonwealth, to become just a province of Europe.' Gaitskell's warning against a United States of Europe then and his stress on the need for vigilance about it emerging by default has remained with me as a guiding principle ever since. It is easy to forget that the debate from 1961 to 1962 surrounding the Fouchet Plan amongst continental Europeans in the run-up to our own UK debate in summer 1962 made it perfectly valid for these concerns about the future of the Common Market to be championed domestically in our debate about joining. The view claimed by and large by supporters in the UK of joining was that the future was at most that of a European confederation of member states. The view claimed by those opposed outright to joining, was that it would lead to a federal United States of Europe. Those same echoes can be heard in the debate which will gather momentum in 2013 on how to limit the ever-greater integration within the EU.

I was too busy as a junior hospital doctor to attend the Labour Party conference in Brighton but I read Gaitskell's speech delivered on 8 October in the following day's newspapers with enthusiasm. I was, however, totally unaware of the effect it had on three people who would later be for some years my political friends and fellow founders of the SDP: Roy Jenkins, Shirley Williams and Bill Rodgers. At that stage in my life I had never met them. But I would have read Anthony Howard in the *New Statesman* a few days after Gaitskell's speech asking: 'Why did the Labour Party leader decide to go as far – sparing the feelings of none of his former associates in the process? . . . The proof of it was to be seen in the well-known faces which could be noticed primly sitting down on the ex-officio benches as the rest of the conference rose to give Hugh Gaitskell the greatest ovation of his career. Men like Jack Diamond and Bill Rodgers (Roy Jenkins had the sense to stand up and make a brave shot at making the best of it) certainly looked angry but they also looked beaten and betrayed.'

They believed that many of the 'ifs' in Gaitskell's speech were not negotiable. 'If we carry the Commonwealth with us, safeguarded, flourishing, prosperous, if we could safeguard our agriculture, and our EFTA friends were all in it, if we were secure in our employment policy, and if we were able to maintain our independent foreign policy yet have this wider looser association with Europe, it would indeed be a great ideal. But if this should not prove to be possible, if the Six will not give it to us, if the British government will not even ask for it, then we must stand firm by what we believe.'

The parts of the speech which I somewhat childishly relished were his rubbishing of my political opponent, the Liberal prospective candidate in Torrington, Mark Bonham Carter, who had held the seat for a short time after a by-election only to lose in the 1959 general election. He was a Liberal Party spokesman on foreign affairs. When Gaitskell singled him out he must have known he was a close friend of Roy Jenkins, also a friend of Gaitskell. Recalling that at the Liberal Party conference the idea of Britain going into a European federation was greeted with wild enthusiasm by all the delegates, Gaitskell said ironically: 'They are a little young, I think. I am all for youth but I like it to be sensible as well. After the conference a desperate attempt was made by Mr Bonham Carter to show that, of course, they were not committed to federation at all. Well, I prefer to go by what Mr Grimond says.' Gaitskell then quoted Jo Grimond, the then Liberal leader, that if you are going to 'control the running of Europe democratically, you've got to move towards some form of federalism and if anyone says different to that they are really misleading the public'. Then Gaitskell exclaimed: 'That is one in the eye to Mr Bonham Carter.' That passage provided me in Torrington with good political badinage but like so much of that type of political attack it is of more interest to politicians and their activists than to the general public. It left me, however, with an abiding political legacy, namely that I would never support the Liberal Party's attitudes to European federalism and integration. Twenty years later, in 1982, I was adamant the SDP should not espouse European federalism and insisted on remaining as the SDP spokesman on foreign affairs when Roy Jenkins, who had just beaten me for the leadership, wanted me to step down and become his deputy. Otherwise it would have left the way open for David Steel to become the foreign affairs spokesman for the SDP–Liberal Alliance in the 1983 election. It also meant that in 1987, I felt I had no choice but to decline to join a merged Liberal and Social Democratic Party. Even if I had been chosen as their leader, I would not have been able to prevent them espousing European integration, as they still do in 2012.

In 1962 the Liberal leader, Jo Grimond, a cavalier and engaging politician amongst post-war party leaders, was always open about what federalism eventually required – a European President, elected directly or indirectly by the European Parliament, and a European Cabinet or Commission to make the key decisions in economic, foreign and defence policy. The Cabinet or Commission would be controlled primarily by the European Parliament and also now by the European Council, forming a second chamber of the directly elected European Parliament. This was something very close to what Angela Merkel proposed in 2012 (see Chapter 10).

Harold Macmillan, at his own party conference in 1962, felt confident enough to tease Gaitskell, depicting him as a poor creature, without any real breadth of view or sense of values, with an old song: 'She didn't say yes, she didn't say no, | She didn't say stay, she didn't say go, | She wanted to climb, but she dreaded to fall | So she bided her time and clung to the wall.'*

The truth is that Gaitskell has been largely proven correct and

*Alistair Horne, *Macmillan, vol. II: 1957–1986* (London: Macmillan, 1989), p. 334.

Macmillan and those Prime Ministers who largely shared his views wrong. It says much for Macmillan's political skills within his own party that by 11 October 1962 an anti-Common Market amendment at the Conservative Party conference was defeated by 4,000 votes to 50. So enthusiastic were the Conservatives that even Edward Heath, their negotiator, feared that it might give the six countries already in the Common Market the impression that the UK would join at any price and thereby weaken his negotiating position.

On 15 December 1962, Macmillan travelled to Rambouillet for another meeting with General de Gaulle. This meeting was disastrous. Macmillan's official biographer describes how de Gaulle became increasingly discouraging about the British application to join the Six* and Macmillan recorded that 'our talk became something of a wrangle. This is very unusual in our relationship.' Reverting, 'rather ungraciously', to the difficulties at Brussels, de Gaulle declared that within the Six 'France could say "no" against even the Germans; she could stop policies with which she disagreed, because of the strength of her position. Once Britain and all the rest joined the organisation things would be different.' Realising that the chips were down, Macmillan let his anger take control and said with indignation that what de Gaulle had now put forward 'was a fundamental objection in principle to Britain's application. If that was really the French view, it ought to have been made clear at the start. It

Ibid., p. 431.

was not fair to have a year's negotiation and then bring forward an objection of principle. De Gaulle seemed rather shaken,' he added. Concealing his disillusionment with de Gaulle, Macmillan pretended on his return that our application was still on the rails.

De Gaulle, however, was far from shaken; his political party had won an absolute majority in the November elections and he felt free to reject Britain's application regardless of the other five countries. On 14 January 1963, he held a press conference at the Élysée Palace and made public what he had expressed in private at Rambouillet. He spoke from a long-considered view of the British nation. Over the decades what runs through his speeches and his writing was a continuous strand of ambivalence about England, hovering between outright admiration and scarcely concealed animosity. De Gaulle knew France had to have one big nation as a partner within the European Community without which it would not be strong enough economically. For that all-important partnership he chose Germany because he believed that France could henceforth always remain Germany's equal and on foreign policy he assumed France would always be in the driving seat. That judgement, upheld by successive French Presidents, has been challenged in major ways ever since the fall of the Berlin Wall.

The German Chancellor, Konrad Adenauer, who was musing about Britain being only an associate member of the Community, was more than ready to go only with France's decisions. To demonstrate that, he had signed the Franco-

German Treaty of Co-operation and Friendship at the very moment of de Gaulle's veto.

There was much truth in de Gaulle's brutal dismissal of Britain's application when he said: 'Britain is insular, maritime, bound up by her trade, her markets, her food supplies, with the most varied and often the most distant countries. Her activity is essentially industrial and commercial, not agricultural. She has in all her work very special, very original habits and traditions. In short, the nature, structure, circumstances peculiar to England are very different from those of the other continentals. How can Britain, in the way that she lives, produces, trades, be incorporated in the Common Market as it has been conceived and as it functions?' Fifty years later there are still recognisable characteristics from his description. But de Gaulle always saw Britain from Paris even when he was living during the war in London. As a supreme nationalist he was still striving in the 1960s to redeem France from the ignominy of Marshal Pétain's decision to surrender to the Nazis.

A glimpse of the complexity and the driving forces behind de Gaulle as a leader of France is evident from a vignette of the time. Paul Reynaud, a former Prime Minister and President of France, wrote critically about the French veto of Britain's application in *Le Monde* on 24 January 1963. 'France isolated, the Entente Cordiale ridiculed, disorder in the Atlantic Alliance, the irritation, if not the enmity of the United States towards us, when it is their presence in Europe that guarantees our liberty, the Common Market, the motive force of our expansion, threatened with splits. And why?' Two weeks later Reynaud received a letter and the address on the envelope he recognised as being handwritten by de Gaulle. Inside there was absolutely nothing but on the back of the envelope was written dramatically: 'If absent, forward to Agincourt or Waterloo.' When de Gaulle was asked to address both Houses of Parliament as President he insisted that the ceremony should be in Westminster Hall, refusing to speak in the Queen's Gallery flanked by large paintings of the Battle of Trafalgar and the Battle of Waterloo.

Harold Macmillan spoke to President Kennedy by telephone five days after the French veto. 'President de Gaulle', Macmillan said, 'is crazy. He's simply inventing any means whatever to knock us out and the real simple thing is he wants to be the cock on a small dunghill instead of having two cocks on a larger one.' Macmillan by then had reason to be grateful to Kennedy for salvaging his political reputation in the UK by agreeing earlier at their meeting in Nassau on 19 December to sell US Polaris submarine missiles to replace the US airborne missile Skybolt, which Kennedy had cancelled days before (see Chapter 7). The British ambassador, David Ormsby-Gore, a personal friend of Kennedy's, had on the flight from Washington persuaded the President to reoffer Skybolt as a 50:50 development partnership, unbeknown to Macmillan, but Macmillan would have none of it, remarking that 'while the proposed marriage with Skybolt was not exactly a shotgun wedding, the virginity of the lady must now be regarded as doubtful'; in fact, 'the girl had been violated in a public place'. As his biographer put it, this was just the style of raffish Edwardian wit that particularly struck a chord with Kennedy's own sense of humour.* Macmillan had also given the Americans his experience of fighting in the First World War and the immense human sacrifices in a way designed to appeal to Kennedy, the author of *Profiles in Courage*. Whether or not Britain continued with US nuclear missiles was irrelevant to de Gaulle's decision despite much that has been written about Nassau confirming Britain as being an American Trojan horse in French eyes. Well before Macmillan's meeting with Kennedy in the Bahamas the die had been cast in de Gaulle's mind and no amount of juggling on Anglo-French collaboration over Polaris nuclear missiles or the US advocacy of a dubiously designed multilateral force would have made any difference. President de Gaulle simply had no intention, on grounds of French national interest, of allowing Britain's application to proceed and indeed had told the Council of Ministers on 19 December about his earlier private rejection of Macmillan's pleas. 'I couldn't give the poor man anything and he looked so sad, so downcast, that I wanted to put my hand on his shoulder and say, as Edith Piaf does in her song, *"Ne pleurez pas, milord"*!'

It was left to Edward Heath, who had been Britain's chief negotiator over Europe, to say: 'We in Britain are not going to turn our backs on the mainland of Europe or the countries of the Community.' Harold Macmillan in his diary on 28 January,

*Alistair Horne, *Macmillan, vol. II: 1957–1986* (London: Macmillan, 1989), p. 438.
†Jean Lacouture, *De Gaulle 3: Le Souverain* (Paris: France Loisirs, 1987), p. 357.

after the veto noted: 'All our policies at home and abroad are in ruins. Our defence plans have been radically changed from air to sea. European unity is no more; French domination of Europe is the new and alarming feature; our popularity as a Government is rapidly declining. We have lost everything, except our courage and determination.'

On 14 February 1963, Harold Wilson was elected leader of the Labour Party, Gaitskell having tragically died at the peak of his political power on 18 January. Wilson went to Washington in March 1963 as leader of the opposition intent on impressing President Kennedy, who, in different ways, had enjoyed knowing both Macmillan and Gaitskell. On negotiations with de Gaulle, Wilson told Kennedy: 'We shouldn't do too much appeasing, we should recognise that we had some very strong cards in our hand; while we shouldn't play them, we should at any rate start brandishing them.' On 18 October 1963, Macmillan retired on medical grounds and was succeeded by Sir Alec Douglas-Home, who gave up his hereditary title. On being derided by Wilson as the 14th Earl of Home, he smiled and said one could equally describe the Labour leader as the 14th Mr Wilson.

The 1964 general election was not focused on Europe. In Torrington, the Devon dairy farmers were very hostile to another attempt to join the Six and the Conservative MP for the constituency, himself a farmer, was adamantly against the Common Agricultural Policy. Mark Bonham Carter's Liberal enthusiasm for the Common Market began to wilt. I was comfortable with Labour's policy on the Common Market under Harold Wilson. If anything I became cautiously the most open minded of the three candidates about the Common Market, content to wait while confident that we would most likely eventually join. It was Douglas-Home's laid-back style which won back support for the Conservatives, not much harmed by likening his approach to economics as 'counting matchsticks'. The Conservatives, surprisingly, ran Labour very close in 1964. Nevertheless Labour, after thirteen years out of government, was back in power but without a working majority. This they won in 1966.

Harold Wilson and Edward Heath, as respectively leaders of the Labour and Conservative parties, dominated British politics for the next twelve years. As Prime Ministers and leaders of the opposition from 1964 to 1976, they also developed a barely disguised contempt for each other, the origin of which lay in the European issue. Yet they share the responsibility, the credit or the odium, though in very different ways, for Britain eventually joining the European Community. Their mutual animosity was on display following de Gaulle's announcement that France would withdraw from the integrated command structure of NATO at a Western European Union meeting held in London during the 1966 general election. A French representative had used delphic words about France moving towards supporting an enlarged European Community and his speech was welcomed by Heath, then in opposition. Wilson infuriated Heath in a speech in Bristol by saying of him: 'One encouraging gesture from the

French government and he rolls on his back like a spaniel,' to which Heath replied: 'Lies, stooping to abuse, revolting, poisonous lies, deplorable, personal hostility, nauseating, filthy insinuation – absolutely filthy. God it's a filthy speech.' Political emotions over Europe in Britain have run high ever since.

I personally became aware of the strength of the integrationist movement when I became a member of Parliament in 1966. I had accepted the post of parliamentary private secretary to Gerry Reynolds, a minister of defence. What I did not know was he had been for years an openly avowed federalist. Through Reynolds, I joined the House of Commons 1963 Club, dedicated to Gaitskell's memory. But I did not realise either that the majority of its members did not remotely share Gaitskell's fear of Britain becoming a mere province in Europe. It took me ten years in Parliament to start personally to set very definite and detailed limits to the supranational element within the European Community when in September 1976 I became, in effect, minister for Europe as deputy to the then Foreign Secretary, Anthony Crosland. Those limits had, to some extent, already been set out by de Gaulle, using the 'empty chair'.

In 1965, French ministers, under de Gaulle, had refused to attend Council meetings, and forced on the Community the Luxembourg Compromise, never formally part of the treaties, but which established the right to uphold an informal veto if a vital national interest was imperilled. The wise European Commissioners under the Luxembourg Compromise henceforth began to consult with governments where they knew vital interests might be involved before adopting any important proposal. In this way, while retaining the Commission's right of initiative within the treaties, they kept the balance within the treaty language. As a matter of practice, if any member state felt its vital interests to be at stake even on issues that had hitherto been governed by majority voting, such commissioners would continue discussion until unanimity had been achieved or would drop the proposal altogether. When de Gaulle resigned, gradually the member states allowed the concept behind the compromise to wane. The Luxembourg Compromise was last used by Germany with French connivance in 1985 over cereal prices. It became fashionable to claim that the compromise has since lapsed because it has no treaty basis. But in 1992, when President Mitterrand was having to obtain the agreement of the French Assembly to the Maastricht Treaty and was rightly concerned about his chance of winning the referendum, which he eventually won only by the narrowest of margins, a specific statement was made by Prime Minister Bérégovoy that the Luxembourg Compromise still stood as the ultimate safeguard of French sovereignty.*

After the 1966 election Harold Wilson, with a massive majority of Labour MPs, of which I was but one, began to probe the terms that could be acceptable for both the UK and the Six. To his credit Edward Heath gave him full support as leader of the opposition. George Brown had been moved from Secretary

*Prime Minister Bérégovoy speaking in the French National Assembly, May 1992.

of State for Economic Affairs to become Foreign Secretary after the collapse of economic growth and with it the National Plan in July 1966. Brown had long been convinced that Britain's destiny lay in the European Community and had been shattered as Gaitskell's deputy by his speech to the Labour Party conference in 1962, although, summing up that same debate with some dignity, he had managed to leave the pro-Europeans in the Labour Party believing that their time would come.

It is fair to say that most of the political debate in the UK in the run-up to the 1967 application took the confederal structure of the Common Market as the acceptable reality. There was little evocation of Gaitskell's stance, if for no other reason than most believed that de Gaulle had fought and won the battle over federalism. Little did we understand then that the price of maintaining the structure of a community of self-governing states was eternal vigilance and that the community method was already eroding the frontiers of the state and was not recognising any limits.

Wilson and Brown made exploratory visits in 1967 to the European capitals but somehow it never looked very serious. While the US President, Lyndon Johnson, was telling Wilson in November that 'your entry would certainly help to strengthen and unify the West', de Gaulle was saying: 'The Common Market is incompatible with Great Britain's economy as it stands [and] with the state of sterling, as once again highlighted by the devaluation.' Eventually de Gaulle vetoed this second application on 27 November 1967. It was felt that the British had embarked on an ill-judged diplomatic venture and de Gaulle's renewed veto caused little sense of shock or surprise on the Continent. Even in the UK it seemed inevitable. If Wilson's initiative had any benefit it was in preparing opinion inside the Labour Party for the referendum on staying in the Community in 1975, rather as Macmillan's initiative in 1962 had prepared the Conservative Party for entry under Edward Heath in 1973.

In the May 1967 debate in the House of Commons Heath, in opposition, as always sensitive to the integrationists' mood in Brussels, put up an interesting marker for his future attitudes by saying: 'There can be no doubt that the logical conclusion in a complete market is to move over *de facto* or *de jure* to a common currency.' After the debate 260 Labour MPs, including myself, voted to join and only 35 voted against. The question of the pound as a reserve currency was, however, just starting to become an issue for any future negotiations for entry. When Heath won the general election in 1970 few people had any doubt that European unity was going to be the leitmotiv of his Prime Ministership and so it proved to be.

If Harold Wilson had won the 1970 election, as he fully expected to do, and had he negotiated on the White Paper which his government had prepared on the terms of entering, he would have negotiated in earnest to succeed. In government Wilson, however, would have given every bit as much ground in the negotiations as Heath and possibly, after much posturing, even more. Wilson's one constant characteristic, watching him over the years, was how he saw opposition and government as two quite different challenges for a political leader. In opposition he saw the Labour Party as fragile and fractious with its loyalties weak. Keeping it together was an absolute priority. In government the party, he sensed, enjoyed being in power and he felt he could be, and often was, a robust leader. He felt able to strain its loyalties over US policy towards Vietnam and over trade union reform with the White Paper *In Place of Strife* in 1968. He was depicted as being weak by the Conservatives over the trade unions but he backed Barbara Castle's reforms to the point at which they were both all but disowned by his entire Cabinet including Roy Jenkins. Wilson, who once talked of Britain's frontiers being on the Himalayas, was an internationalist. He passionately opposed apartheid in South Africa; even on the Commonwealth he was emotional but on the argument that signing the Treaty of Rome meant losing sovereignty he was his usual pragmatic self. He revealed this before he even became leader when speaking in a debate in Parliament on 3 August 1961 over possible entry, saying: 'The whole history of political progress is a history of gradual abandonment of national sovereignty.'* That was not the language of a person who would ever be likely to come out in principle against entry. For Wilson it was the negotiation which mattered and making the terms the issue was to provide him with a public position to hold the Labour Party together from 1970 to 1974 in opposition. In government again his personal

*Philip Ziegler, *Wilson: The Authorised Life of Lord Wilson of Rievaulx* (London: Weidenfeld & Nicolson, 1993), p. 131

support with Jim Callaghan as Foreign Secretary in the 1975 referendum for continued British membership of the European Community was the crucial factor and the renegotiated terms were peripheral, but neither man ever accepted an integrationist agenda and they were very careful at all times to protect the self-governing nature of the UK.

Harold Wilson retired as Prime Minister in 1976 having won three elections. Despite having much talent he had very little of real substance in his record to match his rhetoric about forging a modern Britain but at least he settled the question of British membership of the Community for forty years, maybe more. Historians will judge that he achieved the full-hearted consent for Europe from the British people that had eluded Edward Heath. Heath, however, had had the nerve to force entry into the Community through a very reluctant Parliament but Wilson in the referendum campaign in 1975 invited the electorate to vote to retain the status quo of continued membership. He thereby justified his opportunistic support for a referendum in 1972 to help maintain the unity of the Labour Party, a unity that was lost in the 1980s, but regained with great enthusiasm from 1990 until 2010.

Chapter 3

Entering and living within the European Community

Edward Heath's victory in 1970 came as a shock to most people. The opinion polls had predicted a 12 per cent lead for Labour and the bookmakers at one stage even had Labour 20:1 on to win. So confident were we of victory the week before polling day that at a late dinner at my home in Plymouth with Roy Jenkins, then still Chancellor of the Exchequer, and Peter Jenkins (no relation), a perceptive columnist then writing on the *Guardian*, the sole topic of conversation was what jobs Roy and I expected to have in the next Labour government. Roy said that following talks with Harold Wilson he would be Foreign Secretary. He had told Wilson that he would only take the job if he, Wilson, was fully committed to Britain entering the EEC. 'Not just committed, dedicated' came Wilson's reply and he was apparently dismissive of any difficulty over the terms in the negotiations. Roy also said that immediately he got into the Foreign Office he would break what he described as Labour's absurd, almost craven, silence over Vietnam. He planned to openly criticise the Americans while at the same time moving fast towards Europe. This was a revealing choice of priorities.

The Europe-first aspect was one that was soon to be pursued by Edward Heath as incoming Prime Minister. Of all the post-war governments, except that of Sir Anthony Eden after Suez, Heath's had the coolest relations with Washington. I personally had no belief in the Vietnam policies of Lyndon Johnson or Richard Nixon and had quietly admired how Wilson had kept his distance without creating too much damage. It did not win us friends in Washington, particularly with Wilson's rather eccentric attempts at mediation. There were no gains, however, for Britain in gratuitously condemning the American position and neither Sir Alec Douglas-Home, Harold Wilson or Edward Heath adopted that option. They were all content to follow the path of supporting the American case that the war was a defence against communist aggression and not to dissociate Britain from the US, as France had done by then. The French, however, were nursing their own wounds after their defeat at Dien Bien Phu.

In Parliament it was obvious that entering the European Community was the new government's dominant priority. The speech made by Anthony Barber, its chosen negotiator, before he succeeded Iain Macleod as Chancellor, was little different, stressing the difficulties and the opportunities, from that prepared within Whitehall for George Thomson, Labour's negotiator, to deliver. Public opinion, however, was still against entry with only 22 per cent positively in favour. As a West Country MP with a fishing port in my constituency the atmosphere for the negotiations had been set by a disgraceful sleight of hand from the original Six. In June 1970, when the UK, Ireland, Denmark and Norway were literally just about to apply, the European Commission had agreed in principle that all fish in western European waters should become 'a common European resource'. This had but one purpose, to prise out of the new applicants 90 per cent of the fish which lay in their waters. The Commission's statement had no authority from the treaties but it was assumed in Brussels that this Common Fisheries Policy (CFP) would now become part of the *acquis communautaire*, the body of existing EU law that all new applicants are expected to uphold. Britain should have disputed this vigorously immediately the action was taken and it would have had the full support of all the applicant countries and some of the existing members. Sadly, once again the softly-softly approach to negotiating favoured by the Foreign Office won the day. Europe was the loser, for it meant that Norway said 'No' in its referendum and still remains outside the EU. Norway, rich because of North Sea and Arctic oil and gas, is the most generous nation in terms of overseas aid. It is committed to the UN and NATO and, deeply democratic, a country that would strengthen the EU were it ever to become a member. There is little chance, however, its politicians will be able to convince a majority of its people to join while anything like the present CFP remains in place.

Conservative MPs with fishing ports in their constituencies were pressing hard early in 1971 for the government to live up to the reassurances it had given at the end of 1970 that the UK had 'reserved its position' and would 'take proper account of the interests' of the fishermen. By May Geoffrey Rippon, who was the government's new negotiator, was privately telling his own party's MPs that there was 'no question of accepting a *fait accompli*' on the fisheries policy. But it proved all a façade; Edward Heath had no intention of fighting the British fishermen's case and we entered without changing the CFP in any major regard.

The all-important political atmosphere, particularly in France, over considering the UK's application had been transformed by the new President of France, Georges Pompidou. Formerly a banker with Rothschild and General de Gaulle's special envoy to Algeria, and then Prime Minister, he had become French President after de Gaulle's resignation following his defeat in the 1969 referendum. This referendum de Gaulle had called somewhat quixotically on the relatively minor issue of regional government. Immediately President Pompidou put the 'empty chair' crisis behind France and did not fear the opposition of dissatisfied Gaullists.

At an EEC meeting in The Hague on 1–2 December 1969, the first after de Gaulle had stepped down, agreements were concluded on financing the CAP and to open enlargement negotiations to include the UK. The Werner Plan, the product of a committee sitting in 1969 and chaired by Pierre Werner, the Prime Minister of Luxembourg, on monetary union was published one year later. The feeling inside the Community of

Six was again more integrationist and the mood for major reform seemed back, with anything looking possible including a European currency. In London the Treasury made its first assessment of monetary union in 1971, telling ministers privately: 'It should be noted that this has revolutionary long term implications, both economic and political. It could imply the ultimate creation of a European federal state with a single currency.' The Treasury went on to say: 'There must be no mistake about the final objective. The process of change is irreversible and the implications, economic and political, must be accepted from the outset.' There was no attempt to hide from ministers that 'at the ultimate stage, economic sovereignty would to all intents and purposes disappear at national level and the Community would be master of overall economic policy' and the Treasury predicted that the economies of the members of EMU would be 'as interlocked as the states of the United States'. Little of this emerged in public, for the reason that Heath had one priority – to win over a hostile public, and he had no wish to frighten the voters with federalism, let alone a European currency. But Heath's action, while politically prudent, was based on not telling the full truth and eliding the facts. The British people never trusted him on Europe, and rightly so.

Edward Heath, who had been contemptuous of the Labour government's 1970 White Paper, because he believed it exaggerated the likely economic costs of membership, was never worried himself about the political implications of a single currency but he chose to be circumspect in public. At the time, according to reports from the British ambassador in Paris, he went as far as to warn Robert Schuman, France's Foreign Minister, 'of the importance which would be attached in Britain to the lines along which political unification was progressing. He did not imagine they were likely to proceed so fast or in such a way as to frighten the British.' At the time our man in Paris was Christopher Soames, the former Conservative Minister of Agriculture and Winston Churchill's son-in-law. Heath had persuaded him that he was of more use to his country staying as ambassador, which he had been appointed by George Brown, rather than returning to Parliament. Soames wrote to the head of the diplomatic service, Denis Greenhill, in April 1971, about the prospects for British entry and assessed, correctly as it turned out, that the decision maker was France and President Pompidou, saying: 'The French still do not expect any serious pressure from their partners. They believe that in the last resort the Germans will acquiesce in what they decide and that the Italians can be fixed. The Belgians they patronise and the Dutch they admire but disregard. So it comes down to an Anglo-French understanding.'

Heath believed that only he and Pompidou talking directly could settle the entry question and in May 1971 he travelled to Paris for a crucial two-day meeting at the Élysée. He had first met Pompidou in 1962; both were economic technocrats, having been bankers, as well as politicians and this helped them to settle one of the most difficult questions, namely Pompidou's concern about sterling as a reserve currency and his wish for equality of status for the currencies of the member states. Heath promised to reduce the UK's sterling balances and later agreed to 'an orderly and gradual rundown' and that he would maintain the existing rate of sterling. He also confirmed that as members of the enlarged Community the UK would play its full part in the progress towards EMU. So in 1971 for the first time a British Prime Minister committed the country in principle to joining a single currency. It was a commitment that was never whole-heartedly made again by any Prime Minister until in late 1997 Tony Blair accepted the principle of joining the single currency but decided to postpone calling a referendum, much to the dismay of Roy Jenkins and Edward Heath. Why Blair really pulled back we may never know. The simplest explanation, and one I favour, is that it was because he was not sure of winning after the very close referendum result on a Welsh Assembly despite putting his new personal authority behind the proposal. He was also worried that if entry into the euro backfired economically early in this first Parliament it could mean Labour only being a one-term government. From the start, he was determined to lead the first Labour government to serve out two full terms. Eventually, of course, Labour had three terms, remaining in power until 2010.

In Paris, in 1971, Pompidou stressed that what was needed was an historic change in the British attitude. In his auto-biography Heath describes Pompidou as regarding his own country and Britain as the only two countries with what he termed a 'world vocation' and saying quite explicitly that, if the political and intellectual prestige of Britain were added to those of the Six, the Community would be greatly enriched. For Edward Heath his own task was to convince Pompidou that this was also what we wanted to see. By the end it was Pompidou who said to a surprised press: 'Many people believed that Great Britain was not and did not wish to become European, and that Britain wanted to enter the Community only so as to destroy it or to divert it from its objectives. Many people also thought that France was ready to use every pretext to place in the end a fresh veto on Britain's entry. Well, ladies and gentlemen, you see before you tonight two men who are convinced of the contrary.'

Heath adopted from the start a geopolitical approach to entry. The UK faced a fundamental political choice in his view, and economic and trade questions had to be weighed in that balance of advantage. In the process of negotiation some of the detailed issues were swept aside and the terms Britain had to accept were not ideal. Summing up the negotiations one of our distinguished diplomats, Sir Oliver Wright, ambassador to West Germany from 1975 to 1981 and to the United States from 1982 to 1986, later wrote: 'Heath was so desperate to join the then Common Market that, as the official report of the negotiations reveals, his instructions to our chief negotiator were to "swallow it now".'

The most offensive detailed aspect of the negotiations to British interests still remained, the ill-judged CFP. Edward Heath was determined to sign the Treaty of Accession in January 1972 and so enter after ratification by all nine member states on 1 January 1973. He wrote to the Norwegian Prime Minister to try to persuade him to accept at least the principle of Brussels control over all fishing waters in return for an assurance from the Commission that Norway would be given an 'unlimited period of transition'. For Heath the British fishermen, numbering some 20,000 at the time, and their industry were something that had to be sacrificed and he accepted a face-saving derogation for ten years which allowed our fishermen exclusive rights for the first 6 miles and more limited rights out to 12 miles. When Geoffrey Rippon came to defend this in the House of Commons he claimed falsely that we retained full jurisdiction out to the 12-mile limit. Con O'Neill, the senior civil servant in charge of the negotiations, knew that this was untrue and had already minuted that allowing the rest of the Community to have access endangered our industry, which was then the largest in Europe, and that we risked the same overfishing that had destroyed the fishing waters off France, Belgium and the Netherlands. O'Neill's prediction that the cost would be 'borne almost entirely by the home industry, purely to the benefit of foreign fleets' was correct in all its particulars. It left a legacy of distrust behind with fishermen and their MPs about the ways of Whitehall and the duplicity of ministers. But in this case officials in the Foreign and Commonwealth Office had given their political masters the truth and it was the politicians who misled Parliament. It was the issue of fishing that defeated the Norwegian Labour government in its referendum and the hostility of the Norwegians was palpable when at the request of their government I went over to speak for the 'Yes' campaign.

New Zealand butter and cheese were very sensitive issues in the House of Commons but here President Pompidou promised Heath he would be helpful. Understanding our emotional ties and that a small country like New Zealand had much less scope to adjust than, say, Australia or Canada, the French did soften their negotiating position on New Zealand butter. On fish the French had good grounds for believing they could manipulate the system in their favour and so they were adamant against any concessions. The French were correct in their assumptions and ever since France has done well out of the CFP.

The most difficult question in the negotiations was to estimate how much the UK would be paying into the Community Budget, how much we would get back and the all-important balance. Some in the Treasury feared the imbalance would be unsustainable and so it proved. At least Britain won a let-out clause in the negotiations stating that if unacceptable situations should arise 'the very survival of the Community would demand that the institutions find equitable solutions'. This was used by Harold Wilson in his somewhat limited renegotiations in 1975 and again more importantly in the negotiations over the refund begun under James Callaghan in 1978 and brought to a successful conclusion by Margaret Thatcher as Prime Minister in 1984.

By the spring of 1971 the Heath government had become unpopular. As economic growth fell, high unemployment figures began to build up along with unrestrained price rises. The government refused at this time to intervene to help industry and the famous U-turn on industrial policy was only to come a year later. The government also began to face a serious revolt amongst some of its own MPs on entry to the European Community. It began to appear credible that even with the support of the Liberal Party it would not be able to carry the House of Commons for the principle of entry and, embarrassingly for me, it became ever clearer that the votes of some of us on the Labour benches who supported entry might be needed if the British application was not to be rejected by Parliament.

Three personalities in Parliament began to shape opinion against Europe: Enoch Powell, Michael Foot and Tony Benn. The most interesting and intellectually compelling was Enoch Powell. As a member of Harold Macmillan's government he had supported the application to join the Common Market. Later as a member of Heath's shadow Cabinet, when asked on the BBC programme *Any Questions* on 18 March 1966 about the pros and cons of entry, he said: 'There aren't any cons, provided we can get ourselves into the Common Market.' It was not, however, until Heath sacked Powell from the Shadow Cabinet after his 'river of blood' speech on immigration in Birmingham on 20 April 1968 that he began to speak out vehemently against the Common Market. By 1969 his speeches were becoming more explicit and Tony Benn in his diaries records Denis Healey, then Defence Secretary and not keen on any new application being made, saying: 'It would be better to wait in the hope that Enoch Powell would make an issue of it with Heath and split the Tory party rather than us.'

I had watched Powell, with respect for his intellect, on a legislative committee on the Territorial Army in 1966–7. I had had a fascinating private dinner in the early 1970s with him and two friends, both Labour MPs, to discuss the European Community. That evening I saw that the flaw in one of his arguments came from where he started. From then on he argued with impeccable logic. The flaw, if there was one in Powell's arguments, could usually be found at his first premise. That was often the case over immigration.* On the Common Market his official biographer sums up that initial premise well in writing that Powell simply did not believe Britain had to 'choose between America, Europe or the Commonwealth: she did not need any of them'. I believed then and still believe today that Britain needs all three.

Michael Foot, though on the left of the Labour Party, was the man whom Enoch Powell admired more than anyone else in the House of Commons, believing that they had the same combination of logic and passion. Both certainly had passion in abundance and it dominated their thinking but logic was not a characteristic I associated with Foot while observing him from Plymouth as both boy and man. Foot had little time for America but he was as sentimental over the Commonwealth as Hugh Gaitskell. He had, hitherto, consistently opposed the Treaty of Rome. Starting life as a Liberal he became a strong supporter of Socialist International, and the fight of the International Brigade

*Simon Heffer, *Like the Roman. The Life of Enoch Powell* (London: Weidenfeld & Nicolson, 1998).

against Franco in the Spanish Civil War was an abiding memory. One of the reasons why Foot admired Frank Cousins, the former leader of the Transport and General Workers' Union and a strong campaigner for unilateral nuclear disarmament, was that he had actually fought in Spain. Foot's emotional attachment to Spain I later exploited when he was a senior figure in Jim Callaghan's Cabinet and I was shaping the papers for the Cabinet's all-day discussion on the European Community in 1977. In order to attract his support I deliberately championed and highlighted the commitment of the European Community's foreign ministers to enlarge so as to include Spain, a commitment first entered into at Leeds Castle in 1977.* In 1972, however, Foot had not yet agreed to serve on the opposition front bench and he was speaking from the traditional position of dissent on the Labour front bench below the gangway. Foot was the grist to Powell's mill. They joined forces on the floor of the House of Commons to oppose entry, just as they had a few years earlier combined to destroy the cross-party reform package for the House of Lords. Using all the tactical means available to probe and delay the Heath government's legislation they ensured all the issues surrounding sovereignty were endlessly discussed.

Tony Benn, by contrast, was on the opposition front bench and, like Powell, had supported joining the European

*'The European Community', memorandum by the Secretary of State for Foreign and Commonwealth Affairs, 26 July 1977 (copies available in the David Owen Archives at the University of Liverpool and at the National Archives, Kew).

Community in government in the late 1960s. But Benn was preparing to switch his political position in line with the shift in the centre of gravity on this issue inside the Labour Party. While Benn too had passion intellectually he was never in the same league as either Powell or Foot. What he had for a politician was just as useful, an instinct for the movement of opinion within his own political party. I had approached Benn in the tea room of the House of Commons in May 1971, because he was still nominally in favour of our application to join, to see if he would sign a declaration on Europe with Willy Brandt, the then German Chancellor, as one of the signatories. Denis Healey and Roy Jenkins had signed and the declaration was to be carried as an advertisement in the *Guardian*. Benn made it plain to me that his opposition was not to entry but to the manner of the decision and he declined to sign on the basis that Britain should only go in after another election or a referendum. I had also been asked by the group of MPs promoting the *Guardian* advertisement to approach Jim Callaghan. We agreed he must be informed so that he did not feel left out. But we felt on balance it would be better if he did not sign.

It was the first time I had dealt with Callaghan on a big and sensitive political issue. I was surprised to find that we soon reached a subtle formula. Callaghan would say that he had been approached but refused to sign on the grounds that it was better for Shadow Cabinet members to stay outside such an initiative. He would also say he had not been given the wording of the declaration and therefore had no view on it. The advantage of this from our point of view was he could not say he had refused to sign because its form of words were meaningless, the usual way of diminishing the importance of an initiative.

It was clear that a significant section of the Labour Party led by Callaghan was now preparing to shift its ground on Europe. This represented a deep threat to Harold Wilson's leadership for it contained many of the people, middle-of-the-road trade unionist MPs, who had turned against Wilson over trade union reform. Four days after the Heath–Pompidou breakthrough meeting in May 1971 in Paris, Callaghan spoke in Southampton in what was irreverently labelled the '*Non, merci beaucoup*' speech. It followed on Pompidou's reference to French being the language of Europe and Callaghan said, tongue in cheek: 'Millions of people in Britain have been surprised to hear that the language of Chaucer, Shakespeare and Milton must in future be regarded as an American import from which we must protect ourselves if we are to build a new Europe.' It is an interesting side issue to that speech that forty years later there is now no doubt that within the EU English is destined to be the language of Europe. The credit for this is due largely to the worldwide acceptance of English, but it is still a highly significant development and a strong argument why Britain should not give up the struggle for its own conception and definition of what the Europe of the twenty-first century should become. It is also a cautionary tale for those who believe that Europe can never be designed to better coincide with Britain's interests.

Callaghan in that same speech drew on his experience as

Chancellor of the Exchequer and began to explore whether the Werner Report's advocacy of a single currency would mean a federalist Europe. This was at a time when Heath was still able to claim that decisions on this subject would have to be taken unanimously with a veto retained. Callaghan challenged the logic, saying: 'I understand there is to be a confederation of member states whose ministers will retain full powers of decision. That is to say, they can disagree with decisions taken by other countries and so can prevent action by the EEC countries. This is a contradictory position for, if there is to be a successful economic and monetary union, then member states will have to subordinate their own fiscal, taxation and monetary policies to a central governing body.' These were prophetic words anticipating not only the eventual structure of an autonomous European central bank that was to emerge in the Maastricht Treaty, but the design flaws in that treaty and the crisis in the eurozone that began in 2009 and is still with us in 2012. Only in the light of the various failed experiments with currency stabilisation, such as the European Monetary System (EMS) and its all-important Exchange Rate Mechanism (ERM), were the French ready, at Maastricht, to concede to the German Bundesbank that independent bankers should control the eurozone's interest rate and thereby its exchange rate and ultimately its unemployment rate. Yet it is this very issue of the European Central Bank to which the French returned in the 2012 presidential debate between Nicolas Sarkozy and François Hollande. President Hollande in the election had promised to reopen a very sensitive issue, not fully dealt with in the draft Fiscal Compact Treaty (see Chapter 10)

The political impact of Callaghan's speech on Harold Wilson was profound since he recognised that it was a direct challenge to his leadership of the Labour Party. Wilson acted quickly to put himself in line with the changed party mood. The political correspondent of the *Financial Times*, David Watt, had earlier anticipated this switch, writing: 'If the leader of the Labour Party starts at this late stage to discover a sudden burning indignation on behalf of the Caribbean sugar producers, Scottish fishermen and New Zealand farmers, many of us will be quietly sick, but quite a lot of the Parliamentary Labour Party may find it convincing.' In his wind-up speech at a special Labour Party conference on Europe in London, Wilson did rediscover New Zealand farmers and came out against the terms of entry. Some Labour MPs including myself felt very sick but many more of my parliamentary colleagues were highly relieved that they now had a green light to take the political gloves off and oppose the Conservatives outright on the terms of entry into the Community.

The question for myself as one of the minority of Labour MPs in favour of entering the Community on the broad terms on offer was whether to follow Disraeli's famous dictum 'Damn your principles! Stick to your party' or upend it and stick to my principles. No-one knew at the time whether there would be a free vote on the principle of entry without any instructions from party whips. Over a weekend in late June I had several discussions with

Willie Whitelaw, then the Leader of the House of Commons, as we were both attending an Anglo-American Parliamentarians' Conference at Ditchley Park. Whitelaw not only made it clear he was arguing for a free vote but said that Heath had deliberately used words which had left open the door on conceding a free vote in the autumn on the principle of entry. He also said the Cabinet wanted as large a vote as possible in October, after which they would be responsible for their own legislation.

Eventually in the autumn, when Heath knew he could not win with his own votes, he conceded a free vote but by then it was too late for us in the Labour Party. The majority of the Labour shadow Cabinet and of Labour MPs were now determined to have a three-line whip. Defying that whip along with sixty-eight other Labour MPs I voted on 28 October to support entry. There was a cross-party majority of 112. Yet on the detailed legislation, four months later, in February 1972, the majority had fallen to eight. Had every Labour MP joined the thirty-nine Conservative and Ulster Unionist MPs who voted against the principle of entry, Britain would not have been able to sign the Treaty of Accession in Brussels on 22 January 1972. With unemployment rising, Heath was sarcastically described by Wilson in the House of Commons as the 'first dole-queue millionaire to cross the Channel since Neville Chamberlain'.

Much has been written about the legitimacy of the parliamentary process that took us into the Community without a referendum. Yet no fair-minded reading of the six-day House of Commons debate finishing on 26 October can support that there was a conspiracy of silence on the issues involved. Every aspect of the loss of sovereignty was explored and the deficiencies in the terms exposed. The significant shift in legislative procedure whereby Community regulations automatically had legislative effect in our country without passing through our parliamentary procedures was strongly criticised and many MPs personally anguished over this aspect. The issue of whether the European Community was becoming a federation or represented a confederation was also discussed without much light being shed on the exact meaning of the words, but again no fair-minded person can deny the majority 'Yes' vote was made up with most MPs favouring a confederation. In 1970 I had belatedly become a student of American history, having recently married a US citizen. I read then the famous 'Federalist Papers', a series of articles promoting the ratification of the US Constitution, for the first time and the abiding impression I was left with was how different the history and evolution of the United States of America is from that of the nation states that make up the European Community. Also worthy of note is how long it took for the US to move to its present federal structure with a single currency and powerful Federal Reserve bank. For the first 150 years after the 1788 Constitution called for monetary union the country 'was wracked by bitter regional disputes over monetary policies and institutions'.* Americans

*Hugh Rockoff, 'How Long Did It Take the United States to Become an Optimal Currency Area?', City University Business School Conference on Monetary Unions, 14 May 1999.

were not even ready to become the 'single people' called for in their Constitution until after the Civil War ended in 1865. In 1861, when the Civil War began, the United States was divided into three currency areas: Demand Notes or 'greenbacks' in the north-east, Confederate dollars in the south and gold in California. In 1900 the US firmly committed itself to the gold standard. In 1913, after the 1907 banking panic, the Federal Reserve system was established with regional banks each issuing their own currency, the dollar having a different value in shops separated by the state boundary.

In the 1971 parliamentary debates there was a tendency for speakers in favour of entering the Community, such as myself, while highlighting the safeguard of the veto and inter-governmental authority, to pay too little attention to the underlying risk of a momentum building up to demand more majority decision-making and greater integration. But in fairness that momentum was only beginning to restart after being repulsed for more than ten years by de Gaulle. With ratification of the Single European Act in 1987, under Prime Minister Margaret Thatcher, the single largest increase in qualified majority voting took place over the single market. Until then the Community looked like remaining an economic confederation and intergovernmental decision-making was far more dominant than supranational. I referred in my own speech in 1971 on the principle of entry to the reluctance of many MPs 'to give up power from this House; they do not wish to give up any power that we exercise as a nation and put ourselves into the decision structure of other nations because it involves compromises. It involves not always getting one's own way. It is, however, foolish to try to sell the concept of the EEC and not admit that this means giving up some sovereignty. Of course it does, and I believe it rightly does. I believe this is one of the central appeals of it.' Extensive coverage was given to that debate in newspapers, on radio and on television, and few people can honestly claim, looking back, that the facts were not available. In parliamentary terms all the constitutional proprieties had been upheld. But public opinion was never won round. Far from obtaining 'wholehearted consent', which is what Edward Heath had called for to endorse membership, the European Community remained unpopular.

The case for a referendum had been made by Tony Benn for some time, first in general and then in May 1970 specifically for entry into the Community. But it never took off in terms of the public demanding it of their political leaders. The Labour Party appeared by the spring of 1972 to be resigned to Britain's membership despite the tortured hours of debate with very small majorities on the legislation. Most of the sixty-nine Labour MPs who had rebelled, including myself, were now voting against the government's legislation despite feeling a deep sense of shame in doing so. Shabby party political advantage had reasserted itself and I felt pretty miserable voting against.

Suddenly the question of a referendum burst unexpectedly on the political scene. It came over whether the Labour Party should support a Conservative backbench amendment to the

European Communities Bill supporting a consultative referendum prior to entry. The Labour Party conference had voted against a somewhat similar referendum motion at Brighton the previous year. At the Shadow Cabinet on 15 March there were only four votes in favour of voting for the Conservative amendment and Harold Wilson spoke against a referendum. Fatefully, next day President Pompidou announced there would be a referendum in France on the question of enlarging the Community to include Britain. The Labour Party National Executive Committee (NEC) then voted on 22 March to support Tony Benn's initiative in favour of a referendum. On 24 March in an example of crazy political timing Edward Heath unexpectedly announced that for the first time ever, the UK would admit the principle of periodic referendums in Northern Ireland on the issue of union with the South.

When the Shadow Cabinet met on 29 March the political climate had changed and a combination of political opportunism and some quiet manoeuvring meant that they reversed their position of only a fortnight before, voting for the Parliamentary Labour Party to support a consultative referendum. Roy Jenkins was immediately determined to resign as deputy leader. I put a memorandum* to him looking in some depth at the case for the pro-EEC Labour MPs accepting voting for a referendum and listing the conditions necessary for its fair conduct. These included allowing MPs to campaign on either

*David Owen, *Time to Declare* (London: Michael Joseph, 1991), pp. 196–200.

side of the issue, which was one of the conditions which came into effect in the actual referendum of 1975. Privately, Jenkins argued, with immense passion, that the referendum amendment might well pass. He felt it would be more difficult to win a referendum when we were still out of the Community and that a 'Yes' vote would have to endorse the unknown. Also he warned that whatever people's intentions at the start of any referendum campaign, the mood of antagonism in the Labour Party to those of us who were continuing to argue for entry could reach such a pitch that we would run a substantial risk of being expelled from the party. If, however, a referendum was held after a general election, he argued, the 'Yes' vote could be won for it would be to stay in the Community and voters would have already experienced membership. This meant that winning public opinion over would be much easier. My supportive views on a referendum not withstanding, these were fairly compelling arguments and I was determined that Jenkins should not be left alone and isolated on this issue. I was in sufficient doubt as to a referendum's advisability to be content to accept his judgement and resign with him. Rarely is there a right time to resign. In this case I resigned primarily because I was beginning to despise myself for hiding behind a few brave Labour MPs who had ensured, by abstaining or occasionally voting for the government, that the legislation which I favoured for Britain to enter the Community went on to the statute book.

As for Harold Wilson, he had been subjected, as he saw it, in pursuit of party unity, itself a not ignoble priority for any party leader, to vitriolic personal attacks. An example was a *Times* newspaper leader, 'What can one say of such a man, save that he should never be Prime Minister again?' All this was deeply wounding to someone with a strong patriotic streak and who already suffered from a syndrome prevalent amongst politicians of 'press paranoia'. To Wilson it was he who had had to withstand the 'mud, filthy mud' while we pro-marketeers in the Labour Party were lauded by much of the Tory press as people of principle and probity. In fairness, it must have been galling for him. He was bent on personal survival as leader of the party, but also on keeping the party together. Roy Jenkins had come to represent more of a threat to his leadership than Jim Callaghan, with some attacking speeches on domestic policy issues, and so Wilson moved quickly, as he had done with Callaghan the year before, to face down his deputy's challenge. This was the explanation for Wilson's change of mind on the referendum in the shadow Cabinet in a matter of weeks. He knew that by switching to supporting a referendum he was isolating Jenkins in the Labour Party. Having, hitherto, been ready to see Jenkins as his successor he was now in effect forcing his resignation. Wilson also instinctively knew, as I had argued in my own memorandum on a referendum, that the time for this constitutional innovation had come and that, Heath having breached the principle over Northern Ireland, constitutional referendums were now in the UK to stay. In his advocacy of the referendum Tony Benn, as so often, had anticipated the Labour Party's mood change. He had launched what Callaghan had called 'a little yellow life raft on which many of us would be glad to clamber'. In terms of Labour politics the promise of a referendum had become the only way to hold the party together during the forthcoming general election. It was also an essential glue in its aftermath when, to the surprise of many Labour MPs, particularly some pro-marketeers, Labour came into government again in 1974.

A referendum was also the device which John Major attempted to use as Prime Minister to keep the Conservative Party civil war within bounds over the euro before the 1997 general election. He was only able to force it through his own Cabinet, against the opposition of his deputy Prime Minister, Michael Heseltine, and his Chancellor of the Exchequer, Kenneth Clarke, in the immediate run-up to the 1997 general election because public opinion was so strongly against the single currency, resulting, in large part, from the creation of the Referendum Party by the rich businessman James Goldsmith. The same commitment to a referendum was then reluctantly made by Tony Blair and by the leader of the Liberal Democrats, Paddy Ashdown, so keeping the question of joining the euro largely out of the 1997 general election.

Looking back, Edward Heath's calling of a general election in the midst of the miners' industrial action in early 1974 was a foolish response to the power shortages and the three-day week. His campaign theme was 'Who governs Britain?' but this only served to invite the judgement 'You don't'. Within weeks the miners' strike had been settled by Wilson and forgotten by a public only too glad to get back to watching television uninterrupted by power cuts. Voters, by a very narrow majority, were content to return an older, greyer, and perhaps wiser, Harold Wilson to sort out membership of the European Community as Prime Minister, with Jim Callaghan as Foreign Secretary. The two men solemnly went through an exercise labelled 'renegotiation' while cleverly reserving their position on the merits of entry. They then recommended acceptance from a position of apparent objectivity on what they called the new terms, which were little different from those agreed more than three years earlier. The country, somewhat surprisingly, then voted overwhelmingly to stay within the Community. It is a fact, but a rarely stated one, that the referendum was not won by the enthusiastic 'Yes' campaign of pro-marketeers but by the capacity of these two streetwise middle-of-the-road Labour leaders to convince mainstream Labour voters. The European Community was presented under the old adage 'Better the devil you know than the devil you don't', which was posed against an unstated but widely held fear that withdrawal from the Community would be very uncomfortable for an economically weak Britain. The polls, which had been strongly against even three months before, turned in favour of staying in the EEC before the referendum was called and then barely shifted during the campaign. A largely pro-Community press helped characterise the somewhat fanatical, freakish approach of the 'No' campaign, dominated by Michael Foot and Enoch Powell, so that it gave an image of xenophobia and of refighting the

Second World War. The polarisation added to the impression that the campaign had mattered, but what had really mattered was the Labour Party machine shifting its position to favour staying in the EEC. The new Conservative Party leader, Margaret Thatcher, campaigned for a 'Yes' vote, as did Jeremy Thorpe, the Liberal Party leader, so all three party leaders favoured entry in 1975.

Another feature was the political pragmatism displayed by the European Community and Commission during the run-up to the referendum, something not usually associated with Brussels. Helmut Schmidt, the wise German Social Democrat and Chancellor, also went out of his way to play up publicly the significance of the renegotiations even though the process stuck in his gullet and he was disparaging in private. Schmidt attended and wooed the Labour Party conference, showing humour and solidarity. In the process he greatly reduced a latent but waning anti-German feeling among older voters. All this manoeuvring was greatly helped by a cyclical change in world food prices, whereby for the referendum period food prices fell and the outlook appeared far better for the CAP, which would otherwise have been an embarrassment capable of exploitation by those arguing for a 'No' vote.

The 1975 European referendum proved a successful constitutional innovation, convincing many that on major constitutional questions it should be used in future, particularly when there was controversy crossing party political lines. Eight years later the Labour Party's call in the 1983 general election to come out of the Community without a referendum appeared to many party supporters, therefore, as illegitimate. The old precedent that each parliament was sovereign had changed; the people, having once been given the choice in a referendum, were not about to surrender it and let only Parliament decide this issue. After the 1997 general election endorsed a referendum on the euro to replace the pound, pledges were given in the next three general elections. By 2012 the conventional wisdom is woe betide any party that tries to pull back from a referendum on entry to the euro.

In September 1976 I moved from being Health Minister to the Foreign Office. Only then did I begin to realise that the country's problems, let alone the Labour Party's, with the European Community were not solved and were just about to begin again. As I absorbed the detail it became ever clearer to me that we really did have a lousy deal. Not only because of the CAP, which we had always known worked against British interests, but because the Community finances were out of control with big surpluses building up in milk products, olive oil and wine. Even worse, the projection of the UK budgetary contribution was due to rise at a pace which was unacceptable. We would soon find the UK making the largest contribution to the Community. It was clear that Britain faced a grinding acrimonious debate to recoup lost ground. Yet talking to Foreign Office officials, with some notable exceptions, I found those senior diplomats who had been involved in the negotiations dismissive, even light hearted, about these economic realities. It was as if they could not criticise their own handiwork and as if the past negotiations were sacrosanct and not to be disinterred. This is one of the many reasons why Britain's negotiating team in Brussels should not be dominated by the diplomatic service and why we need a cross-fertilisation in leadership from the civil service, albeit usually best led politically by the Foreign Secretary provided that person broadly shares the Prime Minister's views on Europe. The two are inextricably linked in the negotiating process and pulling all of these complex issues into 10 Downing Street, as was done under Tony Blair from 2001 onwards, led to the chaos of the Constitutional Treaty and the messy, and in many ways far too integrationist, Lisbon Treaty.

On 21 February 1977, I became Foreign Secretary after the tragic death in office of Tony Crosland. Now I had the necessary authority to define a tough new negotiating strategy where we would over a period of years reduce the budgetary imbalance. My problems with the senior Foreign Office diplomats were never over southern Africa, Israel or any of the world's flashpoints. They overwhelmingly concerned the European Community.

There is nothing wrong in a genuine clash of opinion between ministers and officials; indeed it is often healthy. The problem arises if there is resistance to implementing what ministers, after discussion, determine. Too many of the senior diplomats then serving in European capitals were already battle scarred from the previous sixteen years of on–off negotiations and as a consequence were reluctant to embark on any course which put

Britain at serious loggerheads with a majority of the Community member states. Fortunately the British ambassador to the EEC, Sir Donald Maitland, while being strongly committed to the idea of European integration, nevertheless retained both a diplomatic robustness and a loyalty to me personally as his political boss. In the new circumstances he accepted that I as the new Foreign Secretary with Cabinet support had the right to chart a different negotiating strategy and define what constituted the national interest.

As far as European integration is concerned, in my experience there were influential diplomats who carried into their public life a tendency to think that Europeanism represented a higher calling than the more mundane task of supporting their government in fighting the British corner in Brussels. They were tempted down the path of believing in and advocating the doctrine of the inevitability of integration. In justification of such inevitability they went back to the intentions of the founding fathers, men such as Jean Monnet, Paul-Henri Spaak and Alcide de Gasperi, and played up their statements and downplayed or ignored the repeated rejections of their dreams by the turn of political events. The failure to establish a European Defence Community, the reinterpretation of the Rome Treaty with the Luxembourg Compromise forced on the Community during President de Gaulle's period in office, the continued controversy over the issues that underlay the negotiations over the Fouchet Plan were all brushed aside. Ministers then were rarely briefed positively about the UK's rights and about how to maintain the limits to integration that had been already set ministerially, let alone how to establish new limits. With rare exceptions a tough negotiating position had to be dragged out of them. One notable exception was discussions in the Foreign Office over the European Assembly Elections Bill. The House of Commons was incensed that Treaty amendments giving the Assembly important new powers over the EC budget had been implemented in the UK through an Order in Council under Section 1(3) of the European Communities Act 1972. So we responded by putting provision in European Assembly Elections Bill that UK implementation of any other treaties (or equivalent) giving increased powers to the Assembly would require primary legislation. This has been the law ever since.

Diplomacy should represent far more than just splitting the difference. It involves knowing when to hold firm, when to build alliances and when to trade off support for seemingly unrelated negotiating objectives. The greatest danger for the British Foreign Office was that it was progressively bypassed from 1982 to 2010 by the ever stronger involvement of successive Prime Ministers in the working of the EU. The reduction in its influence and power began during the period when Francis Pym and then Geoffrey Howe were judged to be ineffective by Margaret Thatcher and as the power of Charles Powell, her private secretary in Number 10, grew. There was a readjustment under Douglas Hurd with John Major returning some power. Yet the concentration of power in Number 10 became virtually total under Tony Blair. This did not produce beneficial results. The most worrying demonstration of this in recent years was the deplorable diplomacy surrounding the negotiations just prior to the unveiling of the rapid reaction force at the Nice summit in December 2001, when the French Foreign Ministry at the Quai d'Orsay outpointed the British position at every turn.

In the first half of 1977 the UK held the presidency of the European Community for the first time. The then Cabinet had no enthusiasm for moving from indirect representation in the European Assembly, provided by backbench MPs in the House of Commons and a few peers, to directly elected members of the European Parliament. However, under the terms of the treaties already signed, we were committed to bringing in direct elections for the European Parliament. The opposition in principle to the move was correct in believing that direct elections might stimulate moves toward Eurofederalism. Perhaps its greatest potential danger was to divorce national parliamentarians from the democratic developments of the European Community. Yet while this argument had much with which I agreed it was one of the issues that in all logic had been settled by the 1975 referendum. I recommended to Cabinet the regional list system of proportional representation and a majority of the Cabinet preferred this to first-past-the-post voting, not because they wanted proportional representation for the UK, which most disliked intensely, but because they could see that the large European constituencies voting along the normal system of first-past-the-post would result in Labour, because of its then unpopularity, losing more seats than they would under a proportional system.

Ever since direct elections for the European Parliament came into operation there have been constant pressures to develop cross-European political parties and to use European Community money to foster this development at the expense of single-country political parties. If this had been accompanied by a readiness for the European Parliament to limit its scrutiny to the supranational part of the treaties and leave scrutiny of the intergovernmental activity to national parliaments that would have been logical and politically more acceptable. But the European Parliament has all the time pushed, with the connivance of the Commission, to extend its scrutiny to foreign affairs and defence, and to economic issues concerning tax. The most recent example was in 2012 with the pressure to introduce a Europe-wide transaction or Tobin tax (see Chapter 8).

The new President of the Commission in 1977 was Roy Jenkins and he felt the President of the Commission should be present at the upcoming G7 Summit. It was Britain's turn to host the meeting and Jim Callaghan, having chosen the intimacy of No. 10, wanted only the heads of government of the G7 countries (Canada, France, Germany, Italy, Japan, the UK and the US) to be at the meeting with their foreign and finance ministers. The French President, Valéry Giscard d'Estaing, was also then strongly opposed to the President of the Commission being represented. Neither country wanted to give the impression that the President of the Commission was a head of government and nor did I, but I did not want Callaghan to be depicted as vetoing Jenkins's attendance out of petty spite. I also felt that if the G7 was to survive as a small body and the Community to enlarge, having the President of the Commission present would mean we would be better able to resist demands for more European countries to be represented in that forum in future. Eventually a compromise was struck and Jenkins was invited but only to the sessions on trade, where the Commissioner for Trade was the sole representative in international negotiations for all the Community member states. Giscard d'Estaing, by way of a protest, refused to come to the opening dinner, to which Callaghan had invited Jenkins. At the next G7 summit in Bonn, the Commission was present throughout.

At the end of July 1977, an all-day special Cabinet meeting on Labour's European strategy was held. Callaghan asked me to supervise the writing of the papers personally and not leave them to the Foreign Office. Looking back over the last thirty-five years it is salutary to read the papers produced. They were firmly pro-European, but anti-federalist, and made much of the democratic and political arguments for enlargement of the Community to include Greece, emerging from a junta of military leaders, and Portugal and Spain, from the fascist leaderships of Salazar and Franco respectively. At a lunch with Jenkins and his supporters, who had been meeting from time to time over the past five years, I was given an insight into the tensions that lay ahead for the Labour Party over Europe despite the referendum. It was the first time this grouping had met since I had become Foreign

Secretary and Jenkins President of the Commission. He had been partially briefed about the Cabinet papers and launched into oblique and coded criticism of people who were backsliding on Europe, without mentioning whom he was attacking. Essentially he objected to stressing enlargement because it could lead to a loosening and slowing of the momentum towards union. I had not much objection to being criticised; he was after all as President of the Commission now representing different interests and these, I pointed out, were not, from now on, necessarily always going to be identical with British interests. The commissioners swear an oath of allegiance to the European Community. My job was to uphold British interests, Jenkins's as President of the Commission to uphold Europe's, but he never publicly expressed the view that the Commission should become the government of Europe.

I was telephoned by David Watt, who was writing about the Cabinet meeting for his *Financial Times* column the next day. He was a close friend and gave me the impression that he already knew exactly what was in the Cabinet papers. He put it to me that it was being said by my supposed friends that I was chickening out of my commitment to the European Community. This was such a travesty of what I had produced that I overreacted and rebutted my critics point by point, in the process revealing more to him than I should have done about what was actually in the Cabinet papers. The next morning in the *Financial Times* there appeared a very good précis of the papers I had put to Cabinet and the criticisms of my position by some of my pro-market Cabinet colleagues. When called over to No. 10 to explain the article to an angry Jim Callaghan prior to the meeting, I thought the best thing to do was to be totally honest and I apologised, explaining how frustration had led me to say too much. He was rather nonplussed to find a Cabinet minister actually admitting responsibility for a press story and became sympathetic to the position that I had been put in. Nevertheless, annoyed by the leak, Callaghan nearly cancelled the Cabinet meeting.

Tony Benn accurately describes in his diaries what then happened 'at one of the most remarkable Cabinets he had ever attended'.* That Labour Cabinet defined the position on the European Community which has in broad terms been followed by every succeeding government, whether Labour, Conservative or the present Conservative–Liberal Democrat coalition: 'Yes' to Britain's continued and constructive membership, specifically 'No' to the integrationist wish eventually for a single state, a United States of Europe. It should have been possible to look back and say 1977 was the point when the UK began to stop the drip-drip of continuous integration but even under the Prime Ministership of Margaret Thatcher the true record has been of slow but unchecked further integration. It is this progression in 2012 that has reached the point when a new restructuring of Europe to grapple with the problems of the eurozone has become essential. (see Chapter 10).

*Tony Benn, *Conflicts of Interest: Diaries 1977–80* (London: Hutchinson, 1990), pp. 201–6.

The informal Foreign Affairs meeting was held every six months in the country that held the presidency. In the spring of 1977 it took place at Leeds Castle and firmed up the principle of Greek, Spanish and Portuguese entry. This was despite the French fear of Spanish agriculture competing with their agricultural industry in the south, and despite Commission fears of the EEC being dragged down by the old-fashioned protectionism and the statist structure of Spanish industry. This meeting showed the Community at its best, strengthening nascent democracies and developing market economies. In order to reach agreement on enlargement a deal was later done in effect between Valéry Giscard d'Estaing, Helmut Schmidt and Jim Callaghan. Giscard d'Estaing could have Greece in first and honour his obligation to Konstantinos Karamanlis, their new Prime Minister, who had been exiled in Paris. But France would have to agree to give up its objections to Spain and Portugal entering the Community soon after. There were powerful echoes of that same democratic imperative in the immediate political response of the EU soon after the fall of the Berlin Wall in the early 1990s to admit, in principle, the former communist countries of eastern Europe. Some of the initial enthusiasm for enlargement faded during the wars in the former Yugoslavia from 1992 to 1995 but the most important of these countries – Poland, Hungary and the Czech Republic – were eventually admitted in 2004, along with Slovakia, Slovenia and the ex-Soviet Baltic states. Yet some delay was understandable given the immense financial burden which West Germany had to undertake to overcome the communist legacy in East Germany from 1990. There was, however, an EU political decision after NATO's bombing of Serbia in 1999 to hasten the admission of Romania and Bulgaria, who had given political assistance regarding the Russian military overflying their countries.

In the 1970s the Community, through the Foreign Affairs Council, started to develop a new policy framework called Political Co-operation. It covered foreign policy issues, including disarmament, and even the Mutual and Balanced Force Reductions talks in Europe and those parts of the US–Soviet Strategic Arms Limitation talks which affected Europe. It took the sensible form of discussion aimed at widening consensus and co-ordinating our response as a community in other world forums. In discussion over southern Africa my colleagues were very helpful to what the US Secretary of State, Cyrus Vance, and I were trying to do in Rhodesia before it became Zimbabwe. Regarding Namibia a UN Security Council contact group of five nations was formed involving the US, UK, German, French and Canadian foreign ministers. In the summer of 1978 those ministers, including myself, negotiated directly in Pretoria with the newly elected South African President, P. W. Botha, and his Foreign Minister, Pik Botha. These negotiations gave rise to the UN resolution on which twelve years later Namibia was granted its independence. In all this, European co-ordination was useful. Today Political Co-operation could be restored for a wider single-market Europe of thirty-plus member states, leaving the highly integrated Foreign

Affairs and Security Policy with more qualified majority voting, for those who are already part of eurozone Europe or aspire soon to become members.

Margaret Thatcher won the general election on 4 May 1979, and in its first few months the new Conservative government, in marked contrast to what was to follow in subsequent years, initially developed a heady pro-European stance under Peter Carrington, the new Foreign Secretary. Most unwisely they agreed to lift the carefully organised zero-increase farm price settlement which the Labour government, with the support of the European Commission, had left behind in the early summer of 1979 and accepted the exact farm price increase which I had rejected out of hand only a few weeks before. No doubt the same Foreign Office diplomats persuaded Lord Carrington using the same arguments I had refused. But under the British system these same diplomats were allowed but not obliged to reveal to him that this was the lever by which the previous government had hoped to prise open a budgetary agreement at the European Council meeting in Dublin.

By October 1979 Margaret Thatcher, still in 'be nice to the Community' mode, found herself bargaining at Dublin with no leverage on farm prices. She was totally rebuffed as a consequence on the British budgetary contribution and her mood and attitude to the Community changed almost overnight. She then had to rely on tough words alone for some months while the other Community member states adjusted to the political necessity of moving their negotiating position in the face of legitimate obduracy from a head of government determined to defend a vital national interest. At Dublin Margaret Thatcher would not use the Community language of 'own resources', saying, 'I am only talking about our money, no-one else's; there should be a cash refund of our money to bring our receipts up to the average level of receipts in the Community.' The next European Council was not until April 1980 in Luxembourg and the British started threatening to withhold contributions to the Community Budget. The problem with this lever was that it was illegal whereas vetoing the farm price review, a tactic which had been used by other countries in the past, was not. Despite some help from the Italian Prime Minister, Francesco Cossiga, Britain was only offered initially a one-year solution, later increased to two. Thatcher then, despite being urged to settle by Helmut Schmidt and Roy Jenkins, still President of the Commission, rightly refused. The matter was referred to the Foreign Ministers Council and Peter Carrington managed to achieve a three-year rebate with a promised major review to start by mid-1981. Reluctantly Thatcher accepted. To her it was all best summed up in Rudyard Kipling's poem 'Norman and Saxon':

The Saxon is not like us Normans. His manners are not so
    polite.
But he never means anything serious till he talks about
    justice and right.
When he stands like an ox in the furrow with his sullen set
    eyes on your own,

And grumbles, "This isn't fair dealing," my son, leave the
Saxon alone.

It can be seen in retrospect that it was Thatcher's budgetary
settlement in 1980, not the referendum in 1975, that allowed
Britain's membership of the European Community to become a
settled issue with public opinion, even though the Labour Party
had to be heavily defeated in the 1983 general election to begin
to come to terms with this reality. The rebate issue corrected an
injustice; the budgetary issue recurred but it never again reached
the same intense level of dissension, in part because as the British
economy improved it became more understandable why our
contribution was higher than that of most other member states.
It was undoubtedly a 'Thatcher triumph' but as so often in
diplomacy the ground had been laid over many years, in this case
over six years, and it had taken three Prime Ministers, Harold
Wilson, Jim Callaghan and Margaret Thatcher, with their
different manners and their different negotiating styles, to
convince our European partners that this issue had to be
resolved. Agreement was eventually reached, not just because of
the fuss we were causing, but because the long-running
disagreement was destroying the unity of the Community.
Heads of government know that in practice unity cannot be
built against a background of perceived unfairness. Yet the issue
has resurfaced in 2012 with much talk of ending the British
rebate, a demand heightened by Tony Blair's readiness to give
up part of the rebate in December 2005. That British concession

was for £7.1 billion spread over seven years, which was claimed by No. 10 at the time as being approximately £1 billion off the British rebate each year. This was because of the complicated way in which the rebate was calculated; it meant even after the concession the rebate would still rise in value in gross terms in the years ahead. Blair used the argument, with some justification, in 2005, that Britain being the country pushing hardest for further enlargement, he could not refuse providing some money to pay for it.* But it meant once again conceding ground on a principled position before serious reform of the CAP budget had taken place.

I returned to the Council of Foreign Ministers on frequent occasions between 1992 and 1995, while I was the EU peace negotiator in the Balkans, to find a much more structured grouping as part of the post-Maastricht Common Foreign and Security Policy. It was never going to be easy for the then fifteen member states to build and sustain in defence and international affairs the intergovernmental power structure to support a common policy while five different ethnic wars took place in the former Yugoslavia. In January 1993 the US gained a new President, Bill Clinton. We in Europe soon discovered how he would grandstand in the Balkan wars while seeking consensus and promoting co-operation, ruling out using force through NATO to enforce any settlement – first the Vance–Owen Plan of 1992, second the European Action Plan of 1993 and finally

*Anthony Seldon, *Blair Unbound* (London: Simon & Schuster, 2007), pp. 410–14.

the Contact Group Plan of 1994, involving the US, the UK, France, Germany and Russia. Only after the massacre at Srebrenica of over 8,000 Muslim men and boys by the Bosnian Serb army in the summer of 1995 was the US ready to use NATO to enforce what became the Dayton Accords. This agreement was endorsed in Paris by Bill Clinton, John Major, Jacques Chirac and Boris Yeltsin alongside President Slobodan Milošević of Serbia, President Franjo Tudjman of Croatia and President Alija Izetbegovi of Bosnia. This experience led to demands in Europe for a revival of the European defence debate of the early 1950s, which will be discussed in Chapter 6.

Chapter 4

Devaluation, snakes, deutschmarks and the ERM

The British have through the centuries been keener on economic liberalism than their continental neighbours. Adam Smith's *An Inquiry into the Nature and Causes of the Wealth of Nations* was published in 1776, the same year as the American Declaration of Independence. It has had a profound influence in the UK as well as in the US but it has not markedly influenced continental Europe. Meanwhile, European monetary union has a long history from which there are many lessons to learn, going back to Emperor Charlemagne. One place to start learning is 1922, when at the Genoa Conference the gold exchange standard was discussed. Britain returned the pound to the gold standard at a high fixed rate in 1925 until it finally crumbled in 1931. The British experience with the gold standard vindicated John Maynard Keynes. His view was that we in Britain should be able to choose our own inflation targets, enjoy interest rate autonomy and retain control of our own national monetary policy. At the Bretton Woods conference in 1944, the UK was one of the few nations present that saw internationalism as a constraint on employment policies and in part as a consequence the eventual agreement was firmly intergovernmental. Keynes was even doubtful that Britain should ratify and so influential was he that we might never have ratified had the Americans not made acceptance of Bretton Woods a condition of their 1946 loan to the UK.

The Labour government's reluctance to even contemplate devaluation immediately after the Second World War was maintained under Clement Attlee and his Chancellors of the Exchequer, Hugh Dalton and Stafford Cripps, for too long. Eventually devaluation took place, on 18 September 1949. It had been championed by Hugh Gaitskell and had been agreed on 29 July by the Cabinet, overcoming a totally misplaced belief that the UK could maintain the existing rate indefinitely. Under the terms of the Bretton Woods agreement there was provision for the British government to readjust. Experience shows, however, that rather than readjust politicians have vested in the value of the pound emotions and patriotic feelings, in order to deflect market sentiment, that are wholly inappropriate to rational adjustment and objective data. In the spring of 1952 Rab Butler as Chancellor of the Exchequer in the new Conservative government favoured a Bank of England scheme for floating the pound, blocking the accumulated sterling balances but making sterling freely convertible and letting the exchange rate rather than the reserves take the strain.* Churchill favoured 'setting the

*Roy Jenkins, *Churchill: A Biography* (New York: Farrar, Straus and Giroux, 2001), pp. 851–2.

pound free' but Eden opposed the change and it was only twenty years later that we floated the pound. Had Butler had his way I believe the British economy would never have gone through such a long period of relative decline as it did.

My first exposure to politicians believing that they can withstand persistent market speculation on currency movements occurred when the Labour Government refused to devalue under Harold Wilson from 1964–7. It was widely believed that had the Conservatives won in 1964, Reginald Maudling, their Chancellor of the Exchequer, would have immediately devalued. My first big parliamentary occasion as a newly elected MP was the Budget on 3 May 1966. Jim Callaghan was Chancellor of the Exchequer, and stood confident as always at the dispatch box producing like a conjuror out of a hat a new tax – selective employment tax – which was to take effect in September. It looked to me like a clever wheeze. In theory with regional variations it could have had the effect of a regional devaluation. I had little knowledge of the internal arguments in government between the newly created Department of Economic Affairs and the Treasury on how deflationary the Budget should be. The Treasury wanted to slow the economy immediately but had been forced to postpone this until September. The Conservative shadow Chancellor, Iain Macleod, warned perceptively that the Budget was not deflationary enough. I realised after that Budget that I had to start reading economics textbooks and try to learn about a subject which was clearly of vital importance to my new political life in the House of Commons.

Then the seamen's strike damaged confidence in the British economy. According to Harold Wilson's famous description the strike was run by 'a tightly knit group of politically motivated men'. It ended on 1 July 1966, the day the Steel Nationalisation Bill was published. The economic press was still full of reports about a fall in international confidence affecting sterling when Frank Cousins, the former head of the Transport and General Workers' Union, who had been brought into Parliament in a by-election, and made Minister of Technology in 1964, resigned in order to fight the imposition of an incomes policy. On 13 July Harold Wilson announced that steps were being taken to reduce demand at home and to cut back spending overseas. The currency markets thought that this meant the long-postponed devaluation of sterling was imminent and speculation started. Soon a dramatic run on the pound developed and in Labour circles there was much talk of 'the gnomes of Zurich'. For the first time since coming into government in 1964 devaluation was again discussed by the Cabinet only to be once again rejected.

On 20 July Harold Wilson announced a deflationary package and the stop–go cycle of the British economy which I, as a Labour candidate, had often criticised before the 1964 election under the slogan 'Thirteen years of wasted Tory misrule' was back, this time with a massive stop. A six-month statutory standstill in wages and dividends was announced, which would be followed by another period of restraint and a twelve-month price freeze. Public expenditure was to be cut back.

Economics, I was beginning to realise, is not a pure science but rather an applied science, depending as it does so much on human behaviour. A few of us Labour MPs questioned the basic premise of our government's policy. It was not an easy thing to do and we were soon accused along with others who advocated devaluation 'of selling Britain short'. In Cabinet the word 'devaluation' was not one to be uttered. For Harold Wilson advocacy of devaluation was the equivalent of hauling down the Union Jack. Nevertheless the economic storm clouds were gathering. In 1967 the dockers in London and Liverpool came out on strike over the government's de-casualisation scheme. Jack Dash, a small communist docker from the East End, became a public figure. Vital exports were stuck in the docks. The Arab–Israeli Six Day War had ended with the Suez Canal blocked and the balance of trade figures were still severely distorted. On top of all that, in November there was much talk about Britain being about to be granted a new international loan. The October trade figures showed a trade gap of £107 million, the highest then in our history. Speculation followed and the Bank of England lost as much as £90 million in one day defending the then £1 to US$2.80 rate of exchange.

A Labour MP who had long argued for devaluation put down a private notice question in November 1967 to ask the Prime Minister to make a statement on the rumour that a £1,000 million loan was being negotiated with foreign banks. None of us in the House of Commons knew that the Cabinet had that morning agreed to devalue by 14.3 per cent and to also accept the consequential deflationary package. Representation was made by the government to the Speaker to disallow the question. Not having been told about the Cabinet's devaluation decision, he refused. When Jim Callaghan rose to speak he declined to say much, relying on 'It would clearly be wrong for the government either to confirm or to deny a press rumour of this kind'. Iain Macleod, the shadow Chancellor, made a helpful intervention but Callaghan was in an impossible position and when he sat down there was immediate and massive selling of sterling. The Bank of England was the only one buying sterling and it could not stop a massive run on the pound. Devaluation followed and the new sterling exchange rate against the US dollar was set at $2.40 to the pound. The Labour government after devaluation never had the same authority and in particular the Prime Minister, Harold Wilson, was never allowed to forget his explanatory statement that 'it does not, of course, mean that the pound here in Britain, in your pocket or purse, or in your bank, has been devalued'.

The new Conservative government, elected in 1970, appeared as if it would reverse the trend towards inflation and rising levels of unemployment. But Edward Heath was soon facing the same problems that had bedevilled the economy through the 1960s. First the doctors gained an inflationary award by arbitration and then the power workers through a court of inquiry were awarded a 15 per cent increase. Unemployment was rising and in March 1971 Anthony Barber, Chancellor of the Exchequer, spoke about the exchange rate. 'The lesson of the international balance of payments upsets of the last few years is that it is neither necessary nor desirable to distort domestic economies to an unacceptable level in order to maintain unrealistic exchange rates, whether they are too high or too low.' This seemingly more open-minded approach to fixing the exchange rate reflected these international upheavals and helped convince some experts that European monetary union was now going to be set aside. But this was not to be. The European Council decided to adopt the Werner Report and as a Stage 1 to hold exchange rate fluctuations amongst Community countries with narrower margins than those in force for the US dollar. Then on 9 May, before this European arrangement could be brought in, Germany floated the deutschmark. On 15 August President Nixon declared the dollar no longer convertible to gold and thereby compelled all the world's currencies to float. Exchange rates were, however, refixed under the Smithsonian agreement in December 1971 with widened margins of permissible fluctuation against a currency's parity or central rate. After this the Community thought it possible to restart the Werner proposal and the 'snake in the tunnel' came into force on 10 April 1972 with the original Six.

The British government, somewhat surprisingly, in view of the Chancellor's earlier statement, decided for European political reasons, rather than those of economic management, to join the 'snake' in May 1972. This had established a maximum permitted margin of fluctuation between any two participating currencies of 2.25 per cent. Within a mere six weeks of market pressure on the pound, because there was so little confidence in the government's strategy, sterling was thrown off the 'snake' and on 23 June the pound floated. The Chancellor told the House of Commons that sterling would float 'as a temporary measure'. In the event that temporary measure lasted for eighteen years until Britain entered the Exchange Rate Mechanism in October 1990. Those still within the 'snake' floated as a group, but even among the original six countries it started to fall apart relatively fast. Italy left the 'snake' in February 1973 and the French suspended their participation in January 1974, letting the franc float. The 'snake' was now seen as only an informal grouping of Benelux, Germany, Denmark and two non-EEC countries, Sweden and Norway. In September 1974 the French proposed a *relance monétaire européenne* but it was rejected by members of the 'snake' because of its technical complexity and because they did not believe that the margins with the unit of account and the level of the US dollar could be both effective and kept secret.

Against that short history of international monetary chaos and disagreements it was wholly in tune with the mood of the time that in the first national referendum of June 1975 the official document sent out on behalf of the 'Yes' grouping, led by Roy Jenkins and Edward Heath, set the tone for a campaign in which the threat of European monetary union reappearing was dismissed out of hand. The exact words were in the 'Money and Jobs' section: 'There was a threat to employment from the movement in the Common Market towards an Economic and

Monetary Union. This could have forced us to accept fixed exchange rates for the pound, restricting industrial growth and so putting jobs at risk. This threat has been removed.'

I genuinely – along with many others – thought that EMU was dead. Yet as so often over Europe where further integration is concerned, just when one battle, in this instance implementing the Werner Report, appeared to be over, another one flared up. On 10 July 1975 the French came back into the 'snake' and announced that France regarded it as a Community mechanism and wished to strengthen the mechanisms so as to prepare for economic and monetary union, which was openly stated as their motive. When France tried to get the IMF executive board to welcome its decision rather than note it, as was the usual practice, the French minister complained to Community colleagues because not all member states supported it. The franc then came under pressure in the exchange markets since inflation in France had been double that of Germany. France not wanting to exhaust its reserves, under President Giscard d'Estaing on 15 March 1976 the franc left the 'snake' for good.

In the UK the most significant happening was Jim Callaghan's first speech as Prime Minister to the Labour Party annual conference. On 28 September 1976 he dramatically changed the economic prospects for the UK, saying that we could no longer spend our way out of recession. 'I tell you in all candour that option no longer exists and in so far as it ever did exist, it only worked on each occasion since the war by injecting a bigger dose of inflation into the economy followed by a higher level of unemployment as the next step.' The next day Callaghan rang President Gerald Ford and warned him that the UK would need a stand-by loan from the IMF and a safety net for sterling. It was the beginning of twenty-six years of monetary discipline and the fact that this discipline was accepted first by Labour made it easier for successive Conservative governments to apply similar disciplines. Somewhat to my surprise I was a member of an informal grouping, almost a seminar, which the Prime Minister had created to discuss UK monetary policy and which included the Governor and Deputy Governor of the Bank of England. It proved a fascinating and educational experience, as did membership of the Cabinet Economic Committee.

In October 1977 Roy Jenkins, as President of the Commission, reignited the debate about European monetary matters in a speech in Florence. Thereafter the German Chancellor, Helmut Schmidt, and the French President, Valéry Giscard d'Estaing, took the issue under their wing. It did not come as a total surprise, therefore, to Jim Callaghan and me when, over dinner with the other heads of government at the European Council meeting in Copenhagen on 7 April 1978, Schmidt developed his ideas for a new monetary system for Europe. But what did surprise me, Callaghan and in particular the Treasury official who had come to Denmark specifically for this issue was the boldness of the actual proposals. We in Britain had been tending to explain what was being envisaged as 'window-dressing' for the continuation of the existing 'snake' so as to make it easier for France to participate again in a European currency system very similar to the old. It soon became clear that Schmidt's scheme was capable of developing into far more than just a deutschmark zone. While Callaghan wanted currency stability, he was more worried about the US dollar and felt that concentrating on the European currencies was too narrow a focus. Also he claimed that in Schmidt's system a strong deutschmark would pull the sterling exchange rate up and do political damage to the British economy in the run-up to an election.

When, next morning, Schmidt, Giscard d'Estaing and Callaghan met for breakfast it was clear that France was going to join and Callaghan reserved the British position. Talking privately to Callaghan over that period, I inferred that he was not prepared to risk the row in the Labour Party that would undoubtedly come if we were to join the European Monetary System (EMS) before the election. The irony was that in these early days, Margaret Thatcher, in opposition, was giving the impression of being in favour of the EMS.

At the Bremen European summit on 6 July the EMS plan was moving forward. On the flight over I felt Callaghan was becoming much more ambivalent about the political consequences of not joining the scheme though he still felt that internal Labour Party politics made joining inadvisable. I sensed that, with a G7 summit imminent, he knew he would not be in a strong position to argue for worldwide currency stability measures, something he was always very keen on, while being seen by others to be dragging his feet on the European proposals. Moreover, the Americans seemed increasingly favourable towards the EMS.

At the G7 summit in Bonn President Carter was less enthusiastic towards the EMS than we had anticipated. Agreement on a co-ordinated worldwide package was, with difficulty, reached by the Seven, with Schmidt, despite Bundesbank opposition, conceding a higher target for German growth than at one time looked likely. Whether this co-ordinated economic expansion programme could have achieved its objectives will never be known because it was dealt a massive blow by the oil price rise in early 1979. Probably all G7 summits on global economic management have tended to exaggerate the capacity of governments to do more than create a climate for a different approach. By the start of the twenty-first century month-by-month practical co-operation between the G7's finance ministers and the heads of the US Federal Reserve, the European Central Bank, the Bank of Japan, the Bank of England and the Bank of Canada provided a useful but modest mechanism but the early enthusiasm for international monetary interventionism had waned considerably. That is, until Britain was hit by the collapse of Northern Rock in 2007, a precursor to the full-blown global crisis that was developing by 2008, whereupon Gordon Brown succeeded in mobilising a G20 meeting in London into co-ordinated action.

All through 1978 British officials were involved in discussions about the development of the EMS, even though Callaghan had made it clear to Schmidt and Giscard d'Estaing that he was not going to join. Callaghan passed a note across the table to me during the Cabinet meeting on Thursday 21 September 1978 to ask if I would have lunch with him at the Athenaeum to discuss our joint trip to Kano in Nigeria. Walking back through St James's Park he brought up the issue of the EMS, slightly concerned about the attitude of Denis Healey, the Chancellor of the Exchequer, who had made different speeches on the subject recently. The Prime Minister reiterated his view that the Labour Party would not wear entry to any exchange mechanism and that consideration would have to wait until after the election. I then suggested the possibility of formally joining the EMS but not the actual Exchange Rate Mechanism (ERM), an idea put to me a few days before by a very bright senior diplomat, Michael Butler. This meant depositing some gold in the EMS but in effect standing aside from the fundamental mechanism, namely the commitment to keep one's currency from fluctuating beyond certain bands in the ERM. Pondering this for a moment, Callaghan asked me what I thought Healey's attitude would be to this idea and then cleverly suggested that I ask Foreign Office officials to first square Treasury officials. The Prime Minister then sold this somewhat ingenious approach with Healey to the Labour Cabinet in early November by first getting everyone to accept that the UK wanted a zone of monetary stability and that we should commit ourselves to helping to achieve this while emphasising that we would not accept any obligations restricting our own freedom to manage the sterling exchange rate as we thought fit.

I doubt many of the Cabinet, except Peter Shore, really understood that they were agreeing to join the System but not the Mechanism. The Parliamentary Labour Party was very uneasy about the whole EMS issue and over a hundred back-bench Labour MPs signed an early day motion against it. At a meeting there was an attempt to restrict the Prime Minister's freedom to sign up for any arrangement; but he insisted vigorously on the government's right to settle for a compromise. The Irish government had cleverly winkled extra financial support out of Germany and France as its price for signing up to the ERM at the EEC summit in early December, which meant the punt decoupling from the pound. With the launch of the EMS, in Paris, Valéry Giscard d'Estaing presented us with the first minted ecu, a symbol rather than a currency. Eventually Parliament agreed that the UK would be associated with the development of the European Currency Unit (ECU) and we made up our national share of its gold deposits and committed dollar reserves. This ensured that the necessary procedural hurdles were passed by the Callaghan government for full membership by any future government if it was felt appropriate. When Britain joined the ERM in October 1990, no new legislative authority was required and entry was fixed up quickly and conveniently over a weekend. A precedent was also set for going along with European Monetary Union in the Treaty of Maastricht but remaining outside the eurozone.

After the election in May 1979 the Conservatives remained in favour of the EMS and in the 1979 European elections on 8

June the Conservative manifesto, approved before the general election by Margaret Thatcher, was forthright. 'We regret the Labour Government's decision – alone amongst the Nine – not to become a full member of the European Monetary System. We support the objectives of the new system, which are currency stability in Europe and closer coordination of national economic policies, and we shall look for ways in which Britain can take her rightful place within it.' *Plus ça change, plus c'est la même chose* – and a very different stance to that which Margaret Thatcher later developed to most things European.

The early 1980s did not show much enthusiasm for arguments about the ERM. There were far bigger issues transforming the political debate. The Labour Party was splitting itself asunder; this was not the normal left–right division but a total *volte-face* in Labour foreign and defence policies established in three post-war governments. Having been Foreign Secretary a mere eighteen months before I was being asked to reverse every vital policy that I had espoused in the national interest. I am still occasionally surprised today when I find people who think that I should have been ready to advocate such policies, despite disagreeing with them, on Labour platforms in the 1983 general election. The pace and extent of Labour's policy change were most clearly manifested in three party conferences held in less than a year. A special conference was held in Wembley in May 1980. I reluctantly attended with no intention of speaking, but listening to the speeches, particularly that of Jim Callaghan, I felt I had to speak since no-one from the shadow Cabinet was challenging the passage in the statement before the conference in which the Labour Party was basically endorsing unilateral nuclear disarmament. This was something Labour had only ever done for one traumatic year after its 1960 conference, and the pledge was reversed the following year by Hugh Gaitskell after a bitter fight. My spontaneous speech provoked uproar when I said: 'Peace is not won by one nation pursuing its own policy in total isolation from others. It is in pooling, in making a bargain, in making a deal, in negotiating with the Soviet Union from a position of strength, not a position of weakness.' Hardly anyone else challenged the document and it was overwhelmingly passed with no recorded vote.

The next conference was the regular annual one, held in Blackpool in September, and I spoke again, challenging the motion that the next Labour government should include withdrawal from the European Community without a referendum as a priority in its manifesto. I said to the conference that it was 'a constitutional outrage, first to go to the British people and let them decide in 1975 and now not even to give the British people a chance to determine their own destiny'. This motion also went through by a significantly large majority.

Another special conference was held at Wembley on 24 January 1981 to endorse the proposed electoral college, consisting of trade unions, parliamentarians and constituency parties, for electing Labour's leader. Once more I spoke from the floor, arguing that 'to allow the block vote to choose the future Prime Minister of this country is an outrage. It is a disgrace and this conference ought not to accept it.' The significance of the electoral college was that once this procedure chose the Labour leader it would entrench the policies to which I and others took exception. We calculated that it would take two general election defeats at least before unilateral disarmament and opposition to the European Community would cease to be party policy, and so it proved. The electoral college took away from the parliamentary party its previous right to choose the leader and it rejected the only real commonsense alternative of allowing all the members to make the choice. It instead empowered the activists on the left, in the trade unions and the constituencies' general management committees. I knew that personally I would not be ready to fight as a Labour candidate with these manifesto commitments.

The SDP was in effect launched the day after this Wembley conference with the signing of the Limehouse Declaration at my home in the East End of London. Although we only formed then the Council for Social Democracy it was not long before I and others resigned from the Labour Party. But I decided, after much thought, not to quit politics. There was a fight that needed to take place on the doorsteps of Britain to convince the voters that there was a progressive alternative to these left-wing Labour policies. We decided to fight for the principles of social democracy and I became an SDP MP on 2 March 1981. In doing so I became free to champion not just continued membership of the European Community and the retention of the UK's nuclear deterrent but a market economy as distinct from the old mixed economy. There was a liberation of thought that came with the new party and in 1981 I tentatively started to develop the theme of the social market. The SDP felt free to support trade union reform, and we began to advocate, as well as support, many of the structural reforms, the deregulation and the modernisation that were starting to be introduced under Margaret Thatcher. At the same time the SDP was championing the NHS, an anti-poverty strategy and greater environmental concern. Many of our proposals for linking tax and welfare benefit reforms, for getting rid of tax concessions that benefited the better off and a more targeted provision were introduced by Labour after 1997.

The SDP always supported the UK joining the ERM. As leader of the SDP I was particularly keen to join in 1985, before Nigel Lawson began shadowing the deutschmark. We now know that in November of that year Lawson made his first and most substantial attempt to persuade Margaret Thatcher to join the ERM.* Lawson thought the ERM offered a way of reducing exchange volatility and uncertainty, but without the British government losing the power to adjust the exchange rate and fix interest rates. Both those powers are lost by any country that enters the euro under EMU and it is why both Lawson and I later joined together in New Europe to oppose joining the euro. It was important, Lawson felt, for the critical sterling–deutschmark rate to be maintained at a competitive level in

*Nigel Lawson, *The View from No. 11: Memoirs of a Tory Radical* (London: Bantam Press, 1992), p. 888.

1986 if export-led growth was to be achieved. I too felt that the disciplined framework the ERM provided could have helped Britain keep a competitive position. In effect, it offered an external means of imposing a greater degree of internal consistency on the way successive governments had approached monetary policy. The SDP was worried that continuous depreciation had only added to inflation and had softened our awareness of our persistent economic decline. Later the SDP began to advocate greater independence for the Bank of England on monetary policy, something wisely adopted by Labour in government in 1997.

Thatcher had changed her position from supporting the EMS in 1979 and by 1985 was firmly against joining the ERM. She did not want to lose her 'freedom for manoeuvre' and only agreed that the government should be ready to join 'when the time is ripe'. What was interesting was that in the UK from 1980 to 1990, when we did join, no political party leader or Treasury spokesperson, either Conservative, Labour, SDP or Liberal, was opposed to entering the ERM in principle. The arguments were far less passionate over the ERM than later over the euro and in the main this was because parliamentarians knew that membership of the ERM, as opposed to EMU, was not irrevocable. As with membership of the 'snake', if the conditions inside became disadvantageous any government was free to come out.

This distinction between the design of the EMS and that of EMU, where membership is designed to be permanent with national currencies abolished, is often not stressed enough. The

EMS and EMU also represented very different conceptual designs: the EMS was a largely technical way of trying to achieve monetary stability, whereas EMU is, first and foremost, a political decision to lock currencies together by merging them into one. Nor is enough attention given to the nature of the political agenda that lies behind EMU. It is predominantly advocated by those who have always been in favour of the concept of an integrated single European state.

One person who has never blurred the distinction between the EMS and EMU is Nigel Lawson. Even as Financial Secretary in 1981, while starting to be pretty open minded about joining the ERM, he was adamantly against EMU. In his intelligent and informative autobiography, *The View from No. 11*, he records a paper from the Treasury on participation in the ERM written by the then second permanent secretary, who was one of the very few senior Treasury officials at that time in favour. Claiming that the climate for sterling's participation was more favourable than it had been in recent years, it went on to state some conditions that would strengthen the case for entry: first, the oil market should continue to be relatively settled; second, UK and German policies and economies should continue to converge; third, the negotiations over the Community budget should be nearer to being settled; and fourth but most important, the US dollar should fall against the deutschmark. These conditions, the paper concluded, might well be fulfilled some time in 1984. In the event in 1985 Thatcher simply vetoed ERM entry by saying: 'If you join the EMS, you will have to do so without me.'

Lawson admits this decision of the Prime Minister did not absolve him from any mistakes he may subsequently have made, but that it undoubtedly made the conduct of economic policy more difficult, and thus errors more likely. In particular, it was more difficult to handle the effects of the 1986 oil price collapse and prevent sterling from falling too far. Lawson concludes that entry in November 1985 would have dampened pay and price increases in the internationally exposed sector of the UK economy and he would have been freer to overcome Thatcher's resistance to raising interest rates in 1986. He goes on to identify two further advantages that he was not aware of at the time: namely, this would have been unequivocally an act of economic policy and not influenced by the Conservative Party's division over the future of Europe, and it would have given the UK five or six years with the deutschmark providing a low-inflation anchor, prior to the inflationary strains of later reunification. The 'ifs' of history can always be used for self-justification but they can also provide valuable insights for future decision-making. In my judgement also it would have been far better for us to have entered the ERM in late 1985 rather than in 1990.

It is perfectly reasonable to oppose both the ERM and EMU but some of the arguments are different economically and constitutionally and will always remain so. An example of this is that Denmark has stayed happily within the ERM up to and after the referendum in 2000 when it voted against joining the euro. Also Sweden, despite having fulfilled the criteria, still holds off entering the euro, and not just because it is fearful of a 'No' in a referendum. By 2012 many Swedes who had previously been enthusiastic for entry were openly arguing to stay out for at least five years and maybe longer. This emphasises that while the economic case for Denmark and Sweden staying out of the eurozone may be different from that of the UK, where one of our deep problems is with the difference in the UK economic cycle from that of the continental economies, and also the far greater weight played by the US dollar in our economy, nevertheless these three economies see the so-called 'fast track' of the euro likely over the years ahead to be a 'slow track' of lower growth than outside.

Having ignored Lawson's views on the ERM, Thatcher was in no mood a few weeks later to treat seriously his specific objections to making any new treaty commitments in what was to become the Single Act (in French, *l'Acte unique*) covering European Monetary Union. Prior to the meeting of the European Council due to be held in Luxembourg in December 1985, Lawson sent her two memos of historic significance. The first one, dated 14 November, said: 'The inclusion of EMU as a Treaty objective would be a political commitment going well beyond previous references to EMU, which have been non-binding European Council resolutions or solemn declarations.'* On 28 November he minuted her again: 'There should be no reference in the Treaty to EMU, since this – which implies progress towards a common currency and a common Central

*Lawson, *The View from No. 11*, p. 833.

Bank – would be no more credible to outside opinion than the commitments entered into in 1971 and 1972 and is, in any case, politically unacceptable to the UK.'

Thatcher in her memoirs recalls some of Lawson's warnings but asserts that the formula she accepted and added to the phrase 'Economic and Monetary Union' was an important gloss. It was described as 'co-operation in economic and monetary policy', she claims, unconvincingly, and that this would signal the limits the Act placed on it.* She thought she had surrendered no important British interest but regrettably this emphatically was not the case. Once again, it showed words do matter. Sir Geoffrey Howe, as Foreign Secretary, did not raise any objection to this formulation and despite being advised by Charles Powell, her private secretary, who was always against EMU, Thatcher nevertheless by default conceded words supportive of the objective of EMU. It was this wording which was later incorporated in the new Single European Act in 1988. Thatcher cannot convincingly argue that this was the price for achieving her principal objective, the single market, for the 'internal market', as it was then becoming termed, was already agreed and ready to be put in place. It is almost incomprehensible how such a major and unjustifiable new concession was ever extracted from a Prime Minister who was utterly opposed to the very principle of monetary union and against the advice of her Chancellor of the Exchequer. It, however, emphasised the importance for

*Margaret Thatcher, *The Downing Street Years* (London: HarperCollins, 1993), p. 555.

Margaret Thatcher of having a Foreign Secretary who did not share the integrationist European ethos of the Foreign and Commonwealth Office as Howe did.

The 1985 EMU wording gave the newly reappointed President of the European Commission, Jacques Delors, the legislative authority he wanted to bring about a single European currency. Thatcher's surprising concession was then compounded at the European Council in Hanover in June 1988 by her agreeing to establish a committee of the Community's central bank governors in their personal capacities, to be chaired by Delors. Again she was uncharacteristically satisfied by the others agreeing to drop all mention of a European central bank in the announcement. Neil Kinnock, then leader of the opposition, spotted the issue, to his credit, in an exchange on the floor of the House of Commons when he reminded everyone that the Prime Minister had said that a European central bank is 'not on the cards'. He went on: 'As it is obvious, as President Mitterrand has pointed out, that a central bank follows from monetary union, is it not clear that the Prime Minister is facing both ways?' In response Thatcher merely reiterated: 'With regard to the European central bank, we have taken part in the Single European Act, which went through the House and which said that we would make progressive steps to the realisation of monetary union, and we have set up a group to consider that. Monetary union would be the first step, but progress towards it would not necessarily involve a single currency or a European central bank.'

What all this illustrates is how the integrationists' objectives are achieved not just within the European Community but in the internal discussion within the government of the UK. All too often the advice of some key diplomats and lawyers in the Foreign Office is that a suggested form of words is just meaningless and can be accepted. Then EU committees are established and when their reports are received the next step is for advisers to argue that there is no danger of imminent action, then that one can accept dubious wording since it is only an agreement in principle, and not to specific action. Yet this agreement in principle is then included in statements or declarations of objectives and this is later cited as a justification for incorporation into a first draft, albeit it is explained as tentative, for the wording of a suggested treaty. Gradually such wording, having become part of the political debate in member states, develops a semi-official status within the EU and a supportive following, which leads to it becoming binding legislation unless a country is ready to hold out and veto wording at a late stage. Almost always in the early stages it is argued that to veto the process will be unnecessarily provocative and it would be better to wait for a more opportune time. This is not, as it may sound, a paranoid description but an objective record of an aspect of the community method already described. It is what has happened time after time.

Another specific example of this process came on 19 June 1983 when the heads of government met at Stuttgart. They agreed the Solemn Declaration on the European Union as part of relaunching the Community. The declaration dealt with everything: economic strategy; the EMS; economic and monetary union; economic cohesion; external relations and developing countries. Completion of the internal market was, surprisingly, not given great prominence, being included as part of the section 'Development of Community Policies'. By any standard this declaration will be one of the most significant documents in the entire history of the European Union. But it was never seen as such at the time by the UK, whether the government, Parliament or the press. The declaration was described in the government's half-yearly report to the UK Parliament on developments in the European Community as the 'Genscher–Colombo Declaration', 'not a legal instrument and involv[ing] no Treaty amendments or increases in the powers of the institutions'. How wrong that proved to be. That declaration paved the way not just for a single market with far more extensive qualified majority voting, but even more importantly, and wrongly, for the false claim that a single market needs a single currency. In 2012, now that the euro has been hit by a crisis, we are hearing what some of us have always argued: that, to succeed, a single currency needs a single country.

A lesson to learn is that having people to represent Britain in the Commission who agree in their heart and head with the government's policies towards Europe is vitally important. Margaret Thatcher paid too little attention to this and she was too cavalier in appointing people to the Commission who did not share her views on Europe. In October 1984 it was the single market which was the British government's key priority. Thatcher had dinner at No. 10 with Jacques Delors with the sole objective of persuading him to give her Cabinet colleague Lord Cockfield this portfolio. Delors agreed to do this but used the opportunity to cleverly retain for himself the economic and monetary affairs portfolio, which he correctly saw as the motor for integration. That was the portfolio Margaret Thatcher should have demanded for the UK. In addition she should have sent to Brussels a commissioner who was a political heavyweight in the Conservative Party and who reflected her own opposition to monetary union. Cockfield was an excellent choice for dealing with the detail of the single market but he was also a self-acknowledged federalist. He established a relationship of trust with Delors and had every right to claim to be with Delors the joint architect of the single market. He was, however, part of the momentum built up in the Commission in Brussels to combine two elements, the Solemn Declaration on European Union and the internal market in a Single Act Treaty. This again is typical of the way integrationist ideas develop and then become acquiesced on in capitals of member states. Thatcher claims that right up to the beginning of the Luxembourg Council she thought she could rely on Chancellor Helmut Kohl's recent conversation with her that the Germans were totally opposed to any wording to cover economic and monetary union in the revisions of the treaty. That was not to be the case.

Policies in politics are rarely as important as personalities. What had begun as a personal and fairly private problem over entering the ERM between Margaret Thatcher, Nigel Lawson and Geoffrey Howe became after the Luxembourg Council a political weakness for the whole government. On the crucial issue of European Monetary Union the government began to lack coherence. The three were at loggerheads over the ERM and EMU and the resignations of both men that followed destroyed the Prime Minister's authority. It also precipitated her rejection by most of her own appointed Cabinet and by the crucial number of MPs who had the power to force her resignation. As Prime Minister, Jim Callaghan made clear to me when I became Foreign Secretary that in his view the Prime Minister, the Chancellor of the Exchequer, the Foreign Secretary and the Home Secretary should never disagree in Cabinet without the other three knowing beforehand and having privately tried to settle any difference. No government in my experience can long survive a serious and open conflict between a Prime Minister and two of those senior Cabinet colleagues without serious damage and usually resignations. The Tony Blair–Gordon Brown joint presidential relationship was destructive to the Labour government's performance and credibility in the long term. But Brown never had, for any length of time, another very senior Cabinet Minister on his side against Blair, which makes it all the more surprising that Blair conceded so much to Brown.

Margaret Thatcher's conflict with a Chancellor with whom she had so much in common on market economics and monetarism manifested itself most obviously over Nigel Lawson's policy of shadowing the deutschmark, a policy which is now widely acknowledged to have failed. Its failure in 1987 began to influence my thinking towards the advisability of keeping floating exchange rates and to becoming far more critical of the merits of all the various mechanisms for achieving exchange rate stability.

The Conservative government's economic policy in the run-up to the 1987 general election generated a pre-election boom. Sterling depreciated by 20 per cent in 1986. The Louvre Agreement in February 1987, involving concerted international intervention, seemed sensible and led to a strengthening of sterling. The Budget that followed, however, was inflationary and irresponsibly so, with Nigel Lawson refusing to revalorise excise duties and in a blatant electoral bribe taking two pence off the standard rate of income tax. In a policy designed to make the electorate feel good in the short term, the Chancellor seemed to have exchange rate targets of $1.60 and DM2.90 to the pound and it was assumed that the Bank of England was intervening along broadly those guidelines, having both a floor and a ceiling. Shadowing might have provided an electorally helpful period of exchange rate stability in the run-up to the election; the problem was that it continued afterwards, when Nigel Lawson both wanted and expected Margaret Thatcher to agree to enter the ERM. When she peremptorily refused to do so he should not have continued to shadow the deutschmark. Eventually the scale of intervention needed to keep the pound down became so high that it had to be uncapped in March 1988.

To Thatcher, who, despite some briefing to the contrary, was fully involved in this earlier shadowing policy, the lesson was 'there is no way in which one can buck the market'. To Lawson the lesson in his biography was not that the intervention had been inflationary, as many commentators have come to believe, but that 'the overall stance of policy – taking both exchange rates and interest rates into account – was not tight enough'. In retrospect, after the Wall Street collapse of October 1987 monetary policy should have been tightened and sterling, as the Bank of England wanted, should have been allowed to rise.

The UK had tried to be a member of the European 'snake' and that had lasted six weeks; sterling had tried to shadow German currency and that had lasted barely a year. In sum two failed experiments. There was still one to go, ERM. By the time the ERM experiment failed as well in 1992, like many others I concluded on economic grounds that we must be in no hurry to join a single European currency and that it had to prove itself beyond any shadow of doubt before we could safely contemplate entry. This judgement was compounded by a growing realisation of the political and constitutional implications of further integration on the back of any single currency provided for in the Maastricht Treaty.

The aftermath of the 1987 general election was a difficult one for me personally. Within days the SDP was locked in a divisive debate about merging with the Liberal Party. Having been a social democrat by inclination within the Labour Party from 1959 to 1981, and by name within the SDP for six years, I decided to continue, with two other SDP MPs, John Cartwright and Rosie Barnes, as a social democrat for at least the whole parliament for which I had been elected. I had never at any time in my life been attracted to becoming a Liberal, despite my family link to the Lloyd George Liberal Party in south Wales. The reasons are many and varied but one, given the focus of this book, will be obvious: I had never been nor was ever likely to become a believer in a federal Europe. That policy of progressive integration, in place since Jo Grimond had been leader of the Liberal Party, was one of the distinctive hallmarks of being a Liberal. The city of Plymouth, my birthplace and political base, had also never given any significant support to Liberals since Leslie Hore-Belisha, the MP for Devonport, left the Liberal Party to become a Conservative in 1945. Despite the Liberals doing well in local elections and gaining MPs in both Devon and Cornwall, the Plymouth electorate has stood out for a straight choice, Labour or Conservative. This is not unrelated to the fact that Plymouth stood out for Cromwell against the surrounding West Country's political support for the King. The city has since 1945 swung solely between Labour, Social Democrat and Conservative MPs and between Labour and Conservative councils. Though it embraced the SDP on its post-war council estates between 1981 and 1987 it swung massively back to Labour in 1992, when there was no SDP candidate. For me to have joined the Liberal Democrats in 1987 would not only have been to abandon many of my basic political beliefs but would, I judged, have made it impossible for me to hold my parliamentary seat in 1992, which I was confident I could still have held as a Social Democrat. I decided to stay and die with the SDP, which became for these few years more like a think-tank than a political party. In the dissolution honours list just prior to the general election, I became a member of the House of Lords, as has been the tradition for former Foreign Secretaries, but as a crossbencher rather than a party politician.

One policy the SDP adopted in the late 1980s, ahead of its time, was the advocacy of an independent Bank of England. We did not know that Nigel Lawson, when Chancellor of the Exchequer, had sent a five-page memorandum to the Prime Minister in November 1989 advocating exactly that. The new Labour government in 1997 wisely made independence of the Bank of England one of its first acts, but foolishly linked it to stripping the Bank of its regulatory powers and creating the ill-fated Financial Services Authority. The successful management of the economy in Labour's first term in office was greatly helped by the working of the Bank of England Monetary Committee while the Chancellor retained the power to set the inflation target. The minutes of the committee were published to ensure an accountable mechanism, which has enhanced the credibility of the UK's position outside the euro.

A major lesson on curbing the integrationist momentum within the EU is not to allow EU committees to be established on a wide agenda if you are not prepared to move at least some way down such an agenda. It was clear that the Delors Committee, which started work in September 1988, was bound to give a substantial boost to Economic and Monetary Union. In

April 1989 the three stages for the achievement of EMU were identified in the Delors report:

- **Stage 1** All EU member states to join the ERM within the narrow band.
- **Stage 2** Fewer realignments within the ERM and banks to become independent.
- **Stage 3** Irrevocable fixing of exchange rates; European Central Bank to establish and run a single currency.

Given the intelligence of its principal author, Jacques Delors, it was a clever package, but not just on economic grounds – it was highly political. By eliding the ERM with EMU it downplayed the essential difference between the two; namely that ERM was a non-binding agreement between independent Community member states whereas EMU involved a permanent supranational institution, the European Central Bank, at best with strong federalist implications and at worst providing an escalator to a United States of Europe. A trap was set in that report. For it was a fatal mistake to endorse even Stage 1, let alone Stage 2, while Stage 3 remained in the Delors report. Margaret Thatcher, who did not believe in a single currency, should have rejected the Delors report with all its stages and only after its rejection had been formally established should she have considered joining the ERM.

The Madrid European Council in June 1989 was the point for decisions on the Delors report. Prior to it Nigel Lawson and

Geoffrey Howe sent two memos and had two meetings with Thatcher urging her to commit to join the ERM and not go on relying on the by-now jaded formula of joining when the time was ripe. At the last meeting they both told her that if she did not move at Madrid they would both resign from the Cabinet. In the event she moved a little on the ERM but despite that within months she had forced them both out. In a strict interpretation of what she actually said it can be argued she only moved an inch but in terms of the way the press reported it she moved a mile. The Madrid formulation on the ERM also helped John Major, as Chancellor, to later persuade Thatcher to join. Major had taken over from Howe as Foreign Secretary when Howe accepted being moved to Leader of the House. John Major then took over from Lawson as Chancellor when the latter resigned after one clash too many with the Prime Minister over economic policy. Yet once again, behind all the rows and drama over the ERM in the UK, the other heads of government at the Madrid summit ensured a major victory for EMU in that an agreement was made to hold an intergovernmental conference (IGC) for treaty amendments to implement Stages 2 and 3, and the ground was laid for the Maastricht (IGC) of December 1991.

While Major was still Chancellor and before he became Prime Minister, the second permanent secretary to the Treasury, a very able civil servant called Nigel Wicks, seeing which way opinion was moving both inside the Conservative Party and more generally with public opinion, suggested to Major that Britain might negotiate an opt-out. What eventually emerged was similar to what Jim Callaghan had done over EMS and the ERM in 1979. Now the UK would sign up for a treaty on EMU as Callaghan and I had done for the EMS, and opt out of the single currency as we had opted out of the ERM.

Before Major persuaded Thatcher that ERM entry should no longer be postponed he had in June 1990 proposed the 'hard ecu', a basket currency mechanism, as a common or parallel currency which would operate alongside national currencies. That seemed to me a logical evolutionary step to run in association with the ERM, but it came politically too late and never attracted the German Bundesbank, the one institution that might have advocated it from a position of strength and been able to halt the political pressure from Chancellor Kohl to give up the deutschmark for a single European currency. This pressure, we now know, involved Kohl constantly ignoring the facts and the caution expressed by his officials.

The UK entered the ERM on 5 October 1990 and chose a rate of DM2.95 to the pound, effectively the market rate and around the average rate adjusted for inflation for the previous decade. The rate was not negotiated with the Monetary Committee in Brussels but soundings were taken. The Bundesbank favoured a lower rate of DM2.90, which surprisingly was not chosen; however, being only very slightly lower, it would not have made any difference to the crisis in 1992. The Banque de France, perhaps not surprisingly given its wish to retain a competitive edge for the French economy, wanted a higher rate of DM3.00. The broader 6 per cent band was chosen, which allowed the pound to fluctuate between DM3.12 and DM2.778. Thatcher said of ERM entry from Downing Street: 'We have done it because it is right', wording which has become the mantra of every Prime Minister since. The problems for the UK have stemmed from the fact that much of the time they have been 'wrong'. She insisted on simultaneously announcing an interest rate cut. The *Financial Times* praised entry as shrewdly timed. The non-specialist press was also mainly in favour as were the Labour Party, the Liberal Democrats and the by-now collapsing SDP. Yet within just less than two years that decision, so widely praised, had led to a dramatic and costly UK withdrawal. For the third time a UK experiment of attempting to tie its currency to that of its Community partners had come unstuck.

Within the ERM inflation, which was at 10.9 per cent in October 1990, fell very rapidly, reaching 1.7 per cent after sterling had left in January 1993. The discipline of the ERM did therefore probably work in substantially reducing inflation. The recession, which owed more to Nigel Lawson's period in office, lasted throughout Britain's period in the ERM, although it was beginning to lift before we came out and it lifted a little faster afterwards. If there is a simple answer as to why the debacle occurred it must be the failure to realign our currency as was allowed for in the mechanisms of the ERM, and that failure had its roots in the politics as much as the economics of the period.

In the debate on the Queen's Speech on Tuesday 13

November, five weeks after ERM entry, Geoffrey Howe, annoyed by government attempts to portray his recent resignation in the press as an argument about style and not substance, used his right to make a personal statement in the House to unleash a full-frontal attack on Margaret Thatcher. It was the speech of an assassin and every word was sharpened to penetrate ever deeper. He ended by saying: 'The time has come for others to consider their response to the tragic conflict of loyalty with which I have perhaps wrestled for far too long.' After the speech, outside the Chamber of the House of Commons, Michael Heseltine announced on cue that he would challenge Thatcher for the leadership of the Conservative Party and all the tensions and divisions within that party over Europe began to unravel.

On Monday 19 November, while Thatcher was in Paris attending an international conference, the result of the first ballot among Conservative MPs was announced. She had failed by four votes to secure the requisite majority. It was a sensational rebuff. Even though Heseltine was fifty-two votes behind her, under the complex rules the contest automatically then went to a second ballot because she had not been able to achieve the required majority of fifty-six. The so-called 'Tory wets', most of whom were also strong believers in the European Community, after having been reviled from 10 Downing Street over all those years, had had their revenge in the secrecy of the ballot box. Motives were mixed but in addition to the cumulative dislike of Thatcher's personality and policies and fear of losing the next general election, there was an underlying belief that her stance on Europe had dramatically changed and that it was no longer just rhetoric but a reality that she did not want Britain to remain in the European Community. Many Conservative MPs felt she was ready to force matters to breaking point and was looking for fights in the Community as an excuse to leave. This was too much for some, who, though natural Thatcher supporters, had nevertheless believed all their political life that membership, for all its difficulties, was still in Britain's national interest. On Thursday 22 November at 10.00 a.m. Margaret Thatcher resigned as leader of the Conservative Party.

John Major became Prime Minister, beating both Heseltine and Douglas Hurd. He showed signs of having the necessary quiet determination at the negotiating table that Britain was going to need in the Maastricht European IGC in December the following year. He persuaded Chancellor Kohl that he had to win an opt-out from the single currency and could not live with a social chapter in the treaty, but he would go along with everything the Germans wanted in terms of introducing EMU and the new euro currency. It was a deft negotiation, initially accepted by his party. The intense party backlash came only after the Conservatives, surprisingly, won the 1992 general election.

On Monday 17 June 1991, at a meeting of foreign ministers in Luxembourg, a Dutch presidency paper was presented in which, for the first time in the history of the European Community, an explicit reference was to be made in a treaty to the 'federal goal' of European union. The paper also proposed a further round of intergovernmental negotiations in 1996 on a new federal constitution. Douglas Hurd, as Foreign Secretary, immediately rejected these words on behalf of the British government and fortunately spoke for the majority of governments. It was helpful that at long last the integrationists in the EU had broken cover. But the fact that they felt emboldened enough to seek to build in an explicit goal for what had hitherto been for them implicit in the Treaty words of 'an ever closer union' was a warning of pressure to come. It was, however, premature as a political initiative and they should have recognised this, particularly when some of Jacques Delors's federalist proposals at the earlier Rome summit had been turned back. Even so, some commentators, diplomats and politicians in the UK, ready apologists for anything coming out of the integrationist wing, tried unconvincingly to pretend that the word 'federalism' in this context only meant decentralisation.

This short political controversy provoked by the Dutch, and the quick rejection of their choice of the word 'federalism', had one advantage: it meant that for the next ten years it became a little harder for diplomats and commentators to argue that the Treaty of Rome had within it an inherent commitment to a federal United States of Europe. But they did not stop trying.

In the run-up to Maastricht I listened by chance to Douglas Hurd speaking to an empty House of Commons on a Friday morning explaining how it might be acceptable to have some qualified majority voting (QMV) in the Foreign Affairs Council. He was attempting to justify its use for minor matters like what colour to paint vehicles operating in a European humanitarian field operation, but I could see this as yet another step on a very slippery slope. I wrote to John Major and he fortunately saw the dangers of this QMV issue opening up for the Common Foreign and Security Policy (CFSP) at the Maastricht negotiations. A less damaging form of wording was substituted in the eventual treaty which made it clear that nothing could happen in the CFSP on the basis of QMV without initial unanimity. But it once again demonstrated that having no defined limits and no clear 'bottom line' was a dangerous negotiating position. In September 1991 one of the last acts of the dying SDP was to devote the entire ten minutes of our party political broadcast as good Europeans to alerting people to the danger of losing Britain's independent nationhood within the EU.

Despite Delors championing what was referred to 'as an all-embracing tree-like treaty', Maastricht ended up with the politicians from the member states agreeing a 'pillared' structure amidst images of a classical Greek temple with a balanced and harmonious design. But it was not to last. The pillared structure had initially three main supports. The first was the supranational integrationist pillar of the European Community, with decisions that could be taken by QMV within the Council of Ministers, where the European Commission had the power of initiation and where the European Parliament filled the main role for democratic accountability. The intergovernmental second pillar covered the CFSP; the third pillar was also intergovernmental, covering justice, home affairs and internal security policy. The two intergovernmental pillars were meant to ensure that policy would be determined by the Council of Ministers with little QMV and with overall direction to be given by the European Council, consisting of heads of government. EMU, with the British opt-out from the euro, was to be a wholly new arrangement with control delegated to an independent European Central Bank, which was not answerable to any existing institution. There was vague wording to suggest that there might eventually be a fourth pillar covering defence, which would obviously be intergovernmental.

Two irreconcilable views on the Maastricht Treaty emerged in the UK. One held that it was the moment when a European Union was established which would move inexorably towards a single federal United States of Europe. This was, somewhat bizarrely, the view of both the most committed integrationists and those opposed to any further integration. The second view, which I favoured, was that it was a moment when, in order to let the single currency through, nations normally wholly opposed to intergovernmentalism allowed for the first time a formal unique design for the European Union and the pillared structure created established new treaty language which for the first time made clear that the EU did not have to move inexorably to greater integration. We were all to be proved wrong; the pillared structure was eroded and the eurozone design was demonstrably flawed. The Treaty of Amsterdam and then the Treaty of Nice that followed just managed to keep some pillared language but the direction of greater integration was maintained. It was the unratified Constitutional Treaty which removed the pillared structure of Maastricht entirely. This proposed removal was one of the reasons why the European public rightly sensed that the Constitutional Treaty was a bridge too far and raised a clamour for its rejection. Two referendums, one in France and one in the Netherlands, turned the treaty down. But the politicians in both countries, aided and abetted by Tony Blair in the UK, reintroduced many of the integrationist advances from the Constitutional Treaty into the Lisbon Treaty. They then refused any referendum even though one had been promised in the UK before the 2005 election.

Looking back, I kick myself for not realising that it was almost inevitable that after Maastricht attempts would continue to be made to expand the supranational content of the EU and to erode the two intergovernmental pillars. In the justice and home affairs pillar, it became accepted that more QMV would happen. In each case a rational argument, it could be said, was being made for the change. There were in Maastricht, and still within the Lisbon Treaty, some defining limits to what had been hitherto aspirational language about leading inexorably to a federal union. The UK could have probably lived with that but in 2009 the edifice came tumbling down. The eurozone crisis revealed that the design was flawed and could not continue unchanged. There was going to have to be much greater integration in the eurozone.

Some Conservatives believed that John Major should have vetoed the whole Maastricht Treaty in December 1990 and called a general election to endorse his rejection before the Gulf War. If he had, Neil Kinnock would very likely have won such a general election and taken the UK much further along the path of integration and probably into the single currency without a referendum. In the 1992 general election no referendum on euro entry was promised by any party – that only came in 1997. The Conservative government would have undoubtedly split before and during such an election on Europe. The image of having conducted a good negotiation at Maastricht, which Major cleverly built on, and his modest but effective handling of the Gulf War or, as some people call it, the first Iraq War secured a surprising win for the Conservatives. The history of the Conservative's disarray over the European Union in the following eight years demonstrates for all to see, however, that there were significant figures from the Cabinet, such as Michael Heseltine, Kenneth Clarke and Douglas Hurd, who would have dissociated themselves or resigned had Major chosen the path of treaty rejection.

On Wednesday 16 September 1992, just a few months after the general election, Britain was forced out of the ERM by pressure on the currency market. It was for John Major, like the devaluation of 1967 for Harold Wilson, the killer blow to his Prime Ministership. Even more important than the fall in support in public opinion polls was the collapse of his authority within his party and with the governing elite in the country. The authority that comes with the office of Prime Minister is in part mystique, in part respect. It is not a purely rational gift and its withdrawal can be just as irrational. But once that authority, which stems from a record of competence, goes it is very hard to recover. The ins and outs of who did what or when on the day and in the run-up period to withdrawing from the ERM have since been recounted in some detail by the two key participants, Norman Lamont, the Chancellor, and Major, and it is possible to analyse what happened.

In retrospect nothing that day could have stopped the UK coming out of the ERM. It would have been wiser to raise interest rates as Eddie George, the governor of the Bank of England, wanted before the money markets opened, but that would not have stemmed the speculation. The ERM was suffering a systemic crisis. What only a few professional currency speculators realised was that inside the ERM the UK was not facing a normal sterling crisis of the type which it had experienced all too many times before. Normally successive governments had responded to a weakening of the pound by pushing up interest rates, with the Bank of England intervening by buying sterling and generally trying to look resolute while indicating a readiness to cut public expenditure. By intervening in this way, the Bank of England was in effect playing cat and mouse with speculators. If the intervention was well managed the Bank could demonstrate to the speculators that they risked losing out and they would stop speculating. Inside the ERM, however, it meant that when, as had happened, sterling dropped to the bottom of its band – DM2.778 – the Bank was obliged to meet demands to be paid for sterling at that rate as long as we remained in the ERM. The speculator had in this system a one-way bet and people like George Soros made a fortune that day by selling pounds at DM2.778 to the Bank but buying them in the market at lower levels. This resulted in the Bank of England reserves falling by $27 billion gross. This was a technical loss in the reserves and over the next few years the Bank could and did rebuild as much of the reserves as it wished by buying and selling in foreign exchange markets. But to the lay public it appeared as if their money had been lost by ministerial incompetence.

The request to Major from Lamont and George to suspend sterling that morning was the correct advice and it was technically the only appropriate response. It should have been acted on immediately but Major chose to share the responsibility by involving some of the pro-Europeans in the Cabinet, Kenneth Clarke, then Home Secretary, Douglas Hurd, Foreign Secretary, and Michael Heseltine, President of the Board of Trade. They should all have had enough collective wisdom to suspend sterling immediately but instead they waited until after the markets had closed at 4.00 p.m. when the obligation to meet all demands ceased. The decision to raise interest rates to 15 per cent in the afternoon was pointless; not surprisingly it had no effect and it was sensibly dropped after membership of the ERM had been suspended. In retrospect raising interest rates a couple of weeks before was the only action that might have postponed the crisis until after the French referendum on the euro. The remarks of Dr Helmut Schlesinger, the president of the Bundesbank, in an article for *Handelsblatt* that surfaced publicly on the evening of 15 September, were disastrous for market sentiment and proved the ultimate trigger, but they did not themselves create the crisis.

Two overriding political events made it virtually impossible for the ERM machinery to function effectively in the summer of 1992. The first was the reunification of Germany and the consequences of Chancellor Kohl's decision, against the strong advice of the Bundesbank, to offer parity to the East German currency with the West German currency. The second was the decision of President François Mitterrand to maintain the *franc fort* policy as an absolute at least until the French referendum on the Maastricht Treaty had been won.

Kohl's highest personal priority was that the French should win their referendum. He had championed the Maastricht Treaty with Mitterrand and had jointly made all the running on EMU. Since the fall of the Berlin Wall in November 1989 Kohl had worked to achieve an understanding with Mitterrand on EMU. Early in 1990, well before the formal reunification of Germany on 3 October, Mitterrand agreed to drop his opposition to reunification in return for Kohl's acceptance that the deutschmark would join the franc in a single European currency, thereby assuaging his fear of a much larger Germany dominating the EU. In this way a core French objective was achieved of removing Germany from the dominant position that it had gained by having control of the strongest currency in the EU. Kohl would not have wanted any action from Mitterrand to risk a 'No' in the French referendum and he knew a revaluation of the deutschmark was opposed by the French, who were only just ready to accept devaluation of the lira, which everyone knew of itself would not destabilise the ERM. The best ERM solution was a revaluation of the deutschmark, which would have allowed the Germans to reduce their interest rates, coupled with a general realignment. The Bundesbank, however, was against Germany revaluing and cutting interest rates and it was still angry that Kohl had ignored its advice on handling the merging of the two currencies in East and West Germany.

The German discount rate had risen by 2.75 percentage points from January 1991 to July 1992. The dollar was weak after a drop in interest rates and this helped to push the deutschmark up. John Major wrote to Kohl on 14 July complaining about damaging reports from the Bundesbank that if countries were unhappy about maintaining their parities against the deutschmark they could devalue. Two days later the Bundesbank demonstrated its independence by raising its discount rate by a further three-quarters of a point to 8.75 per cent. Major wrote again to Kohl, saying: 'The collapse of the dollar has pushed the deutschmark to record highs and forced up other ERM currencies too. The pound has now reached $2, an absurd level. But since the main flight has been into the deutschmark, the ERM has become stretched, with the pound, the French franc and the lira all close to the bottom of their bands.' But Kohl would have been all too aware by then that the polls showed that the French government might lose the forthcoming referendum, with one forecasting a 51 per cent vote against Maastricht. In another letter to Kohl Major was quite explicit: 'I must say frankly that German reunification is at the heart of these problems.' But his pleas for German revaluation were not politically acceptable.

At the meeting of European finance ministers in Bath on Saturday 5 September the most the other ERM countries collectively could get out of a reluctant Schlesinger was that 'the Bundesbank in present circumstances has no intention to increase rates'. But Schlesinger gave the essential clue to the Bundesbank's position in a private conversation* over dinner: 'The Bundesbank might well cut rates after all – but only if a parallel realignment could be arranged.' In effect the Germans wanted realignment before cutting interest rates, and the French would not support realignment.

The Germans had decided to leave the issue until after the French referendum. When Chancellor Kohl privately visited the Bundesbank on Friday 11 September he would have been told how many lire the Bundesbank had bought in. He knew about the concern in London over sterling. He had to choose realignment of ERM currencies or winning the French referendum. He chose to protect the referendum. Politics, not economics, was the breaking force within the design of the ERM, overriding technical arguments and economic considerations.

The risk that politics would eventually do the same to EMU was meant to be avoided by giving the European Central Bank

---

*John Major, *John Major: The Autobiography* (London: HarperCollins, 1999), p. 323.

(ECB) real independence along the lines of the Bundesbank. Yet it was a folly to pretend that even with this mechanism the ECB could be all about economics. Inherently, decisions taken even by an independent ECB are going to be influenced by national politicians, for the ECB's decisions will impact on member countries to the disadvantage of some and the benefit of others. We have seen these tensions develop within and around the ECB on a continuous basis since 2008 and they are still present in 2012.

For the UK in 2012 maintaining a free floating exchange rate is clearly, in the light of experience, the correct course. First, there were the damaging effects of the delayed devaluations of 1949 and 1967 under the Bretton Woods system and our experience with the gold standard before the Second World War. Then the three failed monetary experiments already detailed, the 'snake' in 1972, shadowing the deutschmark in 1986 and membership of the ERM from 1990 until our ignominious exit in 1992. Finally, there has been the eurozone crisis.

In September 1992 the French electorate voted by the narrowest of margins to say 'Yes' to the Maastricht Treaty. Denmark then voted 'No' and this was seized on by the UK Conservative MPs against the euro as the excuse they wanted to abandon the Maastricht Treaty and make it hard for the Danish government to go for renegotiation and another referendum. The powerful German Social Democrat Gerhard Schröder, not yet leader of his party, was at that time against the single currency and might have been tempted to undermine Chancellor Kohl's position if there was a real chance of the single currency being abandoned. But these are the 'ifs' of history. Already greatly weakened politically by the collapse of British membership of the ERM, John Major judged that reversing his political position and refusing to push ratification of the treaty through Parliament was neither a politically feasible course nor an honourable one. So he cajoled and coerced his dissenting MPs and by the narrowest of margins achieved ratification. The Conservatives, pitted against each other, bitterly divided and intellectually exhausted on Europe, became an easy target for New Labour, by now doing very well under Tony Blair. The Conservative government's euro referendum commitment for fighting the 1997 general election was dragged out of a divided Cabinet by fear of Referendum Party candidates making inroads into Conservative seats. When this was matched by Labour and even the Liberal Democrats, the general election was bound to focus on other issues, particularly since Blair gave the strong impression to the *Sun* and other newspapers that he was very sceptical about the euro.

The natural instinct of the electorate to alternate power and the exceptional eighteen years of Conservative government meant that Labour was bound to win, but the size of their victory owed much to disillusionment with a divided govern_ ment. Left to their own decisions, none of the three political parties would have conceded a referendum on euro entry and instead would have left the decision be taken by Parliament alone. Fortunately they did concede because they feared public opinion was becomingly increasingly hostile to the euro and only a referendum commitment could have defused this issue.

In retrospect, the euro referendum safeguard was a vitally important and historic decision which from the perspective of 2012 has probably ensured that the British nation will continue for another thousand years. It certainly paved the way for the 2011 Referendum Act, which aims to ensure that no further transfer of power from the UK to the EU can take place without a specific referendum. But even within this legislation cracks are emerging. It has been argued that it would have allowed the British government, if it had chosen to do so, to have let the draft Fiscal Compact become part of the EU treaties without a UK referendum. Whether the Fiscal Compact Treaty, which lies outside the EU treaties, amended and ratified, will ever be judged illegal by the European Court of Justice depends on many factors. Given its political track record, it is hard to see the ECJ making such a judgment. But the British government has put down a serious marker that it may challenge the legality of the Fiscal Compact. It would be an appropriate challenge to mount if the rest of the EU member states refused to restructure the Union along the lines argued for in this book.

Chapter 5

European foreign and security policy

You are not a citizen of a self-governing nation state if your government is unable in the last analysis to make the critical decisions as to its foreign and security policy. There has never been a time when foreign and security policy could be considered in isolation from the swirl of events internationally, but nor can it be divorced from domestic politics. It can and should reflect an independent national judgement. There is still much truth in the words of John Donne, a poet and Dean of St Paul's Cathedral from 1621 to 1631: 'No man is an island entire of itself; every man is a piece of the continent, a part of the main; if a clod be washed away by the sea, Europe is the less, as well as if a promontory were.'

It has never been easy to reach agreement in Europe on all foreign and security policy issues and there are deep historic and other fundamental reasons for this. Nevertheless in some areas we are finding it easier in Europe to achieve genuine agreement and my emphasis on past disagreements in this chapter is not to exaggerate them but to explain why the UK needs the safeguard of being the ultimate decision maker within a wider area of co-operative policy making. It is all too easy to allow glib talk of a European common foreign and security policy (CFSP) to delude people into believing such a policy exists or can ever exist if we remain a freestanding nation state. We also have to examine the record to show whether for all the elaborate EU machinery in this area developing ever faster, the UK would be better to revert to the more limited Political Co-operation framework for dealing with foreign and security policy that we happily operated under in the European Community between 1973 and 1991.

At the end of the eighteenth century Edmund Burke, warning on how Britain was handling France and Spain, wrote: 'Nothing is so fatal to a nation as an extreme of self-partiality, and the total want of consideration of what others will naturally hope or fear.' This need to consider the hopes and fears of others in forging a consensus has not changed over the years. The habit of dialogue keeps the UN alive. The exchange of information, first in the European Community and now in the EU, has provided the climate for consensus as, indeed, it has done ever since 1948 for NATO. There is no virtue of itself in British exceptionalism but it is an inescapable reality that despite the best of intentions, there will not always be agreement in Europe. We need to understand why there are these differences, understand their nature and define the circumstances when it is necessary for one or more states to block a scheme with which they disagree becoming European policy.

It was a natural development of the European Community that after initially working on trade and economic issues it started a new activity that was called Political Co-operation. This started in 1969 and was not in the institutional framework. It took place in the presidency capital and at first the Commission was not admitted. It was a framework for trying to co-ordinate and develop a consensus on foreign policy issues that affected the member states. It seemed then to most people in Europe, as it does in retrospect, to be a sensible undertaking. Some member states undoubtedly saw it as the chrysalis for a single European foreign policy. The majority saw it as a practical non-ideological development: if we were to work together effectively for international peace and prosperity it helped if neighbouring states could reach agreements. They also shared a belief that geographical proximity was one of many factors that were pushing the member states towards common interests and that it was worth trying to develop the same way of looking at the world in our own region. In October 1973 Political Co-operation, still in its infancy, was severely tested when a surprise attack was launched on Israel by the surrounding Arab states on 6 October, the eve of the Jewish holiday to mark the day of atonement, Yom Kippur.

The Middle East is an area of the world that well illustrates why with such long and different historical involvements it is difficult for European nations to perceive events in the same way. For France, the Napoleonic invasion of Egypt in 1798 was a historic landmark. The Suez Canal, 101 miles long, was built by a French company. It was opened in 1869 and its originator, Ferdinand de Lesseps, accompanied the French Empress Eugénie on the imperial yacht through the canal. Egypt's 44 per cent shareholding was bought for Britain by the Prime Minister, Benjamin Disraeli, in 1875 for £4 million.

Britain dominated Egypt for seventy years from 1882 until 1952, when the Young Officer Revolution laid the seeds for the Egyptian government's seizure of the Suez Canal. Britain had ruled Sudan as an Anglo-Egyptian condominium from Kitchener's Battle of Omdurman in 1898 until it became independent in 1956. Britain's Egyptian and Sudanese policies were influenced by its position in India as the ruling power. From the early nineteenth century British ships gave it a presence and an influence around the Arabian Peninsula, from the Persian Gulf to the Red Sea.

The seeds of later discord in the Middle East were laid when Britain made promises to the Arabs in 1915 which were not fulfilled in the peace settlement after the First World War. In his declaration of 1917, the Foreign Secretary, Arthur Balfour, compromised Britain's pledges to the Arabs by saying that the government viewed 'with favour the establishment in Palestine of a national home for the Jewish people'. Britain, having fought together with the French during the First World War, did not prevent France from expelling King Faisal I from Damascus and accepted the French mandate over Syria. An Anglo-French carve-up of the Levantine Arab provinces led to Britain putting King Faisal on the throne in Baghdad and to creating

Transjordan, now Jordan. Britain then assumed under the League of Nations a mandate over Palestine that was abandoned to a UN-sponsored solution of partition in 1948.

The Suez Canal was nationalised by Colonel Nasser on 26 July 1956. The Prime Minister, Sir Anthony Eden, heard the news while giving a dinner at No. 10 to King Faisal II of Iraq and his Prime Minister, Nuri as-Said. Eden's reaction at a meeting with his advisers that night was 'I don't care whether it is legal or not, I'm not going to let him do it'. Eden believed Britain had the power to impose its will. Britain was the largest supplier of weapons to the Middle East. The British military presence was substantial with troops at bases in Cyprus, Aden, Iraq and Libya. In 1956 it was still just accepted by America that Britain was the major Western power in the region with influence over most of the Arab nations. The French were bogged down in Algeria though still influential in Lebanon and Syria. In France the Socialist Prime Minister, Guy Mollet, had told Shimon Peres, then director general of the Israeli Ministry of Defence, wanting French arms and more nuclear collaboration: 'Now you will see that I will not be a Bevin,' a reference to the pro-Arab views of Britain's Foreign Secretary during Israel's struggle for independence.

Franco-British collusion with Israel to retake the Suez Canal and push Nasser out in circumstances of absolute secrecy and to the total exclusion of America was fraught with risk and a reckless departure for Eden from British diplomacy of working closely with the USA. The Suez debacle ended eighteen hours after the main body of Anglo-French forces had landed on 6 November. Eden telephoned Mollet, telling him that, under intense pressure from President Eisenhower, who resented not being told in advance about the collusion, his Cabinet had agreed to a ceasefire at midnight on the next day. Britain's gold reserves had fallen by £100 million in the previous week and the Chancellor of the Exchequer, Harold Macmillan, said that the exchange rate could not be held, earning him the jibe from Harold Wilson, his shadow on the opposition benches, of being the 'first in, first out of Suez'. The Americans had $1.5 billion ready to lend to Britain on very attractive terms including deferred interest payments but the price was a humiliating ceasefire and withdrawal. Eden resigned on 9 January 1957 to be replaced by Macmillan.

Mollet's government fell in May 1957. In 1958 Charles de Gaulle returned to power and retained France's links with Israel until the 1963 war when he stopped all arms shipments to Israel and moved French policy decisively towards the Arabs. On Eden's death in 1977 his obituary in *The Times* summed it all up: 'He was the last Prime Minister to believe Britain was a great power and the first to confront a crisis which proved she was not.' Suez had other major consequences. President Eisenhower and his Secretary of State, John Foster Dulles, inserted the US into the Middle East as the major power checking the Soviet Union, which had at one point looked like intervening militarily. Nevertheless, Soviet power increased in Arab countries, not least in Egypt. In the UN the moral authority of the UK and

France was temporarily reduced to zero after Suez. Israel, however, appeared to gain in power, with Egypt having to open the Straits of Tiran to Israeli shipping, and a UN observer presence was stationed on its frontier with Egypt, making cross-border raids more difficult. In Iraq the seeds of radicalism were sown for the overthrow of King Faisal and in 1958 the Ba'ath Party came to power, paving the way for the long and evil rule of Saddam Hussein.

The UK in particular but also France misjudged the consequences for not informing or consulting the US over Suez. Of all the post-Second World War readjustments to US power, Suez was the most traumatic for both France and Britain. In its aftermath, the UK turned more to the US. The French followed instead Konrad Adenauer's prediction to Mollet in November 1956: 'Europe will be your revenge.' In 2012 we are still living within the EU of consequences of the different directions taken by France and Britain in their foreign and defence policies after Suez.

Today the cultural legacy in Egypt, Lebanon, Syria and even Iraq is more French than British. Yet neither France nor Britain are power players in the Middle East. That position passed slowly but surely to the United States after it became in 1947 the first country to recognise Israel. The US in 2012 has the Republican Party, as well as the Democrats in Congress, ready to make a strategic commitment to defend Israel. If Israel ever wanted a mutual security treaty the legislative support is there in Congress for such a treaty. Though never formally acknowledged by any US government there is already a moral commitment to sustain Israel underpinned by strong sentiment more than any obvious overwhelming strategic or economic interest.

Against that short telescoped background of complexity, it is not surprising, therefore, that in the EU views frequently differ on the Middle East. In 1973 Edward Heath as Prime Minister chose to side with France, not the US, in a pro-Arab posture in the Middle East. During the 1973 Yom Kippur war Britain applied an allegedly even-handed arms embargo policy, something I opposed. Centurion tanks, manufactured in Britain and on their way to Israel, were held in a UK Customs shed, as was the ammunition for Centurions already supplied and desperately fighting on the Israeli front line. Heath also refused permission for the United States to fly equipment to Israel from military bases in the UK or Cyprus, forcing the Americans to fly instead from the Azores. The fear in Europe that was undoubtedly guiding its foreign policy was of an Arab oil embargo. In the event an Arab embargo only fell on the Dutch, who were felt to be the most pro-Israeli country in the European Community. At the EEC heads of government summit in Copenhagen in December an energy crisis was threatening and it was agreed the nine member states would henceforth bargain collectively. But Heath, to the annoyance of many in the Community, refused to allow British North Sea oil to be used as a collective resource.

The UK damaged its relations not just with Israel in 1973 but also with the USA, given that Heath had prevented the US from using bases in the UK and Cyprus. Coming on top of Harold Wilson's decision from 1964 to 1970 not to support the Americans in Vietnam with troops, the sense in Washington particularly amongst Republican policy makers was that the British could not be relied on, at least over the Middle East.

The first big foreign policy division within the European Community concerned the Middle East, when the French, led by President Giscard d'Estaing, wanted the Community to qualify its support for President Carter's considerable achievement with the Camp David Peace Accords of September 1978. The Dutch Foreign Minister and myself, as Britain's Foreign Secretary, were totally opposed to any statement or action that would weaken Arab support for the accords. Arab countries were only too ready to criticise Camp David as an abandonment of a comprehensive settlement in favour of a separate Egyptian–Israeli peace. This was a view which if supported by the European Community would have become widely held and vigorously propagated in the Arab world. We in Britain believed that for this interpretation to be endorsed by the European Community would have undermined what had been achieved and placed Egypt's President Sadat in an even more vulnerable position. The accords were therefore welcomed by the British Labour government, if not by all British diplomats, as part of a necessary step-by-step process which had been started by Henry Kissinger after the Yom Kippur war. That same British approach continued right up to President Clinton's attempt in the last few weeks of his presidency to achieve a comprehensive breakthrough with the Israeli Prime Minister, Ehud Barak, and the Palestinian leader, Yasser Arafat, in December 2000. By then it was broadly supported by all countries in the EU, showing that there had been a measure of progressive unity in the CFSP towards the Middle East.

Yet during all these years there has been an inner tension within Europe over its attitude to the US being the dominant player in the Arab–Israeli peace process, underlined by the success of Norway, outside the EU, in brokering the secret Oslo negotiations between the Israelis and the PLO. Broadly speaking, the British believed that the US alone had the power to persuade the Israelis towards a fair settlement while France believed the Europeans should be present as of right at the negotiating table. President Mitterrand changed French policy during his fourteen-year presidency to one of greater sympathy towards Israeli security concerns. Meanwhile Germany has become progressively more understanding and friendly with Israel, becoming a significant supplier of arms, in particular diesel-powered submarines. This has meant that gradually a European political consensus on the Middle East has developed to the point that at the start of the twenty-first century it has become fairly well grounded in common positions, which are underpinned by very generous EU development aid to the Palestinians and preferential Israeli access to the European single market. The EU in 2012 is part of the Quartet, along with the UN, the Russian Federation and the USA, aimed at helping to resolve the Israeli–Palestinian peace process. Hopefully this more positive position between the US and the EU will remain, but given past differences it is in the interests of the UK and the US, although not always recognised as being so by the State Department, that all European states retain their right, if the need arises, to prevent an EU position on the Middle East being adopted which any individual state feels runs against its own vital interests.

At the start of 1980 within the European Community it was possible to define in headline terms the different foreign policy priorities which held the potential for serious division in the United States. Germany wanted Franco-German entente, the US defence guarantee and *Ostpolitik*; France wanted national defence, Franco-German entente and an independent foreign policy with European co-ordination; Britain wanted a strong NATO, a quadripartite understanding between Germany, France, Britain and the US and the retention of links with the Commonwealth. In the early 1980s a serious division of public opinion within the European Community developed over NATO's defence posture and governments were challenged by strong public opposition to the deployment of US Pershing and Cruise missiles to counter the Soviet Union's SS20 missiles. I found myself in the 1980s in the midst of a passionate debate that was mainly conducted from within the European left, as I was the treasurer of the Independent Commission on Disarmament and Security Issues, chaired by Olof Palme. In 1980 the Labour Party, by then in opposition, effectively adopted unilateral nuclear disarmament for the second time and became committed to the withdrawal of American nuclear bases in Britain. Reaction against Labour's new foreign and defence policies helped to create the Social Democratic Party (SDP).

The British government, led by Margaret Thatcher, was adamant in support of the US within NATO and held a strong line in favour of deploying new missiles. Thatcher reacted against any hint of unilateral disarmament and was for holding firm in the Mutual and Balanced Force Reductions (MBFR) talks in Vienna. On nuclear policy François Mitterrand as the newly elected Socialist French President went before the Bundestag and argued directly to German MPs, including, controversially, fellow Social Democrats, for the US missiles to be deployed and to be stationed on German territory. His action was decisive in helping West Germany's new Christian Democrat–Liberal coalition government to hold to NATO's support for the deployment of cruise missiles. Political Co-operation, which had earlier moved in 1978, when I was Foreign Secretary, into the field of disarmament, through the MBFR talks, was used for quiet informal discussions even though NATO was the main forum. This informal approach continued as President Reagan began to talk about 'Star Wars', which caused controversy in Europe and meant breaking with the existing Anti-Ballistic Missile Treaty. There was then much doubt as to whether the US could build anti-missile defences. While the nuclear debate continued to be divisive in Europe, Reagan and Mikhail Gorbachev began to meet and find common ground. The fall of the Berlin Wall in 1989 followed that dialogue and allowed West Germany to reap the benefits of its long, patient pursuit of *Ostpolitik* from the time of Willy Brandt.

It would be absurd to pretend that in areas of difference over foreign policy within the European Community Britain is always right and continental Europe always wrong. A spectacular error in British foreign policy occurred over German reunification. It was a very personal policy and it stemmed almost entirely from the then Prime Minister, Margaret Thatcher. It was never shared by the British diplomatic service, nor by the Foreign Secretary, Douglas Hurd. From the moment the Berlin Wall collapsed Thatcher believed that German reunification was a threat to the UK. She was determined to slow it down, believing that it could be a process spun out over ten to fifteen years. Initially President Mitterrand also feared reunification and appeared a soulmate whenever privately he and Thatcher talked the issue over. But he kept his views to background briefings. She spoke openly to the *Wall Street Journal* and was happy for her views to be well known. Once Chancellor Kohl outlined his ten-point strategy on 28 November for German unity, without consulting his allies, it was only a matter of time before France came on board. But it was a major shock to French diplomacy and the Quai d'Orsay view was that on foreign policy Germany, which had hitherto always taken its lead from France, was now ready to announce unilaterally its own foreign policy. In February 1990 Kohl and his Foreign

Minister, Hans-Dietrich Genscher, visited Moscow and convinced Gorbachev of the need for early reunification. The British position was negative and damagingly so, reversing the policy of all previous governments that reunification was a proper objective for German diplomacy. In the summer Kohl then managed to persuade Gorbachev that the unified Germany could stay in NATO. Throughout this time President George Bush Sr was fully supportive of Bonn's diplomacy and while this irritated Thatcher it helped change her position. Britain was represented in the Two Plus Four negotiations, composed of the two Germanys and the four post-war occupying powers, the United States, the Soviet Union, the UK and France, but the real negotiations were between West Germany and the Soviet Union, and particularly between Kohl and Gorbachev directly. It was probably Gorbachev's greatest act of statesmanship that he never countenanced the use of Soviet military power to check the tidal wave of east European dissent.

Africa is another area where the colonial history of different European nations has provided scope for differences in Political Co-operation and then in the CFSP. Over Africa in the late 1970s, however, Political Co-operation enabled real progress. The German and French foreign ministers and myself, with the support of the Danish Foreign Minister in particular, co-ordinated policy on South Africa, Namibia and Rhodesia in transition to Zimbabwe. This European co-operation continued under my successor, Lord Carrington. In another instance, Somalia's incursion across the Ogaden into Ethiopia, Genscher,

Louis de Guiringaud, the French Foreign Minister, and I all agreed with Cyrus Vance, the US Secretary of State, that we should not support Somalia. It was clear that eventually Ethiopia with Soviet and Cuban support would rally and not just push the Somali forces back to their borders but be tempted to cross over into Somalian territory. When that happened we were able to persuade the Soviet Foreign Minister, Andrei Gromyko, to stop Ethiopia. We believed that holding to the Organisation for African Unity's policy of no boundary changes without a prior referendum was vital if the continent was to live with the arbitrary straight lines of the old European colonial boundaries, and this principle was applied with regard to Eritrea and, later on, the splitting up of Sudan.

Problems over South Africa arose in the middle 1980s with Margaret Thatcher's strident opposition to any sanctions against apartheid that would hurt the South African economy. Britain had economic interests in South Africa to protect and when the US Congress disowned President Reagan's opposition to all economic sanctions, Britain came under ever greater pressure in the Commonwealth. In Europe Britain had only occasional support from Chancellor Kohl. Then came President F. W. de Klerk's dramatic change of policy in 1990 from that of his predecessor, P. W. Botha, and his readiness to release Nelson Mandela from Robben Island prison, which meant a repackaging of British diplomacy into something constructive during the rest of the 1990s, helped by Mandela's spectacular reconciliation with the Afrikaners.

France had its own Francophone African policy under Mitterrand. He was content to let Britain go its own way in Anglophone Africa and Germany was preoccupied with eastern Europe. This meant that over Rwanda, though there was an agreement under CFSP procedures to send an EU human rights monitoring team before the violence got out of control, it never happened because of the inadequate arrangements under original CFSP for provision of finance. These were remedied under the Treaty of Amsterdam, which had a clear fallback for financing if member states did not agree on who should pay. There were, however, different positions between Britain, France and Belgium, which also inhibited any specifically European initiative. In a continuing spillover conflict with Zaire, Belgium and France had mining interests and political positions to protect whilst Britain had a traditional friendship with Uganda, which favoured the Tutsis. In Rwanda itself the most serious genocide was well under way while in the UN Security Council France, the traditional supporter of the Hutu minority, who were then in power, became equivocal over the massacring of the Tutsi majority. But neither Britain nor the US supported a UN military intervention of 5,000 troops called for by the Canadian UN commander on the spot. A good development was that at the start of the twenty-first century the British and French foreign ministers paid joint visits to the continent of Africa. Slowly the interests of Francophone and Anglophone Africa have been channelled into a more trans-African European policy. But there has been a tendency for the EU to develop its own African initiatives, neither primarily using the UN nor involving the US.

Differences on military deployment between European states have been a major area of disagreement for many years. In April 1986, President Reagan asked for European support to strike at Libya. Margaret Thatcher agreed to let American aircraft fly from bases in the UK to strike against Libyan targets which were demonstrably involved in the conduct and support of terrorist activities in Berlin. She added a crucial caveat in an attempt to keep within the UN Charter: she was allowing the use of British bases for actions taken in self-defence but not in retaliation. Even so, President Mitterrand refused to allow the American F1-11s to cross French airspace. The Spanish government agreed but only if it was done in a way that would not be noticed and so the aircraft flew through the Strait of Gibraltar. The German government warned that America would not get whole-hearted support from its European allies and much would depend on whether the action succeeded or not. The initial controversy settled.

In the White House it was noticed and remembered that when the chips were down America's constant ally was the UK. That carried, and still carries, a political dividend, often down-played and sometimes denigrated by commentators who do not understand the very personal nature of US presidential power in foreign and defence policy, where the President is Commander in Chief. For Thatcher the Libya affair was an opportunity to show her gratitude for the support she had been given by Reagan and especially by the US Secretary of Defense, Caspar Weinberger, during the Falklands War (see also Chapter 7).

After the Iraqi invasion of Kuwait in 1990, the EU and its member states had common positions on many aspects. There were, however, different views as to whether its member states wished to be fully involved in the military operation. The UK committed itself heavily from the outset under Margaret Thatcher and John Major, again something well understood and appreciated in the White House under George Bush Sr. The French became involved at a much later stage, after Mitterrand overruled his Defence Minister, but most other European countries stayed outside the conflict. There was considerable bitterness in Britain when it became known that the Belgian government had refused to supply ammunition to British forces. In 1991 Mitterrand joined with Major in persuading Bush to undertake the first of what became known as the humanitarian interventions under the authority of the Security Council to protect the Kurds and the Marsh Arabs with no-fly zones in the north and south of Iraq. The French, after a few years, pulled out of this operation and subsequently some European countries, particularly Germany and France, began to circumvent UN sanctions against Iraq. A series of American and British air strikes over four days in December 1998 was openly criticised by France and given little if any public endorsement by other EU member states, which, in the main, contributed to the debacle of the oil-for-food programme.

Looking forward into the twenty-first century, the situation in Libya in 2011, when the EU was again divided and which is discussed in Chapter 6, shows why it is inevitable that profound differences within a large and diverse Europe will appear from time to time. This has happened despite the tortured introduction of the new methods of EU decision-making and its complicated new structures in the Lisbon Treaty. It is fundamental to any restructuring of Europe and to its true character that it accepts, as NATO does, that its member states will retain a capacity for independent action in the fields of foreign and security policy. This needs to be acknowledged even if the countries within the eurozone are ready to accept QMV in an attempt at even greater integration within the CFSP.

Judging the value to the UK in 2012 of the CFSP and its External Action Service, it is important to keep all these past differences in mind. In some difficult areas of foreign and defence policy, worthwhile agreements have been reached but most of these would have happened under Political Co-operation in the old European Community. Recalling those areas where there have been important differences in foreign and security policy is, nevertheless, a reminder that although the aspiration for more agreement has existed throughout, genuine differences of perspective and national interest have still prevented agreement. The reason is quite simple. Europe is not a nation state and there are genuine reasons why it is only nation states who are ready to wield real power backed by military might. The EU does not have the capacity of a unified state to ask its citizens to risk life and limb, or the steadiness to take the ups and downs of wielding armed forces that some European nation states have developed over the centuries when using their fighting forces.

For the UK, if its citizens, as I believe they will, remain determined to stay out of the eurozone, the time has arrived to question whether the cost of maintaining all the pretension of the CFSP remains in the national interest. At the time, in April 2012, when the UK coalition government determined that it had to make a further £40 million cut in the Foreign Office budget, it was asked to make a substantial contribution to fund the EU External Action Service. It is not hard to demonstrate that spending that money on the Foreign and Commonwealth Office would deliver a far better return.

A tendency in the EU has long existed that believes unanimity stems from structure. But however much detailed machinery for joint decisions can be agreed, nothing replaces the feeling of citizens that they are part of an identifiable whole that is their own country. No amount of compromises that underpin new machinery for unity can replace that feeling of belonging to a country of one's own. When the Maastricht Treaty established the CFSP as the second intergovernmental pillar, provision was made in the Treaty for 'joint actions', the term used for specific situations where operational action by the EU was required. It also provided for 'common positions', the term used to define the approach of the Union to a particular matter of a geographical or thematic nature. To undertake this there had to be a unanimous decision but implementation could be by QMV.

In June 1999, the Cologne European Council adopted a common strategy on Russia. In the words of the presidency conclusion, this gave the strategy under QMV 'a horizon extending far into the next century', although the initial period chosen was four years. Russia deserved the full and serious attention of the EU but that could have been done under the framework of Political Co-operation and if it involved a Europe of around thirty-two nations, including Turkey, so much the better. UK policy can gain from the depth of commitment and knowledge of Russia in such a wider Europe. There is no evidence, however, that such policy development needs QMV to succeed. The practical result is that the European Council simply discontinued adopting common strategies for many reasons, one of which was that they opened the doors to QMV. The question, however, remains, and is not purely academic: will the EU in future seek to adopt CFSP decisions under QMV? Common strategies cover complex, deep-seated and controversial issues. This is particularly so for the Arab–Israeli conflict. When it comes to settling the final status of Jerusalem, for instance, the judgement of European states, who have differed very significantly in the past and may well differ in the future, is not, if we are honest, likely to be decisive. We need to remember too how divided Europe was over the Russians' and the Georgians' handling of South Ossetia and Abkhazia.

Under the Lisbon Treaty, it is very clear that we are watching unfold a further EU deliberate strategy amongst some, particularly those in the eurozone countries, to replace a common EU foreign and security policy (that is, one forged by consensus) with a single one (controlled by voting). What is worrying is that the whole exercise is being pushed forward amidst public indifference in Europe and little serious scrutiny. Even in the UK not many realise that widespread adoption of common strategies by the European Council could involve, under the Lisbon Treaty, the EU's foreign and security policy in formal qualified majority decision-making, albeit with the right of appeal to the European Council. This could eventually cover almost every problem and trouble spot in the world. Is this really a UK interest? Negotiations with Iran to prevent it breaking its Non-Proliferation Treaty commitments and developing nuclear weapons began in Europe because President George W. Bush did not want the US to become involved. The UK, France and Germany started the process as E3 with Javier Solana, then High Representative for the CFSP, as the lead spokesman. His previous NATO experience was very helpful. This grouping became P5+1 when the USA, China and the Russian Federation joined the talks, thereby involving the five permanent UNSC members, and at the same time Baroness Ashton took over from Solana. This contact group approach is very sensible and looks likely against the background of tough banking sanctions to be making slow progress. But UK membership owes little to our being a member of the EU.

There are strong grounds for Britain, and France too, to deal with some of these global problems primarily in the UN and not in the EU. Britain's and France's permanent seats on the

Security Council give our two countries a special role that, so far, we have not allowed to be constrained by prior EU decisions. But this will become ever more difficult if the scope of an EU foreign and security policy is to encompass all aspects of the UN agenda. Hopefully Germany and Japan will soon become permanent members of the Security Council along with a few other countries such as Brazil, India and Nigeria. But there is no objective justification for collapsing UK and French member-ship into one rotating EU place on the Security Council as some would like. I understand why for example Spain is prepared for more QMV in foreign and defence policy decision-making in the EU. It might gain more than it stands to lose. This is not an irrational judgement given where modern-day Spain finds itself. It has the third most commonly used language in the world and the legacy of a once great empire. It attempted at Nice to be given the same weighting as the big four countries in the EU but failed and is now on a par with Poland. It sees Italy failing to become a permanent member of the Security Council but nevertheless being a member of G8. In terms of population Spain (47 million) is larger than Canada (35 million), which is in G8 but which is also not a member of the Security Council. On the rotating regional system in the UN for membership of the Security Council Spain will only be a member of it rarely. The Dutch government too faces a somewhat similar choice. Because of its past empire, and centuries-long interest in inter-national law, it wishes to and does play a strong international role.

In the Netherlands too there are attractions in collective EU membership to the UN. Dutch politicians were amongst the leading integrationists in the 1960s and believed in a single federal state until the early 1990s. Dutch public opinion is, however, now becoming less integrationist. A Dutch commissioner, Frits Bolkestein, has so far been the only commissioner to be avowedly critical of integration for its own sake. After the anguished national soul-searching that followed the Srebrenica massacre, despite Dutch forces in UN blue berets being on the ground, there was for a time an understandable lack of self-confidence about pressing a particular Dutch foreign policy and a readiness to rely more than ever on an EU foreign and security policy. But this may be changing after the Dutch referendum in 2005 rejected the Constitutional Treaty and Dutch political parties are emerging that are explicitly not committed to ever greater integration.

There are politicians in Germany who want EU membership for the UN, but others hope that Germany becomes in its own right a permanent member within a few years, albeit without a veto. It certainly deserves to be. Italy has also lobbied hard for permanent membership. Its ambassador to the UN once joked that with Germany and Japan, Italy 'too lost the Second World War'.

While Britain still retains the ability to project power worldwide and contributes more generously to the UN in money and military manpower than most, it will remain one of the five permanent members with a veto. Britain's membership is, of course, the result of the accidents of history and its global position in 1945 at the San Francisco conference that created the UN. Besides Korea and many peacekeeping operations all over the world since, Britain has broadly lived up to its position on the Security Council. Yet for the last fifteen years it has conceded too much to an EU CFSP.

The Amsterdam Treaty, negotiated in June 1997 and ratified in 1999, introduced a number of reforms which, though on the face of it having no great constitutional significance in themselves, in combination were more extensive than many people realise. They were designed to make it much harder for any EU member state, when in a minority, to block a particular foreign and security policy acceptable to the majority. In particular, the new mechanisms came as close as they could to creating a single foreign policy without formally eroding the independence of an individual member state. The Amsterdam Treaty also clarified a number of ambiguities over CFSP, in particular the important matter of financing. The Lisbon Treaty took the decision-making process even further with the High Representative chairing the meeting of European foreign ministers and an acceptance that action can follow if states acquiesce by not taking a formal voting position even if they have important reservations. Advocates of QMV have the superficial intention of quickening decision-making as more member states start to join. But foreign policy decisions are not to be compared with the myriad of decisions necessary to bring about the single market. They are fewer in number and potentially more far reaching in their consequences. It cannot be stressed often enough too that many politicians advocate QMV, not primarily to speed up decisions, but as part of a strategy of moving slowly from a common to a single foreign policy.

By contrast, NATO, for very good practical and constitutional reasons, operates a decision-making structure that requires acceptance by all and has accepted that majority voting mechanisms do not overcome substantive policy differences. Over Kosovo no system of QMV would have overcome the determination of President Chirac to veto bombing targets and show France counted. Never in NATO will America accept any system of majority voting without the protection of a veto, as in the Security Council. What happened with Kosovo was that America leant firmly on Italy and Germany when they advocated a pause to the bombing. When it became necessary to change the targeting strategy to pressurise Milošević by hitting bridges and factories, the Supreme Allied Commander combined consultation with people such as Chirac with the exercise of greater military discretion, though answerable at all times to the Pentagon. NATO structures were robust enough to allow US muscle to be exercised from the Pentagon and the White House – too uncomfortably for some European leaders. But these are the realities of armed conflict; decisions have to be delegated to the military within political parameters.

Within the EU and NATO, Greece all along had a different perspective, as a Balkan state, to its other allies on the wars in the former Yugoslavia. At one time, the issue of Macedonia as the name for the new neighbouring state brought hundreds of thousands of demonstrators on to the streets of Thessaloniki and Athens. A Greek Foreign Minister resigned over the issue. I lived with this problem day by day as the EU negotiator from 1992 to 1995 but I never believed that it would have helped a resolution of this deep issue if decisions had been forced on Greece by QMV. It has still not been fully resolved in 2012. Greek governments of different political parties have recognised, however, the need to avoid disrupting the effectiveness of the organisations to which they belong and they respect majority views while registering their dissent. In democratic politics most politicians know that a little untidiness in decision-making is a necessary price to pay and provides a flexibility that is not found through the pursuit of bureaucratic neatness.

Britain has played a very full part in recent international humanitarian interventions, from its readiness to protect the Kurds in Iraq in 1991, to heavy troop commitments for the UN in Yugoslavia, to involvement under the Australians in East Timor. In Sierra Leone by deploying a British force but working closely with the UN we had a particular success. In Iraq and in Afghanistan from 1998 to 2012 our role has been very controversial, both at home and abroad. Strong voices were raised in the UK arguing against these deployments, and we had our own internal debate, but we remained a decisive military power. In some respects the decisions taken were clearly wrong, particularly in the aftermath of taking Baghdad. These damaged Britain's status and its credibility in the world. But I see no evidence that these setbacks have threatened our position as a permanent member of the Security Council. Nor have they weakened our political will to stay a global power, hence the decision to build two aircraft carriers. Some will suggest that a stronger, more integrated, CFSP would have prevented the UK embarking on the Iraq War from 2003 to 2009. It has certainly proved to be the worst British foreign and security policy for over a century. I have described the mistakes, very personal to both George W. Bush and Tony Blair, elsewhere* and the facts are by now fairly well known and in recent memory. But Iraq, from 1990 until 2009, demonstrated more starkly than any other foreign policy issue how divided Europe was and still is. The UK and Spain were in 2003 the main European proponents of invading, Germany and France its main opponents. Lessons are there in abundance to be learnt. But the better handling of Iraq, by and large, does not lie with the structures.

Some always argue that to stay on the Security Council we must remain a super-sophisticated nuclear weapon state with ballistic missile-firing submarines. That this is the price for keeping our place at the 'top table'. I do not personally believe that keeping this nuclear role is as important as our peacekeeping role, keeping UK representation in virtually every UN member state and remaining involved globally as a 'blue water' nation state. The commitment of the five original nuclear weapon states through the Non Proliferation Treaty is to work towards the

*David Owen, *The Hubris Syndrome: Bush, Blair and the Intoxication of Power*, new ed. (York: Methuen, 2012).

abolition of nuclear weapons. We have reduced the numbers and the size of our nuclear warheads, but only recently did President Obama follow the lead of President Reagan at Reykjavik and put nuclear zero back on the agenda. Over the next several decades the UK position on nuclear arms control is likely to continue to differ from that of France. If the UK was to drop down the size and the sophistication of its ballistic nuclear deterrent, it would not lead to any reduction of our status on the Security Council as a permanent power. If the UK was to take further steps towards nuclear zero in keeping with the NPT, that would not make our Security Council seat more vulnerable. Particularly since everyone knows that the UK would use its veto to prevent any change in its permanent status. The British nuclear deterrent must be justified on other grounds than ensuring Britain's position at the so-called 'top table'. It must be justified on its contribution to our national security and the safety of our people against all the other calls on the UK defence budget (see Chapter 6).

It is also a good time in considering the value of the CFSP to ask whether it makes sense for the EU to have a policy in every part of the globe. There are some areas in Africa where a Commonwealth initiative might make more sense to the UK than a purely EU initiative and where the French similarly might best use their own Francophone mechanisms. The Spanish too may feel at times that their relations with Latin America put them in a special position to take a lead. Some have asked whether, if Norway had been in the EU at the time of the secret

Oslo talks, it would have been obliged to risk a break in its secret diplomacy and let the EU know what it was doing under the provisions first introduced in the Amsterdam Treaty obliging member states to reveal all their diplomatic activity to their fellows. All this underlines that there are sensible limits to the extent of EU activity for it is a regional grouping.

Under the Amsterdam Treaty, procedures for QMV were applied when adopting or implementing 'joint actions', 'common positions' or the taking of any other decisions on the basis of a 'common strategy'. That language was somewhat changed in the Lisbon Treaty but the intent has remained the same, as has the concept of a qualified abstention, whereby a member state can make a formal declaration that allows it not to apply the decision in its own country even though it is binding on the other states in the EU. Procedures also allow for a member state to declare that for important and stated reasons of national policy it intends to oppose the adoption of a decision to be taken by qualified majority. In this case a vote is not taken; but the Council may, by a qualified majority vote, request that the matter be referred to the European Council for a decision which then has to be taken by unanimity. In essence, therefore, the capacity for a member state to ensure that the EU does not adopt a foreign or security policy with which it fundamentally disagrees is retained. Nevertheless the pressure to conform to the majority view has been deliberately heightened. The UK can just about live with this wording, but it needs to be very clear in 2012 that there is absolutely no room for any weakening of the wording. As part of the greater integration of the eurozone, there will be a suggestion for an expansion of the External Action Service. It will be hard to prevent from outside the eurozone. Yet for the wider European grouping in a single market, to add the framework of Political Co-operation that was developing satisfactorily in the European Community makes good sense (see Chapter 10).

Baroness Ashton, the High Representative of the European Foreign and Security Policy, is now charged with building an External Action Service. Already her double-hatted role as a supranational Vice-President of the European Commission and chairman of the European Council of Foreign Ministers, being answerable to the heads of government meeting in the European Council, is throwing up inherent differences and difficulties. Hers is not an easy task. She is building up a foreign policy diplomatic service to run in parallel with the Foreign Offices of other member states. She can draw on a previous Planning and Early Warning Unit, and the former WEU 'think tank'. The EU representatives in non-member states are not 'ambassadors' except as a courtesy title, but if we start to allow the courtesy title to be used, we will only encourage the pretence. Duplication and extra costs are inevitable. There may be some gains eventually in the monitoring and analysis of developments in relevant areas of the world. It may provide fresh assessments, identify areas of focus for the future as well as providing early warning of events with significant repercussions for the EU. But the diminution of the power of initiative of individual member states is coming with a heavy price, not just in cost but in terms of decisiveness and readiness to ensure a real presence in crisis areas. It may be of particular assistance to the smaller EU countries with limits to the scale of their foreign ministries. But with all these EU structures comes pretension, the abiding weakness of European posturing.

The first High Representative for CFSP was Javier Solana. He did not cover all areas in depth or build up an EU Foreign Office. He provided a 'network' as suggested in an early report to the Foreign Affairs Council on the possible working of the High Representative. Such a network was of particular benefit to the country that held the rotating presidency. But this modest and successful approach of providing a network and having the High Representative linking the planning staffs of national foreign and defence ministries, academics and think-tanks suited Solana, having previous experience as a highly successful secretary general of NATO. It also worked for a rotating presidency. Now we have virtually abolished the presidency because it was a symbol of intergovernmentalism. It did not need to rotate only every six months, and it could usefully have worked in groupings of large and small member states. But that route of evolving steadily was prematurely abolished in favour of the dream of a single EU foreign policy. It is interesting to note, however, that the rotating presidency system is still alive and well at working group level.

It will be years before these new structures prove themselves, and I doubt they ever will. Merging the roles of Javier Solana and the then Commissioner for External Affairs, Chris Patten, did have some logic and some sense. But its fundamental weakness is again pretension, an attempt to create a European Foreign Minister and blur the distinction between the intergovernmental and the supranational elements within the EU. To date the Commission appears to be just as involved in foreign affairs and security policy as before. The Commission's President still speaks as much on foreign and defence policy as in the past. The build-up of staff numbers has already ensured that the modest course designed for the High Representative is becoming an excuse to demand more, to argue for a single foreign policy and a single foreign minister. Co-operation with the European Commission in those areas that touch on other commissioners' respon-sibilities, such as trade and overseas development, has improved, we are told, but it is hard to identify any improvements.

The EU, it is always being argued, must have a single foreign policy to provide the one person for a US Secretary of State to ring, as Henry Kissinger once famously, though with his tongue in his cheek, requested. The EU is not a single country nor do we have a United States of Europe and it should not attempt to model itself on the United States of America. In reality, as no-one knows better than Kissinger himself, if the US gets the answer it wants it will take it from the High Representative as truly representative; but if it does not like that answer it will ring around other EU states' foreign ministers in order to win support for its views. Not unexpectedly this will circumvent any undesirable consensus against US policy developing in the EU.

From a US presidential point of view it may at times appear an advantage to have a single European voice but that illusion rarely stays with a President through the experience of four years in office. The single voice they come to recognise is the voice of least resistance, something President Obama has witnessed repeatedly. He is not the first or the last President to stiffen EU policy with direct representation to member states thought to be sympathetic to the US viewpoint. Much of what the US State Department has said ever since President Kennedy about wanting a single European voice on foreign policy is pure political and diplomatic rhetoric. The hard reality is that the US seeks, not unreasonably from its point of view, EU states' compliance on important issues of US national interest. To pretend otherwise flies in the face of all evidence and experience. The EU can act as one on trading issues in world forums and in so doing has influence on the US. An EU operating a foreign policy based in effect on the lowest common denominator of agreement has little and at times no influence. The only way to prevent the EU lapsing into a false consensus is for individual member states to have the right, in the last analysis, to prevent the EU adopting such policies. We are slowly losing that right.

Some in the EU resented William Hague, as British Foreign Secretary, refusing on over 80 occasions on coming into office in 2010, to accept EU decisions that were not formally described as a decision of the EU and its Member States. Eventually his persistence paid off and this form of words was agreed. This was not a narrow pedantic point, however, but the assertion by the

UK of fact and a welcome refusal to continue pretence.

What in reality is a unified foreign and defence policy for a country like Britain? It is not the exclusive preserve of diplomats nor of the military. It stems from political dialogue and sometimes clashes between senior politicians. It reflects the sense of the country's nationhood tempered by realities of the world. That system went badly wrong under Tony Blair from 2001 until 2007. There were no Cabinet structures to limit or challenge Prime Ministerial authority. The absence of Cabinet government is the main, and hopefully enduring, lesson to be learned from the failure of the aftermath of the invasion of Iraq.

Cabinet government was never more vital than in the five days in May 1940 when Winston Churchill, then Prime Minister for only a couple of weeks, was confronted by a request from his Foreign Secretary, Lord Halifax, to start negotiations with the Italians, who were not yet involved in the war and who had offered their good offices to make peace with Germany. Halifax could have been Prime Minister but had declined Neville Chamberlain's offer as the outgoing Prime Minister to hand over to him. Churchill had appointed a War Cabinet of five but to defeat Halifax's proposition he had to have the support of Chamberlain and could not rely only on Clement Attlee and Arthur Greenwood, the Labour members. Churchill played for time and over nine War Cabinet meetings he managed to convince Chamberlain that to open negotiations would be fatal. Hitler would demand a ceasefire during the dialogue and whatever the terms Hitler offered Churchill would never be able both to reject them and restart the war. Churchill sensed that there was a readiness in the British people to stand and fight against overwhelming odds. He knew that this was no time for negotiating but a time for fighting. He had that inestimable gift of a political leader – he knew his own people, its history and he knew its enemy. The same qualities in Cabinet leadership are needed seventy-two years on.

British foreign policy has to have, to adapt General de Gaulle's telling phrase about his own country, 'a certain idea of Britain'. Many people have tried to define what Britain is and what its people want to be. Lord Palmerston famously centred on interests but his belief that they were eternal has not stood the test of time for they have changed as has the world. Lord Salisbury's definition, 'to float lazily downstream occasionally putting out a diplomatic boathook', was all right when Britain was the world's superpower but today it needs more than a boathook and there are many other powerful boats on the rivers and seas. Churchill's Three Circles – the United States, Europe and the Commonwealth – is no bad yardstick but the circumferences of the first two have enlarged and the Commonwealth shrunk. More recently Sir John Coles, drawing on his experience as head of the diplomatic service, defined the UK as 'a major European power with global interests and responsibilities'.

I do not believe that Britain will ever be content to be part of a country called Europe. Public opinion in Britain has, as yet, never allowed the diplomatic elite to focus, as many of them appear to want to do, only on Europe. The British people were not content, even after the 1975 referendum, to become solely European orientated. They had not lost faith in 'blue water' diplomacy. Britain lifted its sights globally in the 1980s and 1990s, helped by a return of national self-confidence following the retaking of the Falkland Islands in 1982. The fourteen-year period of economic growth which started after the debacle of being forced out of the ERM even allowed us to decide to build two large aircraft carriers, a decision that did not change with the need to cut our fiscal deficit in 2010. The incompetence that politicians and the Ministry of Defence displayed over Iraq and Afghanistan did nothing to improve public morale, but it did not lead to a turning away from a global role. The most prevalent feeling was anger at the handling of both wars. The UK economic crisis starting in 2007 and the eurozone crisis from 2009 still have not depressed people's horizons, though the cuts in defence expenditure in prospect for 2013 and beyond will limit our capabilities. Greater realism over nuclear weapons spending cuts will allow us to keep two aircraft carriers afloat with modern planes and helicopters on one carrier at all times. It is a pity that the choice of US fighter aircraft with vertical landing and short take-off will mean dropping the expensive catapult that could have allowed both French and US aircraft to use our platforms, but this is a decision forced on the Royal Navy by cost constraints, not political considerations, and there remains much to be said for more Anglo-French co-operation over nuclear and other defence policies, which does not heed EU structures.

A twenty-first century United Kingdom, hopefully still including Scotland, is obliged to become involved in the global economy and foreign and defence policies. A eurozone will almost certainly remain, even with the UK outside it: Europe is our largest market and until it revives its purchasing power that will be bound to make exporting harder and more competitive. The UK has to learn new skills fast, acquire new markets and adapt faster to the global economy. There is no respite from all this, whatever happens to the euro. Outside the eurozone the UK has to be even more attentive to living within its means. Never again must it build up unsustainable deficits, as in 2008, which left the country so vulnerable to a global economic crisis. Our future prosperity lies in attracting the world's financial industry to London and exporting into world markets as well as an enlarged European single market.

A more focused British foreign policy, working within a single market European Community, can still affect world events for good and more effectively than just being part of EU pretension. Foreign policy must never, as it has done, become alienated from the views of the people of Britain, whose changing interests it should be designed to serve. The people of Britain, I believe, want to have now, and for the future, first and foremost, a British, not a European, foreign Policy – warts and all.

Chapter 6

European defence

You are not a citizen of a self-governing nation state if your government within the EU is unable to prevent critical decisions involving your armed forces which are against the interest of the major defence organisation to which you belong.

In the area of ultimate defence decision-making, even the most successful military alliance to date, the North Atlantic Treaty Organization (NATO), fully accepts that each member nation makes its own decisions. In NATO there is no alternative to developing a consensus and each member state has the safeguard of unanimity. There is no qualified majority voting in any part of the organisation and no handing over of the power of major decision-making to the secretary general or to Supreme Headquarters Allied Powers Europe (SHAPE) through the Supreme Allied Commander Europe (SACEUR), a position so far always held by a member of the US armed forces.

Under the Treaty of Lisbon the European Union's competences cover 'all questions relating to the Union's security, including the progressive framing of a common defence policy that might lead to a common defence'. The last two words, 'common defence', are a bridge too far for me, as is much of the other wording when it is all put together. The High Representative and the member states shall, we are told in the Lisbon Treaty, put this policy into effect using national and EU resources. In areas where there is disagreement over foreign affairs and security policy, the High Representative will in close consultation with the member states involved search for a solution acceptable to it. If this does not succeed the Foreign Affairs Council may, by a qualified majority, request that the matter be referred to the European Council for a decision by unanimity. The treaty also allows the European Council to adopt unanimously a decision stipulating that the Foreign Affairs Council shall act by a qualified majority in some cases not covered by other wording. The Lisbon Treaty goes further, however, in saying that before undertaking any action on the international scene or entering into a commitment which could affect the EU's interests, each member state shall consult the others within the European Council or the Foreign Affairs Council and shall ensure through the convergence of their actions that the EU is able to assert its interests and values on the international scene.

The fact that France and the UK were able to go their own way over Libya shows that the Lisbon language is just about liveable with but it also shows that the EU does not represent anything like a credible mechanism for European defence. The wording of the EU treaties on security is opaque and that very opacity is dangerous. Power still resides in the forging of consensus within the European Council, which is then transmitted through the council to the military structures necessary to command and control any European rapid reaction force. But attempts to undermine within the EU the structure of inter-governmentalism for defence are continuing. The price for upholding this structural integrity on defence is constant vigilance but that vigilance must also extend to how member states themselves insist on democratic control in this area. The way the draft Constitution metamorphosed into the Lisbon Treaty was a process of deliberate deceit in which many of the EU leaders participated. The price of doing that is still present in terms of public disillusionment and anger.

Some argue that there is no dispute that defence decision-making must stay with nation states. Would that that were the case. Regrettably there is much confusion and ambiguity over these matters. This was manifest inside the Foreign Office, in the Ministry of Defence and at the highest level of government in 10 Downing Street during Tony Blair's period as Prime Minister. Blair went to Warsaw and made a much-heralded, and one has to presume calculated, speech on 6 October 2000 in which he called for the EU to become 'a superpower, but not a superstate'. With all allowances for the age of the soundbite these two words, 'superpower' and 'superstate', are inextricably linked and cannot simply be divorced from each other. It is probably impossible to exercise 'superpower' in the twenty-first century as we have come to use that word without being a single superstate.

There have never been more than two global superpowers co-existing at any time since the beginning of the twentieth century. First of all there was Britain and Germany, after the First World War Britain and the USA, and from 1945 the USSR and the USA. Following the break-up of the Soviet Union in 1990, the USA became the only superpower, while in the twenty-first century, by 2012, we are probably reaching the point when we have two superpowers again, as China emerges to join the United States.

The breakdown of the authority exercised by the Central Committee of the Communist Party of the Soviet Union in 1989 had far-reaching consequences. The Russian Federation is much smaller than the USSR. It retained a big arsenal of nuclear weapons and missiles, but its economic power dwindled to such an extent that by the time Vladimir Putin succeeded Boris Yeltsin as President in 2000, he openly talked of hoping to catch up with the GDP of Portugal within fifteen years. The Russian Federation is unlikely ever to achieve the balance of economic and military power that a superstate needs to exercise super-power but it was wise for the UN to accept that it would inherit the USSR's permanent seat on the Security Council. In the second half of this century China may acquire all the characteristics of a superpower but it is haunted by the fear that its past fissiparous history of internal divisions could return, undermining its present unity and status. The transition to a market economy has nevertheless been very impressive and there are grounds for a political transformation as well as the economic one which they are still experiencing.

The EU has in theory the economic potential over the next half-century to come closer to the GDP of the USA even though the gap at this stage appears to be growing. For Europe to come anywhere near to matching US military power will necessitate a massive increase in its military expenditure, which it shows absolutely no sign of wanting, let alone allocating. It will also mean developing a far greater political integration and political cohesion across a wider area than the eurozone. The political decision within the EU to develop a rapid reaction force for humanitarian interventions has the theoretical potential of leading eventually to a European army, navy and air force, but that is most unlikely to be considered as constituting a super-power. Within the EU this is such a deeply contested concept that it will not emerge democratically from its citizens, who show no sign of agreeing to it even if their elites were to advocate it. The nuclear forces of France and Britain, for example, even if merged would be insufficient. They would have to be significantly enlarged and fully integrated, with one command structure and the power of decision vested in a European President with real authority over any European forces, and answerable to a democratically chosen European Parliament. Even were such a United States of Europe to emerge it would be most unlikely to behave as a superstate or superpower.

It is not just that it is hard to envisage such a development in the twenty-first century but when one looks at the disparate nature of the European Union in 2012 there appears to be an unwillingness of most of its people to want the responsibilities or the burdens. The militarism of Germany over past centuries in Europe was crushed by two defeats, and memories of military occupation after the Second World War are still vivid. In place of the German Reich has come a cultural Europeanism and a social solidarity that wants influence in the world but not superpower status.

Common defence, hitherto words with profound meaning, was seen in Europe as exclusively a NATO responsibility until the Maastricht Treaty negotiations, when the words 'common defence' emerged in texts at a time when the Dutch presidency came forward with its short-lived fully integrated package envisaging a federal EU with a defence role. The final text of the Maastricht Treaty, like the later Lisbon Treaty, refers to 'the eventual framing of a common defence policy which might in time lead to a common defence', but there was considerable unhappiness over this wording. In the Foreign Office the then European director, later to become the UK's permanent representative to NATO and then to the UN, Sir John Weston, argued passionately against allowing common defence to be part of the Treaty of Maastricht. He believed that using these words for the EU could betoken serious trouble for NATO's prime position on defence matters at some later date. His objection was pushed to one side on the grounds that ministers could only achieve a few of their priority negotiating objectives and the opt-outs from the single currency and the social chapter were higher priorities than objecting to what was dismissed as a meaningless form of words. Some think there is little difficulty in distinguishing common defence being for NATO but the pressure, particularly from the French, has never varied, namely to make common defence applicable for NATO tasks.

The EU was at this time still formally looking to build on the Western European Union (WEU), even though most military people in the EU recognised it as being on the way to collapsing. In 1948, before NATO existed, the Brussels Treaty Organisation was formed and it was this which became the WEU in 1954. The WEU had fewer constraints on expansion and by 2001 comprised twenty-eight countries with its associate partners, most in NATO, six in NATO but not in the EU and seven in neither NATO nor the EU. The associates came mainly from central Europe and brought a diversity and a coverage which was soon reflected in EU membership. A WEU intervention in the former Yugoslavia had been suggested by the Dutch during their presidency in the latter half of 1991* but there was never any prospect of agreeing. The 'click-in' device envisaged in the Maastricht Treaty whereby the EU could request the WEU 'to implement decisions and actions of the Union which have defence implications' was a long way from reality, let alone common defence. It was only ever to be used on four occasions.

*David Owen, *Balkan Odyssey* (London: Victor Gollancz, 1995).

The first use of the click-in was to help in a policing operation in the EU-administered city of Mostar in Bosnia & Herzegovina from summer 1994 to autumn 1996. I had myself landed the EU with the invidious task of administering Mostar when negotiating on the EU's behalf with President Franjo Tudjman of Croatia on the EU plan for three republics in Bosnia & Herzegovina in 1993. Tudjman had adamantly refused a proposal for UN administration of the bitterly divided city, where Bosnian Muslims and Bosnian Croats were fighting each other for control. When I asked Tudjman if he would agree to EU administration, much to the surprise of his associates he said 'Yes' and I accepted on the spot, obtaining retrospectively the approval, willingly given, of the Council of Foreign Ministers. It proved a thankless task and the EU failed to reunify the city. Another use of the click-in occurred in Albania in 1996–7, when neither Germany nor the UK were ready to intervene to support a WEU intervention, the Americans having already made it clear they did not wish to be involved. Instead, a coalition of the willing was assembled involving mainly France, Germany, Italy, Romania, Spain and Turkey with a UN–OSCE humanitarian mandate.

The Treaty of Amsterdam laid the foundation for the disappearance of the WEU by describing it as 'an integral part of the development of the Union' in that it supported the EU 'in framing the defence aspects of the CFSP'. This was because by December 1998 there was a perceived weakness in the European Union's capacity to intervene in humanitarian situations where the USA was not ready to contribute. The pressure to go beyond NATO with a European initiative on defence came from three different strands in the EU. Firstly, there were those who wanted an EU defence force as part of their overall desire for progressive integration in all fields, in the main the sort of people who had earlier supported a European defence community then rejected by the French. The second strand were those who wanted a powerful EU defence force to challenge US superpower and who believed that American hegemony was something the EU had to counter. The third strand were people like myself who believed the EU would improve its own diplomacy if it could exercise limited military power to run in harness with that diplomacy. This power could be exercised either indirectly through the UN or more directly by projecting limited force within the EU's own control when the USA was not prepared to act through NATO, but was content for the EU to use NATO facilities.

Meanwhile, the experience of dealing with the break-up of the former Yugoslavia between 1991 and 1999 posed a challenge to any notion of common defence within the EU. The Balkans had been an area of historical differences between EU states. Serbia had fought with Britain and France against the German–Austrian forces during the First World War. In the Second World War the Mihailovi royalist forces and Josip Broz Tito's partisans had been supported by Britain when Serbia was attacked by Germany and Italy. Britain had persuaded the US later to concentrate support on Tito, even though a communist, as being the most powerful disruptive force against the Germans.

Though Tito was born a Croat he presented himself as a Yugoslav and despite being disowned by Stalin was a disciplined dictator who held the country together by playing off the different nationalities against each other and imposing his own authority.

Tito's Yugoslavia lasted longer than most people thought it would following his death in 1980. In 1990 NATO's initial position on the outbreak of nationalist tensions was to maintain the territorial integrity of the country. This was in great part a reflection of its determination to prevent fragmentation elsewhere, particularly inside the Russian Federation. This led the European Political Directors at a meeting on 13 July 1991 to reject the paper presented by the Dutch presidency, when the Slovenian and Croatian declarations of independence were only eighteen days old, to explore the option of agreed changes to some of the internal borders between the six Yugoslav republics.* By the following year there were strong differences of opinion in the European Community with Germany already relentlessly championing the recognition of the Yugoslav republic of Croatia as a sovereign state. In December, after the signing of the Maastricht Treaty, the British and French, hitherto adamantly opposed to recognition of Croatia before an overall settlement, a position supported by the US and the UN, changed policy. On 16 December 1991 an expected UK veto in the Council of Foreign Affairs on the EU's recognition of

*Owen, *Balkan Odyssey*, pp. 31–3.

Croatia, when the French had dropped their objections, never materialised. The recognition of Bosnia & Herzegovina in the spring of 1992 was, by then, inevitable and the EU should have linked Croatia's recognition to the immediate deployment of a UN preventive force into Bosnia prior to recognition. This would, at the very least, have moderated, and I believe could have prevented, the subsequent war. Recognition of Bosnia triggered a three-year conflict between Bosnian Serbs, Bosnian Croats and Muslims, the largest ethnic grouping.

Croatian recognition was a classic case of the danger of creating a false EU consensus, undertaken not because member states were convinced of the correctness of the policy but because of European politics. In this case François Mitterrand wanted to solidify the decision to create the euro from the deutschmark, and John Major and Douglas Hurd felt they owed Helmut Kohl and Hans-Dietrich Genscher something after the Germans helped them obtain the opt-out from both the euro and the social chapter in the Maastricht negotiations only days before. Such is European politics, but it does not always make for coherent policy. The absurd claim by the Luxembourg presidency that Yugoslavia was 'the hour of Europe' was overblown and unrealistic. Even more unrealistic was the refusal to contemplate negotiating agreed changes to what were originally regional boundaries within Yugoslavia, rather than simply accepting them as the boundaries of new internationally recognised states.

Croatian recognition, fortunately, did not wreck the Croatian peace settlement brokered on behalf of the UN by Cyrus Vance, as some feared it would, but insufficient numbers of troops in the UN Protection Force (UNPROFOR) and a weak mandate meant the settlement's implementation was made much harder. President Franjo Tudjman gradually eroded the UN's authority in its protected areas in Croatia. Croat forces gradually won back control until their summer offensive in 1995 resulted in a virtually ethnically clean Croatia and a largely independent Croatian region in Bosnia & Herzegovina, a result that left the Bosnian Muslims, after the American-brokered Dayton Accords, controlling less territory than they deserved and considerably less than they would have had under earlier settlement plans.

Despite some mainly private criticisms from the Dutch and the German governments that it accepted too much ethnic cleansing, the EU, particularly France, Britain, Italy, Denmark, Greece, Spain and Portugal, fully supported the ten-province unitary Vance–Owen Peace Plan – VOPP – in the winter of 1992 and they continued to do so against the Clinton administration's opposition in late January 1993 for the next few months, knowing it was the only chance to avoid *de facto* partition.* President Mitterrand was surprised that I, as a former British Foreign Secretary, was prepared to publicly hold America's feet to the coals in this period. He seemed to expect me to fold and acquiesce with the American criticism of the VOPP.

*David Owen, *The Vance–Owen Peace Plan* (Liverpool: Liverpool University Press, 2012).

The VOPP was accepted, subject to agreement by the Bosnian Serb Assembly, in Athens on 2 May, the very day that the US Secretary of State, Warren Christopher, arrived with President Clinton's ill-fated initiative for 'lift and strike'. In effect Christopher argued for lifting the UN arms embargo while bombing the Serbs but still keeping UN forces on the ground in their humanitarian role. This was not bombing for the specific purpose to implement the VOPP, nor was it bombing while offering an alternative plan. The US policy was totally impractical and in fact Clinton disowned it within a few days even while his Secretary of State was in Europe explaining it. On 8 May the Bosnian Serbs meeting in Pale rejected the Athens agreement, despite its being supported by President Milošević and the Prime Minister of Greece, Konstantinos Mitsotakis. They were totally confident that no one in NATO would force them to change their stance, and they were correct.

The British and the French, hearing from the US Secretary of State once again that the US would not galvanise NATO to impose a settlement on Pale, were not prepared to do so on their own, in part because they believed they lacked the capacity. They also felt that other important aspects of Atlantic relations were by now being damaged. So by 20 May they were acquiescing with Spain and Russia in the US ditching of the VOPP in favour, shockingly, of more land for the Serbs. All five countries then championed in the Security Council the ill-fated 'safe haven' initiative that laid the basis for the Serb massacre in Srebrenica in 1995. The nadir of US, British and French diplomacy came that spring in 1993. The Security Council fashioned a false consensus, which so often lay at the root of positions on the former Yugoslavia, which was strong on rhetoric and weak on force. The UN military initially recommended over 30,000 troops to make five Muslim enclaves safe; UN officials were persuaded down to 15,000; the Security Council provided a mere 6,000 extra troops of varying quality. It was a flawed and dangerous folly; the enclaves were neither safe nor havens. The Bosnian government forces attacked outwards and the Bosnian Serb forces inwards. The UN were 'piggy in the middle' without the means to protect the Muslim townspeople from degraded health, poor nutrition and diminished water supplies, let alone protection from sniper fire, mortars and even artillery rounds from the surrounding Serbs, which lasted on and off until the pretence ended, predictably, in July 1995 with the massacre of more than 8,000 Bosnian Muslim men and boys. The Serbs in Srebrenica overran and humiliated a totally insufficient UN force of Dutch troops who a little too easily stood helplessly by.

The EU and UN negotiators, meeting on HMS *Invincible* in the Adriatic, tried again in the summer of 1993 to fashion a different settlement. In December 1993 after months of painstaking diplomacy on the wreckage of the VOPP the European Union put forward its own action plan for three republics in Bosnia & Herzegovina. But the EU had no military capacity of its own to back up its diplomacy. The US, lukewarm about any diplomatic compromise, was unready to support

NATO giving a security guarantee, which the Bosnian government not unreasonably wanted for its own federal republic boundaries against attack from both the Croat and the Serb republics. This predictably undermined the whole initiative. The EU action plan gave the Muslims a defined territory in relation to the Croats and Serbs, which no subsequent plan ever did. As the EU's peace negotiator I suggested to the European political directors in the spring of 1994 that, painful though it was to have to admit it, the situation in the Balkans demanded a contact group somewhat similar to the one set up by the UN in Namibia (see Chapter 3). Thereafter, from 1994, this Contact Group, which from the EU involved only the UK, Germany, France and later Italy, with the US and Russia, took the main decisions in Bosnia & Herzegovina. Its unity was fragile and relations between the European members and the United States were often fraught. The Contact Group presented its map to the Bosnian Serbs in the summer of 1994 but when the Serbs rejected it, these five major powers simply packed their bags and left.

In the early summer of 1995, the US began to shift its policy and after the Srebrenica massacre in July, the US diplomatic and military position altered dramatically. They were ready to commit to NATO bombing Serb positions and tilting the balance of fighting on the ground against the Serbs. This change of military position also involved the US accepting at Dayton many detailed aspects of the Vance–Owen and EU action plans that they had hitherto opposed, as well as the majority views on the Contact Group, which they had never been prepared to fully endorse. The welcome change of policy did, for the first time, allow the US to lead from the front and Richard Holbrooke achieved a considerable personal negotiating success at Dayton. But in the preceding two and a half years US policy, far more than European policy, had meant many lives had been tragically lost and much ethnic cleansing had occurred, creating divisions on the ground that were destined to remain, unfortunately haunting Bosnia & Herzegovina. To this day it still has many appearances of a partitioned state, as I saw for myself in a private visit to the Srebrenica memorial in April 2012

The world saw Dayton as defeat for the Europeans. The Europeans wrung their hands at their own defeat. But that was only because the new CFSP was built on a pretence that Europe could act like a nation state and was ready to confront the Serbs. The EU was not ready to do this over Bosnia or Kosovo. It is still in 2012 in no condition to take on similar armed forces. These tasks are and were only possible through NATO.

Kosovo meanwhile was left to fester, until in February 1999 Milošević was at last challenged, after repeated threats of NATO air strikes, when much of the Muslim population was being pushed out and into Albania by Serbs. The Rambouillet negotiations on Kosovo were chaired by the French and British Foreign Ministers but the US Secretary of State, Madeleine Albright, was a determining presence at all crucial moments in isolating the Serbs and, privately, offered the Kosovo Albanians a referendum within three years. That was the breaking point for the Serbs. In effect NATO's patience had run out before this; its key political leaders by now wanted military action but mistakenly they believed it would be quick and fairly simple. Buoyed up by the success of eventually having used force in Bosnia and believing air power there had been decisive on its own, they expected, as Albright advised her President, that the Serbs would crumble in a few days.

NATO countries then launched seventy-eight days of air attacks against Serbia. It was American leadership, however, that held the divided Europeans together within NATO during what was in formal statements called throughout not a war but a humanitarian engagement. Germany and Italy early on called for a bombing pause, which was a ridiculous position to adopt, and the US helped by the UK and France refused to countenance it. The more serious opposition came from President Chirac of France and some other countries not wanting to bomb many of the targets chosen by NATO's military, as the earlier targeting strategy had proved ineffective. Chirac, in particular, insisted on vetting targets chosen in Serbia as distinct from Kosovo. Greece was opposed to any bombing but allowed NATO forces to come through Thessaloniki to Macedonia. There was no commitment amongst NATO countries, including the US, to even threaten the use of ground troops until Tony Blair argued, rightly, that this option must be kept open. Yet it was the US, while mounting cruise missile attacks on Belgrade, who encouraged the active help of President Yeltsin to pressurise Milošević, after an ultimatum delivered by the former Russian Prime Minister Viktor Chernomyrdin accompanied by the Finnish President, Martti Ahtisaari, to tell the Serb generals to withdraw from Kosovo, even though they felt they had not been defeated.

Within that ultimatum there were important concessions to the Serbs. Firstly, the period of interim Kosovo administration was handed to the UN, which the Serbs had always wanted. There was no commitment to a referendum within three years as promised to the Kosovo Liberation Army at Rambouillet, though it was eventually the pathway for independence. Secondly, the military annex to the Rambouillet negotiations, which involved NATO forces coming into Kosovo through Serbia, was dropped and they came in from Macedonia. This annex had proposed the use of Serbian roads, railways and ports. Not only did this constitute a massive erosion of the Federal Republic of Yugoslavia's (FRY) sovereignty but to many of its paranoid leaders appeared to provide a mechanism for NATO snatching Serbian political and military leaders under arrest orders, whether disclosed or undisclosed, from the International War Crimes Tribunal. Thirdly, the wording introduced concerning the operation of the tribunal in the FRY, which Serb political and military leaders saw as a threat to them personally, was toned down with considerable regret.

All proved wise adjustments. For it was the withdrawal itself that meant Milošević lost the subsequent election and was disowned by his own people. After much to-ing and fro-ing he was offered up by his fellow Serbs for trial at the International

Criminal Tribunal for the Former Yugoslavia in The Hague. Sadly, he was never convicted, as he died while in custody awaiting a verdict.

Whether NATO's action, which was never authorised by the Security Council, was humanitarian within the terms of the UN Charter will long be argued. It certainly stretched the words of the UN Charter to its limits. But it paved the way for future Security Council action authorising humanitarian interventions. It also helped the Balkans towards a long-term peace. By 2012, Serbia under President Boris Tadi had become a candidate member of the EU. NATO's humanitarian intervention in Kosovo also forced the pace at Nice for a European defence and security policy (EDSP). However, it left scars in the Pentagon which made the US military want to resist NATO's offers of immediate help in Afghanistan after the attacks of 11 September 2001.

Even now, seventeen years after Dayton and NATO implementation, it is not possible to be clear about the shape of a final settlement for Bosnia. A more certain outcome looks likely in Kosovo, where NATO brought peace and where a UN administration helped by NATO was able to slowly reach a point where it is possible to believe Kosovo will become truly independent. Some EU states have, however, still not recognised Kosovo. They fear setting a precedent for encouraging splits in other member state countries. This is particularly strongly felt in Spain but also by Cyprus, Greece, Romania and Slovakia.

Any effective configuration over defence in the EU has always been dependent on Anglo-French agreement. Relations between the armed forces of the two countries serving in Yugoslavia became unprecedentedly close. Under Tony Blair, New Labour made it clear, not just in the run-up to the 1997 election but also initially afterwards, that, like its Conservative predecessors, it had no intention of doing anything more than build on the European Security and Defence Identity (ESDI) within NATO. It was also content to rely on the military mechanisms under-pinning the ESDI, the Combined Joint Task Force. These arrangements had been agreed during the middle 1990s after extensive negotiations within NATO during which the concept of the ESDI evolved. It first appeared at NATO's Oslo meeting in June 1992, and was further elaborated at the Berlin NATO ministerial meeting in June 1996.

The first hint of Blair's so-called 'fresh thinking' and his hint that a different UK approach to European defence was in the air came when he talked privately to the EU heads of government in Pörtschach, Austria at the European Council in October 1998. Blair and President Jacques Chirac met in St Malo in December 1998 and published their joint declaration saying that the European Council 'must be able to take decisions on an intergovernmental basis, covering the whole range of activity set out in Title V of the Treaty of European Union'. They went on to say: 'To this end the Union must have the capacity for autonomous action, backed up by credible military forces, the means to decide to use them, and a readiness to do so, in order to respond to international crises.' This wording opened up more questions than it answered.

It was agreed as part of the Treaty of Amsterdam that the ESDI should not prejudice the specific character of the security and defence policy of those member states which see their common defence realised within NATO. Article 17 of the treaty allowed the EU to avail itself of the WEU in order to elaborate and implement decisions and actions which had defence implications. The ESDI was then replaced by the EDSP. President Sarkozy helpfully brought France into a closer relationship with NATO. He also signed a sensible agreement with Prime Minister David Cameron in 2010 covering bilateral defence issues. NATO in 2012 is starting to withdraw from Afghanistan, out-of-area operations have become the norm. Yet still the French persist in wanting common European defence even, it seems, in spite of their bruising relations with Germany over Libya. If the eurozone countries wish to build integrated defence structures it is not something which the UK should block provided it is done within an agreed restructuring of Europe as a whole.

Gradually British governments shifted their ground from believing that NATO should have sole responsibility for collective defence to agreeing a limited role for European peacekeeping. The New Labour government developed this further than the previous Conservative government but it somewhat exaggerated its initiative, which helped push the Conservatives in opposition to back off the progress they had made in office. The Amsterdam Treaty language provided for European humanitarian and peacekeeping tasks and for combat forces in crisis management involving peacekeeping. It is a European structure of decision-making that can be used if and when countries in NATO, such as the United States and Canada, do not wish to become involved militarily. But to move away from NATO command and control structures so as to make a European political point is a fundamental mistake. Even in Libya, where the US took a back seat, its initial contribution, firing over 200 cruise missiles and using attack planes off its aircraft carriers, made a critical contribution to destroying Colonel Gaddafi's sophisticated ground-to-air missile defence systems. The US drone air missile system is another expertise that Europe needs but with Iran having captured a drone plane intact the technology is expected soon to become more widely available.

In Washington there has always been understandable anxiety about the implications of developing a European defence identity. Paradoxically the Kosovo war both deepened and relieved this anxiety. The main fear is that some sections of opinion in the US Congress might take any European defence organisation as a signal to reduce the US commitment to NATO forces based in Europe. Crudely put, the argument is: why should 360 million rich Europeans need 260 million Americans to defend them from 160 million impoverished Russians? The US began within NATO to work out a compromise which would not of itself lead to a decoupling of the North American continent from Europe. Wisely explained, NATO in the twenty-first century is about much more than looking back nostalgically at winning the Cold War. It will work more closely with the Russians if they wish it, and it will be used more frequently at the request of regional organisations, as when the Arab League asked to use NATO to operate a no-fly zone over Libya in 2011. We have yet to see whether it will have a role in Syria. In NATO's 640 million citizens across North America and Europe (which includes Turkey) lies the potential to provide the key underpinning within the terms of the UN Charter for a peaceful, civilised and democratic world and to help the Security Council.

But this potential will only be realised if US anxieties are assuaged as to the meaning of EU autonomous action and ambivalent phrases like a capability for relevant strategic planning, without unnecessary duplication. The shift in policy in St Malo in 1998 has taxed British diplomatic skills, since it has become ever more obvious that France is operating from a different agenda and has different military aspirations. The then US Secretary of State, Madeleine Albright, who responded for the Americans in a speech since referred to as the 'Three Ds', called for the avoidance of 'decoupling, duplication and discrimination' and said the US would examine any proposal on European defence and security with a simple question: 'Does it improve our effectiveness in working together?' That question in 2012 remains unanswered.

As it happened my wife and I had a dinner engagement with Tony and Cherie Blair in Downing Street soon after the St Malo Declaration on Thursday 17 December, the third night that the

US and UK launched new air attacks on Iraq. Over a relaxed, informal, pleasant meal the four of us chatted about many things. We dealt with my opposition to the euro and support for dealing with Saddam Hussein, which was, I think, the purpose behind our meeting. We also covered the St Malo talks and I was reassured by the adamant way in which Tony Blair said that the European Commission, Court and Parliament would not be involved in any new European defence arrangement. In the early part of 1999 I remained confident that the Prime Minister was embarked on a serious, albeit delicate, exercise and that with careful preparation there was a good chance that by building on his good relationships with President Clinton and engagement with President Chirac he could hold the position over NATO and avoid creating divisive tensions with the Americans.

On 24 March 1999 NATO in effect went to war with Serbia, though because of doubts about the legality of the action, since it lacked specific Security Council approval, it was treated formally as a humanitarian intervention. It was for NATO a very different type of engagement to that which they had long planned for against the Soviet Union in the Cold War, and there was no longer the readiness automatically to accept US strategic direction. President Clinton on military matters was the weakest of recent Presidents and the SACEUR, General Wesley Clarke, did not carry the full support of the US Defense Secretary, the chairman of the Joint Chiefs of Staff or the chief of the US Army. It became obvious that there was in the Pentagon a marked reluctance to face American casualties. From the outset this had been a politically limiting factor for this intervention. It was not the best of starts to NATO's tricky engagement. Nevertheless, I supported NATO's action but felt that we should not rule out using ground troops from the start and I shared some of the publicly expressed doubts of my successor as Foreign Secretary, Lord Carrington, who was also my predecessor as EU negotiator in Yugoslavia. It was always obvious that NATO would face a stubborn opponent in the Serbian army, a reasonably well-equipped and disciplined force, as we had experienced in their surrogate action in Bosnia. The dire public warnings the US Secretary of State, Madeleine Albright, had been issuing to President Milošević, both before and after the disastrous Rambouillet conference, of doing nothing over Kosovo, had left NATO with little alternative. Although we did not like being where we were, we could not afford to see NATO diminished in its authority by anything other than victory. The then British Foreign Secretary, Robin Cook, as well as Tony Blair, had understandably gone along with Albright in this highly exposed position with rhetoric which had made NATO action inevitable and yet they, like the Americans, were ruling out deploying troops on the ground. Despite this strategic weakness, NATO, with four million active duty military personnel to call on and a budget of $450 billion, was entering into combat with an economically weakened Serbia, which had military forces numbering a mere 110,000 though with a large police force which also had heavy weapons, many of them deployed in Kosovo. It looked on paper like an easy trial of strength but I could not believe it when I heard that Albright had predicted in Washington to Clinton that it would all be over in a matter of days. To those of us who knew the lie of the land in Kosovo and the problems of relying only on air power, NATO was committing itself to a complex and dangerous engagement. So it turned out to be. Kosovo was to stretch NATO to its limit. I was also very surprised to read in the *Sunday Times* on 28 March 1999 an article by the British Chief of the Defence Staff, General Sir Charles Guthrie. Normally the military do not get involved in political controversy but the article had these words: 'Henry Kissinger, for example, argues that we should not use force in the Balkans, while David Owen thinks that a ground invasion is a prerequisite for success. I do not agree with either.' This article totally contradicts the later British spin from No. 10 that the UK had always wanted to have the threat of ground troops coming into Kosovo and that it was only the US who had insisted that everything could be done from the air.

Milošević's first mistake was the continued forced eviction of the Kosovo Muslims over the border to Albania and Macedonia. This ensured a humanitarian-led outcry, which meant that NATO found it easier to hold a restless public opinion in member countries steady over a far longer bombing period than the Clinton administration had ever envisaged. When after only a few days the Italian and German government ministers advocated a bombing pause the US was reminded just how fragile the European political commitment was. Fortunately, at this stage, the US, at every level was supported by the UK and

France, who would have nothing to do with a bombing pause, knowing that once conceded it would be very difficult to restart.

Weeks later, on 24 April 1999, the NATO heads of government met in Washington supposedly to celebrate the organisation's fiftieth anniversary but in reality to face the worrying situation of NATO forces still bombing from Serbian airspace and the success of the operation still in doubt. The true agenda behind all the ceremonial was a debate about whether to agree to start preparing for the deployment of ground troops. This was something that President Clinton, having unwisely excluded it from the start, was still reluctant to contemplate. Tony Blair was quite correctly pushing Clinton hard to rethink this strategy. I had spoken to the Prime Minister by telephone earlier on this very question in surprising detail when I was visiting Berlin on 16 April. I had told him that the threat to deploy troops would be a necessary element in making Milošević bend even if in deference to the Americans NATO troops did not actually cross the border. I suggested NATO ask its newest member, Hungary, for permission to announce a military exercise involving tanks on its territory. This announcement, I felt, would be taken very seriously by the Serbs as the flat plains shared by the two countries offered the only easy access point for invading tanks. It would force the Serb commanders to spread their forces and not allow them to keep their present total focus on the defence of Kosovo. There were virtually no roads which NATO could use from Albania into Kosovo and the roads from Macedonia were going to be mined and involved traversing tunnels, ravines and other very difficult geographical features for an opposed military advance.

The final NATO communiqué from Washington dealt with a long-standing agreed text with carefully negotiated language over the EDSI which did not move much into the St Malo agenda. It reaffirmed NATO's commitment to building the ESDI within the Alliance and included flexible options for the selection of a European NATO commander and NATO head-quarters for WEU-led operations as well as specific terms of reference for the deputy Supreme Allied Commander (DSACEUR), who was always a European. In only one section did it promise to address the 'identification of a range of European command options for EU-led operations, further developing the role of DSACEUR in order for him to assume fully and effectively his European responsibilities'. It all seemed very sensible but in reality minds were focused on what was happening in Kosovo. Yet within eighteen months this NATO response was to be all but destroyed by the conclusions of the EU IGC at Nice referred to in the preceding chapter.

After eleven weeks of bombing, NATO eventually prevailed over the Serbs in Kosovo without having to fight on the ground. Nevertheless it was not a pure military victory. Instead secret US–Russian diplomacy provided a solution which Milošević embraced to get himself off the hook on which he had impaled himself. It was a settlement over Kosovo's long-term future more favourable to the Serbs than anything offered in Rambouillet and already referred to in Chapter 5. The UN was to administer

Kosovo and no NATO forces would go anywhere in Serbia other than into Kosovo from Macedonia. The settlement was presented by the Finnish President, Martti Ahtisaari, alongside the former Russian Prime Minister, Viktor Chernomyrdin, who had earlier himself visited Belgrade. Milošević accepted immediately and the Serb Parliament followed suit next day, on 3 June. The European Council heard the news with profound relief at its meeting in Cologne and, in a declaration which owed more to wishful thinking than the actual military experience of Kosovo, said that 'the development of an EU military crisis management capacity was to be seen as an activity within the framework of the CFSP and as part of the progressive framing of a common defence policy in accordance with the Treaties'. Yet by then not one of the fifteen EU heads of government could have been under any illusion about the EU member states' military weaknesses, which had been exposed day after day over Kosovo. NATO's victory in Kosovo was totally dependent on US military might and in particular its precision guided missiles. Cruise missiles had actually destroyed two government ministries in a main street in Belgrade leaving surrounding buildings intact.* Had we Europeans in NATO embarked on the Kosovo venture on our own, just as many had advocated we should have done in Bosnia years earlier, it is hard to escape the conclusion that we would have been defeated by the Serbs.

Lord Robertson, the then NATO secretary general and former

---

*David Owen, *Nuclear Papers* (Liverpool: Liverpool University Press, 2009), p. 14.

British Defence Secretary, said in Amsterdam in November 1999 that the ESDI should be based on three key principles, the 'three Is': 'Improvement in European defence capabilities, Inclusiveness and transparency for all allies; and the Indivisibility of trans-Atlantic security – based on our shared values'. Soon after at a joint meeting of defence and foreign ministers the EU referred for the first time specifically to a European Security and Defence Policy (ESDP) and authorised Javier Solana, the High Representative for the CFSP, to be double-hatted and to take over from José Cutileiro as secretary general of the WEU. At Helsinki in December the European Council discussed progress and said: 'Member States would use existing defence planning procedures, including, as appropriate, those available to NATO,' giving no hint of a separate planning process. At Sintra in February 2000 EU defence ministers discussed a paper which did envisage strategic planning within the European Military Staff but which did not entail an operational HQ. The paper said: 'DSACEUR and SHAPE have already been identified as the primary, although not the only candidates, for Operation Commander and Military Strategic Operation HQ.' Misgivings that a separate planning function divorced from NATO was emerging began to be raised within SHAPE by military commanders from Britain, the Netherlands and Germany. They were reassured on this by officials in their own ministries and their diplomatic counterparts. But we were beginning to see the confusion and ambiguities of the various European politicians' aspirations in relation to defence reflected in the negotiations.

At the European Council at Santa Maria da Feira the Portuguese presidency reported on strengthening the common ESDP. It revealed that the Council's legal service was of the opinion that the conclusions of the Cologne and Helsinki European Councils on defence policy could be implemented without it being legally necessary to amend the Treaty on European Union and it was for the member states to consider whether amendments to the treaty would be politically desirable or operational. The Lisbon Treaty language that followed was better in this respect than at one time looked likely but it concealed deep ambiguities about what happened when the EU was divided, ambiguities that were later starkly revealed by the differences over the Libyan NATO no-fly zone between the UK and France on the one hand and Germany and Poland on the other.

Tony Blair never had either the intellectual discipline or the resolve to rule out further EU Treaty amendments on defence. Let us hope David Cameron does not follow the same pattern. The EDSP process was slowed down by EU countries with a history of neutrality worried about public opinion, particularly where their constitutions, as in Ireland, made it necessary to call a referendum. A separate intergovernmental fourth pillar for defence after Kosovo was never achieved but widely discussed. The integrationists knew that any purely defence pillar would be a bulwark against their strategy of creeping supranationalism in foreign policy. Foremost in this category were officials of the Italian Foreign Office, who ever since the Messina Conference in 1955 had been some of the most unabashed supporters of full integration and an eventual single European federal state. This stance changed slightly when in 2001 Silvio Berlusconi, for all his other faults more Atlanticist than most of his predecessors, became Prime Minister for the second time with an overall majority. Early in 2002 he felt strong enough to challenge the Foreign Minister, who was an integrationist, and took over the portfolio himself. Italy began to establish a far more pro-NATO and less integrationist stance in the run-up to the Barcelona meeting on economic restructuring. This meant that the UK had a chance in any IGC of resisting any extension of QMV in foreign and defence policy with Italian support. But Italian officials through all the decades of multiple and revolving governments have been used to playing a key role in the formulation of Italian policy and they bided their time, waiting to fight back against Berlusconi. They were wise enough to know that the direction of greater integration is, from their Italian point of view, what matters and this is more important than the pace of implementation.

Italy, in 2012, is under a technocratic government led by Mario Monti, formerly an effective EU commissioner. He is an integrationist, part of that consensus amongst technocrats who have one single objective from St Malo on, namely of bringing defence policy into the CFSP and killing off any possibility of a separate intergovernmental defence pillar. Maastricht, and all the treaties that followed, did not define foreign policy as a pure intergovernmental pillar because of the past history of the CFSP involving the Commissioner for External Affairs and the Commissioner for Development. This meant there had to be some Commission link with foreign policy and this has been reflected in Lisbon Treaty language. One important provision in the negotiations over the Treaty of Amsterdam in 1997 was to insert in Article 23 of Title V that 'decisions having military implications' could only be taken by unanimity and that QMV would not apply. Armed with this provision Britain acquiesced and dropped the idea of a separate defence pillar. In doing so it took considerable risks with wording in the presidency report on the ESDP at Nice, which applied to the work of the European Political and Security Committee, the Military Committee and the Military Staff, all newly created and intended under the operating principles to act for the 'preservation of the Union's autonomy in decision making'. The treaty language on the CFSP was not amended at Nice to remove all references to the European Commission having any position in relation to any defence policy. This means that the European Parliament has the right to be kept regularly informed by the Commission in the development of all policies, which some argue can include those with military and defence implications. This is a totally new power for the Commission, it is something Tony Blair said had been excluded at St Malo, and it contravenes the British government's earlier claim that its 'central message – that the Commission has no competence, legal or practical, and that parliamentary scrutiny of ESDP should be at national level – is widely shared among Member States'.

As Prime Minister, Blair, worryingly, gave me in writing a qualified endorsement of the Commission being involved in defence before Nice. 'For the sake of coherent activity across all Pillars of the Union, it is helpful for the Commission to be present when responses to crises, including responses over which the Commission has a role (such as economic or trade sanctions), are being considered.' But the Commission is never just present; it has a specified task of informing the European Parliament, and that gives whoever is President of the Commission the excuse they want to speak about the EU's position on defence questions.

The military professionals on both sides of the Atlantic are virtually united in the need for NATO's planning role to remain with an overarching responsibility for the EU rapid reaction force, because this force cannot but affect NATO force levels, equipment and fighting potential. British military and intelligence officers felt very let down by their country's politicians pussyfooting around on this issue. The true picture was revealed by President Clinton's former head of the CIA, James Woolsey, speaking in Washington after the Nice negotiations and on its consequences. 'The one and only thing that the United States asked of our European friends was not to establish a separate and independent military planning capability. And, of course, that is precisely what they did.' That quote encapsulates the key issue, which all NATO professionals fear has been conceded; meanwhile the true meaning of 'autonomy' when used by the French and some others in Europe for the ESDP and what has followed is not just about deploying without American troops from NATO but doing so without American goodwill and even planning a deployment against the interests of the US. Some Europeans say this independence is necessary if the EU is not to be subservient to the US. But it could also be a certain recipe for the US to withdraw more forces from Europe, in the process turning NATO into a mere talking shop and effectively withdrawing any US responsibilities for common defence.

The European heads of government never learnt the lesson of Kosovo. They failed to abandon the illusion of the EU being ready to undertake common defence and concentrate instead on developing the Washington statement with NATO. If they had done that the EU and NATO could credibly have built up the more achievable part of the Cologne Declaration, namely 'the ability to take decisions on the full range of conflict prevention and crisis management tasks defined in the Treaty on European Union, the so-called "Petersberg tasks"'. A very similar message was delivered eleven years later over Libya but once again the European heads of government were not prepared to face up to the unpalatable truth.

The civilians in the Clinton administration in their relief at the outcome in Kosovo were not above claiming, in a false euphoria about the utility of air power, 'You won't see Colin Powell on TV today talking about the Powell doctrine', a reference to his reservations about using military force in Bosnia.

*T. Harnden, 'US to UK: don't let Brussels ruin it', *Spectator*, 12 May 2001, p. 16.

But this political posturing is superficial. With air power becoming ever more accurate, it can be used, as I argued privately and publicly over Bosnia, to tilt the balance in favour of forces already fighting on the ground.* In this case the Kosovo Liberation Army (KLA) was fighting on the ground and was helped by NATO bombing. The Powell doctrine was developed on the back of Operation Desert Storm, following Iraq's invasion of Kuwait in 1990, when Colin Powell was chairman of the Joint Chiefs of Staff. It was premised very sensibly on the belief that military strategies should ensure victory rather than simply the hope of victory. Over Libya, once again the no-fly zone and protection of civilians under the UN Security Council resolution allowed NATO to tilt the balance of fighting.

What Kosovo showed conclusively was that a European Union defence force, relying on its present military capabilities and political leadership, will not have the capacity or political will to deploy sufficient troops or the political realism to use those forces sufficiently robustly to be certain of defeating in combat an equivalent force to that of the Serbs in the region of Europe without US backing. In the process what began by being defined as a humanitarian military operation, targeting and bombing military targets, ended up a strategic military operation, targeting non-military targets with humanitarian war aims, and was brought to a successful conclusion only once Moscow had been co-opted, Russia's clout on Belgrade

*Owen, *Balkan Odyssey*, pp. 102–3, 136.

producing the circumstances under which Milošević forced his military to withdraw from Kosovo and all those refugees who wished to could return. Nevertheless, NATO and the EU have taken a long time to resolve the problems bequeathed to the UN administration in Kosovo and the final end point of a stable, secure and independent Kosovo has not yet emerged.

What the different wars in the former Yugoslavia all demonstrate is that even so-called EU 'Petersberg tasks' can be difficult to fulfil and this was re-emphasised by the understandable reluctance of many NATO countries to deploy forces anywhere other than in Kabul following the initial defeat of the Taleban government in Afghanistan by American and the Northern Alliance forces in 2002. There are painful lessons that NATO peacekeepers have experienced in Afghanistan, particularly when they began to be regarded as an occupying force. NATO withdrawal alongside a US withdrawal is inevitable by 2014. For many involved it cannot come too soon but it will not be a victory and as so often in the past, Afghanistan will have proved the undoing of powerful invading forces.

If Europe pursues autonomous defence then we cannot expect US commitments to NATO to remain unchanged. The logic of the EU saying 'yes' to autonomy means from time to time that the EU will be contemplating force to support a foreign policy initiative where European interests and the American interests are opposed. We need to face these implications head on for they are profound and carry huge risks. Such a growing asymmetry in the transatlantic relationship was dealt with by Strobe Talbott, then US Deputy Secretary of State, speaking in London in October 1999 about the need 'to rebalance our respective roles'. He went on to warn: 'We would not want to see an ESDI that comes into being first within NATO but then grows out of NATO and finally grows away from NATO, since that would lead to an ESDI that initially duplicates NATO but that could eventually compete with NATO.'

Talbott's word 'compete' is the nub of the issue over the ESDP. It will never be in the interests of the US to go on supporting NATO if we allow to grow up in Europe an ESDP that competes with the US. That is happening and the main thrust for it stems from EU foreign and security Policy. If the UK were to move back to Political Co-operation as the basis of its foreign and security policy, it would do much to check EU–NATO competition, which under the direction of French pressure is becoming the only European defence posture. The US will not stay around militarily in central Europe if competition becomes the hallmark of European defence. It may keep bases in Turkey, and perhaps in Iceland, but it will distance itself from eurozone defence pretensions. By the end of this decade it might even have outflanked the eurozone countries and developed closer relations with Russia. A lot will depend on German influence within a eurozone that includes Poland and the Baltic states, and whether these countries will allow past history to be put aside and develop new relationships.

The European treaties in 2012 already make detailed provision for co-operation in the area of defence and security, the most important of which is the 'permanent structured co-operation' in Articles 42 and 46 of the Lisbon Treaty. Also provision is made in Articles 42 and 45 for participation in projects within the framework of the European Defence Agency. Participation of groups of member states in joint operations or tasks involving the use of civilian and military means is provided for in Article 44. This co-operation is open to member states 'whose military capability fulfils higher criteria and which have made more binding commitments to one another in this area with a view to the most demanding missions'. The difference between enhanced co-operation in the field of defence and other fields is that the Council can decide on the establishment of defence co-operation by QMV, whereas enhanced co-operation in other fields of the CFSP requires unanimity. It can be clearly seen therefore that the detailed structures for common defence are far advanced. It is only their implementation that has been held back, largely because of principled opposition from the UK and the fear of other Member states that to cross this divide might lead to a very serious pull-back of the United States from NATO.

In 2012, the Americans are still ready to keep troops as allies on the ground in Europe, something they have done since 1947. It is almost impossible to envisage they might plan and prepare to deploy troops against European, including British, forces. Even over their differences with France and the UK over the Suez Canal, they never contemplated that. If the EU persists with its formal interpretation of autonomy it will not be the

President, senators and congressmen but the professional servicemen in the Pentagon who will judge it incompatible with upholding their national interest for America to be retaining its troops on the ground in Europe. They want to know whether their EU allies are half in or fully in to NATO's defence strategy. Much of the blame for this development at Nice lies squarely on Britain. After the St Malo Agreement between President Chirac and Prime Minister Blair, which first used the word 'autonomous', it was incumbent on the British to stand firm when the French, as they were bound to, tried to chip away at the centrality of NATO to any new design for European defence decision-making. The French were also bound to expand autonomy from meaning 'operating autonomously' to 'planning autonomously'. This is precisely what has happened and the French Chief of Defence Staff, in denying that there is an American right of first refusal, explicitly laid out the procedure on 28 March 2001: 'If the EU works properly, it will start working on crises at a very early stage, well before the situation escalates. NATO has nothing to do with this. At a certain stage the Europeans would decide to conduct a military operation. Either the Americans would come or not.' At one stage, before Nice, officials from Britain tried to get the Dutch and the Germans to act for them in insisting on NATO planning being given the central position because they were so fearful of exposing Britain as having to veto the French position. Not unreasonably they refused and the French got exactly what they most wanted: prime responsibility for military planning and the freedom with it to plan autonomously. Nice could prove to be the most costly British diplomatic blunder since appeasement in the late 1930s. Some ground may have been won back since Nice as some issues were fudged and postponed. But I fear that Nice started a process whereby the US military, hitherto the most enthusiastic part of American policymakers for NATO, began disengaging from European defence. The old Atlantic certainties have gone, some US officers are no longer as worried if their political leaders suggest enlarging NATO for purely political purposes and in the process damage its common capabilities and its cutting edge.

The outgoing US Defense Secretary in the Clinton administration, himself a Republican, warned in December 2000 that NATO would become a 'relic' if the EU developed its own defence force. He was expressing a widespread concern in the Pentagon which preceded the arrival of George W. Bush. It was soon clear that Bush's new Secretary of Defense, Donald Rumsfeld, shared his predecessor's concerns. Returning to government service, having been ambassador to NATO under President Ford and the chairman of the bipartisan Congressional committee which had come out in favour of developing a missile defence system, Rumsfeld made it clear before February 2001 that he expected better of Britain than to acquiesce in the military documentation presented at Nice. As a new President, Bush avoided a confrontation but made his support conditional on Tony Blair's own assessment to him of what the Nice agreements meant. He quoted Blair's interpretation back publicly at their joint press conference at Camp David on 23 February 2001, saying, 'He also assured me that the European defence would no way undermine NATO. He also assured me that there would be a joint command, that planning would take place within NATO, and that should all NATO not wish to go on a mission, that would then serve as a catalyst for the defence forces moving on their own.' The problem was, as the defence specialists in the UK and US teams knew at Camp David, Blair's assurances were not an accurate interpretation of what had been agreed at Nice.

It is the envisaged size of the European rapid reaction force – 60,000–80,000 men, 300–350 fighter planes and 80 ships – which makes it obvious that if drawn down from European countries contributing to NATO, something that has, as yet, not been achieved, it will create a considerable dent in NATO's earmarked force levels. There are still no concrete plans for the rapid reaction force to be additional to the force levels Europe has already promised to NATO. The rapid reaction force was to be deployable in theatre in sixty days and sustainable for a year. Typically, Europe has not met this optimistic target but nor has it met NATO targets. European NATO countries rarely fulfil their pledges on time to deploy forces. Few of their forces are equipped with intra-operable equipment, or are capable of matching in many respects the sophistication of their US partners. But still the pretension persists.

General Sir Rupert Smith, soon after retiring as Deputy SACEUR, with a distinguished career in Northern Ireland, the Gulf and the Balkans, said of any European rapid reaction force, 'at the higher end of the possible scenarios, or Petersberg task list, it must be able to fight as a force. This will require systems to fight the deep battle, that is to say long-range rocket and artillery weapons with the necessary target acquisition systems. In addition within this range of systems, we must also have an evident ability to escalate, to be more forceful because the initial application of forces is only fully credible if it is evidently backed by the means and will to see the job through despite enemy action and setbacks.'* It is impossible to see that capacity being developed in a European rapid reaction force other than at the expense of NATO's capability.

We need to remind ourselves in the UK why the historic decision to form NATO was made after periodic US military involvement in Europe. The US military did not come in on the ground in the First World War until April 1918 but it still made a decisive difference to France and Britain's victory over Germany and Austria-Hungary. Only after Pearl Harbor was attacked by the Japanese in December 1941 could President Franklin Roosevelt, for all his strength domestically, overcome public resistance to being dragged in to another war in Europe. He declared war on Japan after Pearl Harbor, whereupon Germany declared war on the United States. A wiser and less hubristic man than Hitler† would have instead distanced

---

*General Sir Rupert Smith, 'The Development of a European Rapid Reaction Force', One World Trust, 29 November 2001.
†David Owen, *In Sickness and In Power: Illness in Heads of Government During the Last 100 Years*, rev. ed. (London: Methuen, 2011), pp. 27–37.

Germany from Japan's 'day of infamy' and in so doing made it much harder for Roosevelt to come into the European war. President Truman only reversed his predecessor's decision made in 1945, to withdraw US troops when faced by the Soviet threat as it became recognised in the USA in 1946–7. It was a courageous reversal of America's traditional reluctance to station troops abroad when they signed up for NATO and agreed a continued military presence in Europe.

Dictatorship is not just a phenomenon of the 1930s. Yugoslavia was expected to split up after President Tito's death. While it took ten years, there were signs of growing nationalism and once the fighting started it spread quickly. Libya erupted as a result of aggressive military action by Colonel Gaddafi in 2010, despite having been wooed into a constructive relationship with the UK and US in 2004. Syria, likewise, was meant to be under a reformist President, Bashar al-Assad, the son of the previous President. That illusion was shattered in months during late 2011. Globalisation does not just affect the financial and industrial worlds but is a growing factor in the military sphere. For decades we lived in western Europe only under the threat of Soviet missiles. Now countries like Iran have not only shown interest in developing nuclear warheads but have acquired missiles capable of delivering nuclear, radiation and destructive biological materials and chemicals that can encompass half of the EU's land mass.

In theory the European Union is a rich and powerful entity capable of developing its own military power. But it has chosen not to do so and has not shaken off the mood of unilateral nuclear disarmament that swept the European continent in the 1970s and 1980s involving the Netherlands, Belgium, Scandinavia, and the socialist parties in Germany and Britain. To anyone who is not blinded by prejudice Europe has needed over all these years the moorings of an Atlantic alliance. From many different perspectives European public opinion does not wish for the EU to seek superpower status. Only its elite are championing a European military distinct from NATO. The Italian and German governments as already described called publicly for a bombing pause within days of NATO's air strikes commencing against Serbia over Kosovo. The majority of EU countries refused to be involved in the 1991 Gulf War, let alone the 2003 Iraq War and the Libyan no-fly zone in 2011.

These facts are, if we are truthful, revelations of strengths, not just weaknesses. Within the EU there are a few nations who wish and are ready from time to time to exercise power and support the exercise of power with military forces. The British and French are countries that feel like this and they can and at times do stiffen the EU to make it readier to exert diplomatic power and reinforce it with military power. Were the EU to develop in ways that stifled and reduced that sense of nationhood in both countries, Europe would be much weakened globally. But that combination, even when France and Britain are working well together, and joined by Germany and Italy, does not represent superpower. What Europe needs for its foreign and defence policies is realism, policies based less on providing an end-of-meeting press release than on concrete, worked-through action plans and the resources to back them up. It needs to work with the grain of NATO, the most successful military alliance that has ever existed. Pretension is no substitute in terms of military strategy for provision. An EU rapid reaction force is not of itself a bad idea, provided it is embedded in NATO. But that is not the direction in which this force is going. It should not be confined to being deployed in the European theatre, for the UN needs a credible rapid reaction force and a European contribution made available for quick deployment under UN Security Council resolutions, in blue berets, could have much merit.

There are, however, areas of the world where the UN will for various reasons at any one time not be used and where the US will be reluctant to be involved itself or to use NATO. Here on occasions a European rapid reaction force might be acceptable, but its intervention would need solid backing in the regions in which it might deploy, such as central Africa or central Asia. Experience to date indicates too that though the EU might have the command-and-control function, a mixed multilateral force involving the Russians and the Turks would be better placed to create stability in central Asia and likewise one which involved African nations in central Africa. But this force would not be remotely like that which NATO mobilised in Kosovo and in Libya.

When the Berlin Wall collapsed in 1989 there was much loose talk that NATO had been made redundant. Kuwait's invasion of Iraq, the wars in Croatia, Bosnia, Kosovo and

Macedonia and the events of 11 September 2001, followed by the 2003 invasion of Iraq and the war against the Taleban in Afghanistan, let alone the situation in Libya and then Syria, should have demonstrated to the American military as well as EU military leaders that there are tangible advantages in having US troops and European troops with the ingrained habit of working together in NATO military exercises and planning. Under American leadership military coalitions of the willing can be put together to operate effectively in the field but the wiser American commanders know they will do so all the more effectively if based on a command-and-control familiarity bred within NATO.

The other challenge is to involve Russia more with NATO but to do so without weakening NATO's military cohesion or effectiveness. Russian territory now borders the EU. The Russian enclave of Kaliningrad, which is enclosed by Lithuania and Poland, represents a potential area of tension between the EU and Russia. It is an important EU role to help to diversify the Kaliningrad economy and do all we can to help Russia. There have been specific EU initiatives on Russia. Handling EU relations with Ukraine and Belarus is difficult but best done in ways which are sensitive to Russian concerns. Russia has to understand that from time to time NATO and the EU will have different attitudes and different priorities to theirs. The Russian Federation too wants its freedom to act in areas of concern to it in ways which we in the EU will not always endorse.

The danger to NATO's future comes not from it collapsing.

That would be an alarmist prediction. The danger is that NATO slowly withers away after a publicly perceived failure as in Afghanistan. It may still be called NATO, militarily it may on occasions be useful, but it will not be a serious fighting force. The latest, and in many ways the most effective, wake-up call came from President Obama's Defense Secretary, Robert Gates, who was responsible for the 'surge' in Iraq under George W. Bush. Speaking at his last visit to NATO before retiring in June 2011, he analysed NATO's response to and role in the Libyan no-fly zone operation: 'Turning to the NATO operation over Libya, it has become painfully clear that similar shortcomings – in capability and will – have the potential to jeopardise the alliance's ability to conduct an integrated, effective and sustained air–sea campaign.' He asked Europe to remember that Operation Unified Protector, as the no-fly zone was called, was a mission with widespread political support, a mission that did not involve ground troops under fire, and indeed was a mission in Europe's neighbourhood deemed to be in Europe's vital interest. He went on to say: 'To be sure, at the outset, the NATO Libya mission did meet its initial military objectives – grounding Gaddafi's air force and degrading his ability to wage offensive war against his own citizens. And while the operation has exposed some shortcomings caused by underfunding, it has also shown the potential of NATO, with an operation where Europeans are taking the lead with American support. However, while every alliance member voted for the Libya mission, less than half have participated at all, and fewer than a third have been willing to participate in the strike mission. Frankly, many of those allies sitting on the sidelines do so not because they do not want to participate, but simply because they can't. The military capabilities simply aren't there.'

Finally he said: 'In the past, I've worried openly about NATO turning into a two-tiered alliance: between members who specialise in "soft" humanitarian, development, peacekeeping and talking tasks, and those conducting the "hard" combat missions. Between those willing and able to pay the price and bear the burdens of alliance commitments, and those who enjoy the benefits of NATO membership – be they security guarantees or headquarters billets – but don't want to share the risks and the costs. This is no longer a hypothetical worry. We are there today. And it is unacceptable.'*

Any restructuring of Europe starting in 2012 must give attention to future defence arrangements and that is why it is vital to find a way of honouring our commitment to Turkey, an associate EU member state, and come up with a European political structure to which they want to be associated with around the Single Market. I am now convinced that it is better for the UK to sever its connection with the integrated dream of a single European foreign and security policy and resign itself to those who want to pursue it doing so inside the eurozone without us. Instead, the UK should advocate a restructuring that builds a wider Europe involving all the eurozone countries, as a

*Robert Gates, 'Reflections on the status and future of the transatlantic alliance', Brussels, 10 June 2011.

single entity if they wish, in a European Community built around the EU single market and environmental policies and having the less integrated form of Political Co-operation to cover foreign and security policy. I believe the greater clarity within this restructuring would strengthen NATO, not weaken it, and allow for two European structures – one at ease with self-governing member states, the other ready to shed many of the characteristics of self-governing nations.

Chapter 7

Britain and the United States

To mark the Queen's Silver Jubilee, in 1977, I gave a lecture at the request of the then US ambassador, Kingman Brewster, discussing the significance over the previous twenty-five years of the Anglo-American relationship in its historical, political and diplomatic aspects. Writing thirty-five years later at the time of the Queen's Diamond Jubilee, there is still a deep underlying continuity in the trans-Atlantic relationship. Fashions come and go. We were told at the start of the twenty-first century that we lived in a postmodern world, that the nation state was dying. Yet what remains twelve years later is immutable and enduring: a British people who are not prepared to look and trade only across the Channel to the European continent, a people who are Europeans but are still ready to look and trade worldwide and do not see their horizons limited by uncrossable oceans.

In 1950 Ernest Bevin, as Foreign Secretary, said in a statement to the House of Commons: 'I understand the urge towards European unity and sympathise with it and, indeed, I did much to help to bring the Council of Europe into being, but I also understand the new paradox that European unity is no longer possible within Europe alone but only within the broader Atlantic community. It is this great conception of an Atlantic community that we want to build up.' Two years later Sir Anthony Eden, the then Foreign Secretary, said in a speech at Columbia University that if Britain were to join a 'federation on the continent of Europe we should relax the strings of our action in the Western democratic cause and in the Atlantic association which is the expression of that cause. For Britain's story and her interests lie far beyond the continent of Europe.'

To what extent did our perception in the early 1950s of the Anglo-US relationship influence our decision not to be a founder member of the Common Market as it was then called? If it can be demonstrated that our vision of the Anglo-US relationship was so distorted that we saw that relationship as a viable and preferable alternative to the European Community, then for Britain the concept of the 'special relationship' can at least at one time in our history be argued to have been highly damaging. But I hope I have shown in earlier chapters that this was not the case.

In those years the dominant element in the Anglo-US relationship was defence and it is easy to forget how dominant it then was. The Cold War was a reality. The arguments over German rearmament were just beginning. The US had exploded the hydrogen bomb in 1952, and the Soviet Union quickly followed suit in 1953. It was a time when NATO defence was based on American strategic superiority and the threat of massive nuclear retaliation. At times in the 1950s the balance of conventional forces was as much as 5:1 in the Soviet Union's favour. It was a period of perceived danger; European unity was still fragile and any European defence effort alone wholly insufficient.

The US was favourable to British entry into the Common Market from the start. This has remained its consistent position, wanting Britain to be an active European nation. US opposition cannot be blamed in any way for our inactive position as an observer at Messina in 1955. The major factor, as I argued in Chapter 2, against the British presence at Messina was the national mood. Britain still felt the obligations of a major power. The Commonwealth had become for some the 'new Empire'. It was to some extent, for the older generation in particular, a new vehicle to fulfil their nostalgia for imperial grandeur and influence. Another key factor was that Britain was the only western European country to possess nuclear weapons. In 1950, as a consequence of the McMahon Act, Britain started developing her own isotope separation plant at Capenhurst in Cheshire with the capability for uranium enrichment without the benefit of any American technological knowledge. This was despite the fact that much of the American technology used at their plant at Oak Ridge, Tennessee had been developed by British scientists. Even the 1954 relaxations to the McMahon Act did not change the situation, since data relating to the fabrication of atomic weapons was still restricted.

The distinguished French scientist Bertrand Goldschmidt has claimed that, in 1955, the French started negotiations with Britain in an attempt to have the United Kingdom Atomic Energy Authority build an isotope separation plant using the technology developed at Capenhurst. He argued that this initiative was blocked by the United States, invoking Anglo-American agreements which were said to preclude such collaboration with the French because of the military implications. In June 1955 Britain concluded an agreement with the United States covering co-operation on the civil uses of atomic energy. Throughout the 1950s and 1960s Anglo-American nuclear agreements were a powerful factor in Britain's desire to maintain strong links with the US.

There was considerable bitterness in the British and French governments at the attitude of the Eisenhower administration in 1956 to the Suez crisis. They considered that the United States should have supported their intervention and that its refusal to do so had critically undermined their position. These feelings were probably accurate in relation to the American withdrawal of financial support. There is, however, no evidence for the more serious allegations that President Eisenhower had not backed France and Britain when the Russians made vague threats of a ballistic missile attack. Nor is there any evidence of prevarication when Nikolai Bulganin, the Premier of the USSR, proposed to Eisenhower the joint and immediate use of their two countries' naval and air forces under United Nations direction. What evidence there is shows that Eisenhower made it clear to

Bulganin that, if the Russians intervened, he would support France and Britain and that this would mean global war.

The first post-Suez British diplomatic priority was to concentrate on repairing Anglo-American relations. In March 1957 President Eisenhower and the new Prime Minister, Harold Macmillan, met in Bermuda. Eisenhower, seeing his old wartime friend – Macmillan had been particularly close to him in north Africa – was keen to put behind him the whole Suez incident. In exchange for an agreement to station Thor missiles on British territory under the 'double veto' joint control system, Eisenhower agreed to restore nuclear weapon collaboration. The then US Secretary of State, John Foster Dulles, personally persuaded the Joint Congressional Atomic Energy Committee to agree to the 1958 amendment to the McMahon Act, which permitted the release of information on nuclear weapon technology to any ally who had made substantial progress on nuclear weapons. Dulles made it clear at the time that such an agreement related only to Britain and did not include France.

The first French priority was to build up their own independence. In 1953 they had initiated their first nuclear weapon programme, and this was now stepped up. In 1957 the French responded to the Bermuda meeting's further evidence of an exclusive Anglo-American nuclear club with a decision to build their own isotope separation plant and a greater commitment to developing their own nuclear weapon capability. The Americans' official position in 1957 and 1958 was, however, far more flexible on the question of European co-operation than it might have appeared on the surface. They urgently wanted to put their Thor missiles in continental Europe as well as in Britain, and the administration was also at this time prepared to give its NATO allies technical details relating to nuclear propulsion for submarines, though it was dubious whether such an offer would ever have been accepted by the Joint Congressional Atomic Energy Committee. Yet no substantial co-operation emerged, although Italy and Turkey took the already out-of-date Thor missiles. The consequences were seen later when in the midst of the Cuban missile crisis the missiles in Turkey became an important factor in the Khrushchev–Kennedy negotiations, leading to Kennedy promising to remove them in six months provided no leak about his intentions became public. No leak occurred and they were removed.

A Franco-German initiative followed the Bermuda meeting, which is interesting because the implications behind the secret discussions to give West Germany access to nuclear technology could have had the most profound political consequences and repercussions. Franz Josef Strauss and Jacques Chaban-Delmas, then Defence Ministers for West Germany and France respectively, entered into negotiations, which included Italy, for a trilateral agreement whereby Italy and Germany, in exchange for nuclear information for primarily civil purposes, would have contributed to the cost of the French isotope separation plant. These secret negotiations never achieved very much because of the return of General de Gaulle, who unilaterally revoked the military part of the agreement in September 1958. In February that year France had exploded her first nuclear bomb.

On 17 September 1958, with the Algerian situation unresolved, de Gaulle produced a major state document, a memorandum which was sent to Britain and the United States, calling for a new three-power organisation outside NATO. This body would have responsibility for taking joint decisions on all political matters affecting world security, especially those involving the use of nuclear weapons. The whole background and history of this memorandum has been extremely well documented by John Newhouse in *De Gaulle and the Anglo-Saxons*,* and the detail that Newhouse had collected has been substantiated by some of the people most closely involved. The key question was whether de Gaulle really intended to obtain a veto on the worldwide use of American nuclear weapons; but he must have known this would have been impossible, and it is more likely that the memorandum was designed to force a more realistic assessment of nuclear strategy and nuclear-sharing, primarily within Europe. If this was its intention it was far sighted and imaginative but badly expressed. Whatever its intention, and I am inclined to the view that it probably was genuine, the memorandum proved to be a watershed. Anglo-French and Franco-American relations deteriorated sharply and no common ground for negotiations appeared. Perhaps the US missed an historic opportunity to change the whole politics of Europe. Certainly subsequent US administrations softened their

---

*John Newhouse, *De Gaulle and the Anglo-Saxons* (New York: Viking Press, 1970).

approach to collaboration with the French over nuclear weapons policies. Anyhow France, under de Gaulle, subsequently pursued a national nuclear defence policy that, in the short term, owed little to the realities of any Soviet threat. Yet for all its theoretical defects and great expense, the policy proved to have profound long-term consequences in establishing France as a nuclear power in her own right and in re-establishing her military position in Europe and the world. It also served to bind the United Kingdom even closer to the United States.

The next threshold in Anglo-US relations again involved defence and again involved France. At a meeting with de Gaulle in June 1962 Harold Macmillan clearly indicated that after entry to the EEC Britain would Europeanise her defence to the extent of even a European army and a European deterrent. On 19 December Macmillan met President Kennedy at Nassau in the Bahamas to discuss world affairs. It was the sixth such meeting to take place in two years and there was already a strong bond of friendship between the two men, reinforced by the appointment in 1961 of David Ormsby-Gore, later Lord Harlech, as UK ambassador in Washington. Ormsby-Gore was a relative of Kennedy through marriage who got on very well with the President. Kennedy had respect for the way in which Macmillan had supported him a few months before during the Cuban missile crisis and this crisis had sharpened both men's anxiety about Soviet intentions and the dangers of letting Western defences slip. They were superficially a strangely contrasted pair. Yet Macmillan's Edwardian image was a highly deceptive one. He was a tough, agile politician who had welded his party together following the Suez debacle in an amazing manner and was by then the dominant figure in British politics. A strongly committed European, after his visit to de Gaulle to discuss the Common Market he was painfully aware that talks on the subject were doomed.

It was decided that the Skybolt missile project was no longer feasible but the United States would make Polaris missiles available on a continuing basis for the British submarines and that Britain would construct the submarines and also provide the nuclear warheads. To obtain Polaris missiles was for Britain a golden opportunity. It meant purchasing at a relatively low price a proven weapons system whose initial research and development costs had all been borne by the United States. It was essentially a political deal of tremendous significance, born out of Kennedy's guilt over withdrawing Skybolt and executed against the opposition of key presidential advisers, such as the Defense Secretary, Robert McNamara. It owed more to sentiment than to careful evaluation. Nothing new about that; sentiment and personal regard are often the key to all human relations. Presidents and Prime Ministers are not immune from either, nor should they be.

Though the French position was only briefly discussed at Nassau, Kennedy's offer to supply France with Polaris missiles was made in good faith. Significantly, he also widened the offer privately to include sharing weapons technology. Yet only the most optimistic could have thought that there was any real chance of de Gaulle accepting. Psychologically, the whole offer had been handled appallingly. France, as de Gaulle saw her, could not become party to an agreement drafted in her absence by the Americans and British. Kennedy had, however, become committed to broadening arrangements for nuclear weapons control and was ready to conclude bilateral agreements with France as well as Britain.

On 28 December, the West German government welcomed the Nassau agreement, stating that in its view the agreement brought a multilateral nuclear force one step nearer. The West Germans, however, came out unequivocally against an American–British–French 'nuclear directorate' in NATO, stating that they were not prepared to accept NATO powers divided into classes, one with nuclear weapons and the other without. The multilateral nuclear force was later buried, but it was in effect stillborn.

On 14 January 1963, General de Gaulle made it clear in his formal press conference that not only would France block British entry into the Common Market but it would not contribute its nuclear arms, when it had them, to the proposed NATO multilateral nuclear force; nor was it interested in the American proposal to sell it Polaris rockets. Three years later he withdrew French forces from NATO but stayed a signatory to the treaty.

The Anglo-US relationship, despite the relative decline in Britain's power that occurred from the 1950s through to the 1980s, was understandable and not just nostalgia. It was also strongly in Europe's interest right up to the collapse of the Berlin Wall in 1989, for it helped lock the United States into NATO. Europe could survive France going it alone for reasons of national prestige but if Britain had attempted to do the same US troop withdrawals would have soon become a reality. Many times during this period Congressional debates demanded withdrawals and Congress could well have imposed reductions, particularly when US relations with Europe were strained over Vietnam. President Johnson disliked Britain's refusal, under Harold Wilson, to commit combat troops to the Vietnam War and expected more from his ally. The US Pentagon and State Department also disliked a whole series of UK defence decisions to pull back from defence commitments east of Suez. Yet despite those frictions relations with Britain were far better than with France, and fortunately US–German relations were also good.

In 1973 relations with the US were again severely strained when Britain, which had just become a member of the European Community under Edward Heath, was over-conscious of its new European role (see Chapter 5). First, Europe saw the Arab–Israeli war as having direct and adverse consequences on European interests such as its vital oil supplies, while the US saw the war in global East–West terms. Second, the atmosphere of transatlantic discussion had been affected by the US 'Year of Europe' initiative, which was, to put it kindly, *simpliste*. Third, the US government handled its nuclear alert, which involved forces stationed on British soil, at the least, insensitively. The US looked to Britain for support over the Arab–Israeli war but found a different Britain, content to stay safe within the consensus of European Community attitudes to the war. Britain was accused of delay over the US request for landing rights at US Air Force bases for supplies en route to Israel, while Britain refused to sell ammunition for the Centurion tanks it had already sold to Israel, an indefensible decision. Anglo-US relations in 1973 were 1956 in reverse and this time it was the United States which was understandably bitter. If the outcome of the war had been different and Israel beaten or severely weakened, the rupture could have developed into a very damaging long-term falling out between the US and Britain, something for which Heath would have borne responsibility.

Yet it should be admitted that the then British government's attitude was not an aberration arrived at in response to a crisis. Britain had deliberately started to distance itself from the United States, to convince its European partners, particularly France, that it was serious about its European commitment. In 1971 at the Commonwealth Heads of Government meeting in Singapore Britain had also pushed its wish to supply arms to South Africa to such an extent that it came close to permanently damaging the future development of the Commonwealth. It appeared that there was a single priority, Europe, and that this was to be developed at the expense of Commonwealth and US links. Yet throughout this period, somewhat paradoxically, France had been coming closer to the United States. Nothing too overt, but steadily under President Pompidou and continuing under President Giscard d'Estaing, relations, encouraged by

President Nixon, had improved. This was a welcome development, for the extent of anti-American sentiment in France had been damaging for Britain and for Europe. It is a British interest that the US should have good bilateral relations with France and Germany and indeed it should be one of the important consequences of Anglo-US friendship to be able to encourage and foster good relations with all Britain's European partners, but in particular with France. Britain should beware of acting, as is sometimes alleged it does, as a Trojan horse inside Europe, forgetting that France is America's oldest ally and went to its aid in the War of Independence.

Many different words have been used to identify the British role in US–Europe relations: a 'catalyst' or a 'bridge' across the Atlantic are but two. I believe we should be an honest partner on both sides of the Atlantic consistently and courageously; there is little return in trying to curry favour.

In 1974 a new Labour government gave Anglo-US relations a higher priority than they had had since the Kennedy and early Johnson years. Henry Kissinger, Nixon's Secretary of State, struck up a close working relationship with his British counterpart, Jim Callaghan, the Foreign Secretary. The US began to take an interest in Africa, a continent in which it had had little previous involvement. The Kissinger visit to Africa led logically in 1977, under the Carter administration, to the Anglo-US Rhodesia initiative and the two countries were the driving force behind the joint diplomacy of the five-power Namibia Contact Group, which included France, Germany and Canada as well.

The closeness of the contact, the free exchange of information, the genuine debate and dialogue over the complexities that made up the southern African problems were wholly without precedent. As Foreign Secretary I was lucky to start building up a very close personal relationship with Cyrus Vance, Kissinger's successor. That practical co-operation demonstrated that the critics of the UK–US relationship of only a few years before were way off beam.

In an article entitled 'The Special Relationship' which had appeared in the *New Yorker* in September 1977, William Pfaff argued that ever since the end of the Second World War Britain had failed to get to grips with its domestic problems because of a national failure of will and that in this period American friendship had been damaging because it had encouraged Britain to believe that an external solution existed to internal problems. We had sought, Pfaff alleged, a 'special relationship' with the United States to compensate for weaknesses at home and to perpetuate for ourselves a world role to which Britain was not entitled on its own account. He found this an extraordinary phenomenon because historically our mutual relationship has not been particularly friendly. What responsibility at home, he asked in conclusion, had Britain been trying to avoid by attempting to become a member, as he put it, of the American family? Yet US-UK relations continued to prosper despite occasional attacks from journalists and commentators. What they all tended to underestimate is the crucial value of personal relationships at the top of our governments, along with a shared history and language. Humour on occasions too. An identifiably similar legal system provides a framework for business. A cultural affinity through all kinds of music and dance is also often underestimated. These are the intangibles of a personal rapport even when there are differences of policy and of interest.

When Margaret Thatcher came into office relationships were a little strained between herself and President Carter but it did not stop him continuing to offer to supply Trident missiles to replace Polaris, which he had first indicated he was ready to do to Callaghan at a meeting in Guadeloupe called by Valéry Giscard d'Estaing to iron out trans-Atlantic difficulties. The Trident missiles were again a golden deal, like Polaris, for the UK. This offer was then followed by a readiness to sell Cruise missiles to the UK. There were, of course, financial returns for US industry on this and even more so on other deals covering aircraft and weapons, but the mutual value of the exchange was appreciated and understood.

When President Reagan came into office the relationship between him and Thatcher became very close. Over the Falklands War, Britain was helped by both President Mitterrand, who gave us vital information on how to deal with the Super Étendard aircraft and its Exocet missiles, and Reagan, who curbed his UN ambassador, Jeanne Kirkpatrick, keen not to damage relations with South America, and gave the nod to his Defense Secretary, Caspar Weinberger, to give information and equipment to Britain's armed services in ways that went far beyond the call of allied friendship and which proved crucial to

British success. There were differences between Thatcher and Reagan. She was upset, understandably enough, that he neither consulted nor informed her about his plans to invade Grenada, and she grew increasingly worried about his readiness to negotiate away all nuclear weapons while trying to develop a 'Star Wars' capacity to shoot down incoming missiles. However, they were soulmates on the role of the commercial markets in the prosperity of their countries. Furthermore, Thatcher showed in her decision to let the US fly F1-11 aircraft from the UK against Libya in 1986 the sort of solidarity on which the US–UK relationship periodically depends and on which US–European relations often founder. The claims that she and Reagan brought the Cold War to an end between them have been grossly exaggerated by people who should know better, conveniently underplaying the long years of détente, dialogue and negotiation vital for the process of unravelling the ideology of Soviet communism. Such policies had been championed in Europe by successive German Chancellors, Willy Brandt, Helmut Schmidt and Helmut Kohl, almost always supported by the UK.

The UK–US relationship was tested again under John Major and not found wanting in the Gulf War after Kuwait had been invaded by Iraq. The coalition of the willing that President Bush Sr carefully assembled was built on a firm foundation of involvement of Saudi Arabian, Egyptian, Jordanian and even Syrian forces alongside the British and French. Under President Clinton relations with Major were tense for a few years over Bosnia & Herzegovina, discussed in Chapters 5 and 6. The problems in the main lay with the US, not the UK or Europe. It was Major who, for the first time ever, allowed the US a key role in helping to settle the problems of Northern Ireland, an issue that had strained relationships between the two countries for decades. After the massacre in Srebrenica and the new-found US readiness to put troops on the ground in the Balkans, the two countries worked together again very well from 1995 until 2012.

The relationship between Clinton and Tony Blair from 1997 to 2001 was close and forged by Blair's readiness on his first visit to Washington to stand by the President at a time of embarrassment and weakness over Monica Lewinsky. Clinton did not forget such support when it would have been easy for Blair to have distanced himself. Theirs was above all a political marriage, helped by the continued close co-operation over Northern Ireland and on Kosovo. It was reinforced by their mutual interest in modernisation and reform domestically and internationally, a non-ideological point of view, firmly rooted in the modern techniques of focus groups, opinion polls and massaging public opinion. This closeness allowed for differences, most notably over the willingness to introduce ground forces when NATO's bombing of Kosovo was failing.

Many believed that when George W. Bush took office there would be a marked fallback in the intensity of the UK–US relationship. But this was not to be, helped by the events of 9/11 in New York and Washington and Tony Blair's full-hearted response. The two men soon managed to build a relationship which made light of differences over the environment, particularly the Kyoto Treaty and the International Criminal Court. They wisely focused on the big issue on which they were agreed, namely how to fight the war against terrorism. Even when their mutual failure to plan for the aftermath of the invasion of Baghdad became all too apparent, they appeared at ease with each other. The Iraq and Afghanistan policy failures have fortunately not done irreparable damage to relations between the two countries so much as to the reputations of their former leaders, Bush and Blair.

Relations between President Obama and Gordon Brown as Prime Minister were not close but between their advisers, particularly before and during the London G20 meeting in 2008, there was considerable respect and mutual agreement. David Cameron's visit to the USA in 2012 was helped by a successful collaboration over Libya and a similar concern that more needed to be done by Europe to bring an end to the crisis in the eurozone and that both countries should do all they could to help.

I see no incompatibility whatever in the UK maintaining as strong a commitment to the US as ever through the twenty-first century. Relationships will continue to change. But I have never accepted that it is necessary for Britain to make a choice between Europe and America. Fears of a narrow cocooned European Union withdrawing from the world have been shown to be false by enlargement of the EU and the continuation of free trade commitments to the World Trade Organization, the International Monetary Fund and the World Bank. The EU's stance in the Balkans and the Middle East has shown, on the whole, an outward-looking Europe. There will inevitably be tension and conflicting interests between the US and the European Union, particularly over trade matters. Even Britain will at times disagree quite strongly with different US administrations. None of this is incompatible with maintaining the Atlantic Alliance in all its aspects nor, within that, the Anglo-US relationship.

The Atlantic relationship enhances the power of Europe. It does not diminish it. It has also deepened the Anglo-US relationship in a unique way. America inevitably must build new powerful relations with China, India, Brazil and Russia, but so must the UK and Europe. The US does not need to uproot what has gone before, but it needs to know that Europe wants it to be involved. If the EU wants in its more integrated eurozone to pursue autonomy in defence it would be wiser for the UK to work within the framework of Political Co-operation in a European Community. It was defence after December 1941 that brought the US and UK into formalised defence links. Were those critical defence links to go, were the UK ever to become focused on defence in Europe alone, cease to want to be involved in blue water diplomacy, content to be only European, then the Anglo-US relationship would change. It would still be valuable, but it would no longer be crucial to either country. The fact that the relationship has been maintained owes much to history and a little to nostalgia, but most of all to a cold-blooded and fundamentally sound assessment that what is vital to Britain is also important to the US. The UK is a country that, since 1941, has ceased to aspire to become a superpower again. But it is a nation which is, I believe, determined to remain a self-governing country in name and in spirit. The next five years will put that belief to the test.

Chapter 8

EMU

Economic policy-making is different in kind from defence and foreign policy-making in that there is less of a role for government in the management of the economy than in defence and foreign policy. Western democracies have always rejected a command economy or, after 1951 with the defeat of the Labour government, one where government interferes in major ways with the running of a market economy. We are left in 2012 with few absolutes but nevertheless meaningful arguments about the balance. Most people believe there is a definite but limited role for government in the economic management of a market economy, at least in the minimalist position of helping to preserve competition and restricting monopolies. Economic policy means handling a large number of variables which interact with each other: interest rates, inflation, public expenditure, unemployment, wage rates and the exchange rate to name but a few. A fixed exchange rate can achieve stability for international trading. For the UK with an advanced banking system there would be savings in transaction costs were it to be within the eurozone. But transaction costs are coming down as banks use ever more sophisticated electronic methods and the credit card market becomes ever more competitive. To date the eurozone has not demonstrated the cost savings to the consumer that many Commission papers predicted would come with greater price transparency. Instead shopping around in different countries to reduce costs can be done electronically, using credit cards and internet purchasing. Also hedging against currency risks for exporters has become very sophisticated and manu-facturers increasingly use automated procedures when selling into the eurozone which they still use when selling into the large non-euro world trading market. Norway, outside the EU, with its own oil and gas industry and fishing industry, is now second to Luxembourg in being the richest country in the world based on gross national income per capita. Sweden has pulled back from eurozone membership and the Danish people have grown ever more contented to be outside the eurozone. The chances of any British government being able to win a referendum on euro entry are negligible for the foreseeable future.

Outside Europe, Canada went through the global economic crisis of 2008 relatively unscathed. Its position as a member of the North American Free Trade Area (NAFTA) but being determined to retain its own currency, despite sharing a long open trading border with the USA, is instructive. Many Canadians sense that were they to have the US dollar as their currency it would not be long before eventually their country would become the fifty-first state. The present Canadian government appears to want stronger, not weaker, links with the UK. This is a relationship to treasure, built not just in the Commonwealth but in NATO and underpinned by deep affection for the Queen.

The history of monetary unions is that they either collapse over a few decades or those countries within them go on to form a political union and merge to become one country. It may be that the unique nature of the EU will allow for a eurozone for monetary matters while still remaining a union of nation states, but that looks far from certain in 2012. The eurozone is more likely to follow the patterns of the past. I have always resisted the temptation to argue against joining the eurozone as a matter of principle. Such a stance has the benefit of simplicity, and it is what many against the EU in principle want to hear. Margaret Thatcher in March 2002 wrote a book advocating that we should never join the euro and put the case for coming out of the EU and for joining NAFTA. But while we have been able to bridge the Atlantic in NATO, a security organisation, it would be harder, although not impossible, to do so in a trading organisation like NAFTA. Joining is certainly something Britain should not rule out if we were to be welcomed. No-one can pretend to be able to predict the course of history. Who can say whether over a century or more the British might genuinely become Euro-enthusiasts, our citizens might 100 years hence feel content to be governed from Europe with a European Cabinet and a European Parliament determining the macroeconomic, foreign and defence policies? The British people have, however, a traditional caution. Pragmatic evaluation of what we have become and, perhaps more worryingly, could become is feeding an ever stronger mood for withdrawing from the EU. But there is another tradition, that of our merchant adventurers in the West Country, mainly operating from Bristol. That spirit of merchant adventuring, with which I identify, could provide an inspiration for how the UK in 2012 responds to restructuring Europe and our relationship with the EU.

Most people, in trying to define what elements of economic policy they want their government to be responsible for, would choose unemployment first. By the end of April 2012 nearly one in four Spaniards were unemployed. In that same week the UK entered into a double-dip recession and sterling hit its highest level against the euro since August 2009. But it was still 10–15 per cent below its trade-weighted average before the 2008 crisis. Outside the eurozone the exchange rate of the pound floats, adjusting to market pressures and the rates of interest and inflation, all of which can have a profound influence on unemployment. In the eurozone more and more people are asking what was so wrong with periodic devaluations. Why has austerity become the only way forward? Why are the lessons that Maynard Keynes drew from the global crisis of the 1920s and the 1930s to be ignored in the global crisis we have been living through in Europe since 2008?* This European response is not

*Robert Skidelsky, *The Economic Crisis 2008–2011*, Centre for Global Studies, 2012.

mirrored in the USA, where a far more pragmatic economic policy appears to be operating.

Interest rates in the UK are set by the Monetary Committee of the Bank of England and understandably they are set in the eurozone by the ECB. A mechanism which ensures that interest rates are controlled by an independent body and less influenced by political pressure to reduce them prior to an election seems wise. The inflation rate target, meanwhile is set in the UK by the Chancellor of the Exchequer. But in the eurozone, by contrast, it is set by the ECB with no political input. Why are technocrats able to influence the level of unemployment by setting the inflation target while politicians are not?

The institutional bias of the ECB, which it inherited from the Bundesbank, towards disinflation is itself a product of the German people's memories of hyperinflation in the 1920s. The ECB is bound by the language of the Maastricht Treaty, which was drafted when inflation was regarded as the biggest threat to world economic prosperity. The Germans may have thought that they were ensuring a 'hard' currency. Yet the euro helped Germany during a period of serious stagnation. It suited Germany to keep interest rates well below what some other countries, like Ireland, needed to keep their inflation in check.

Setting an inflation target across so many countries, with widely different economies, in the eurozone is a difficult task. Their national economies differ in many key characteristics and it may take many years until they come together. We know in the UK how difficult and sometimes how controversial it is for the Bank of England to fix interest rates which apply across the UK, eliciting howls of anguish from areas of high unemployment where lower interest rates are wanted. But at least in the UK the government has a variety of ways of offsetting the high unemployment levels in the regions. Yet we find that some of our schemes that were useful in the past have had to be given up under the European Commission's wish to maintain a level playing field in the Single Market. Nevertheless, there is some valuable flexibility still remaining in the UK but if we were in the eurozone this flexibility would come under even greater pressure because of the Growth and Stability Pact (GSP), which calls for the countries in the eurozone to keep their national budgets in balance or in surplus and imposes an upper limit on budget deficits of 3 per cent of gross domestic product (GDP). This may be further restricted by the Fiscal Compact Treaty. A system of fines built in as penalties for breaching the limits has, hitherto, been largely ignored, in part because when the limits were breached in 2002 by rich Germany and France it was felt their politicians won a waiver over the objections of the ECB and the European Commission. Now the weaker European governments are coming under very undemocratic pressure to adopt what have been labelled technocratic governments. So far in 2012 we have seen this in Greece and Italy and there is a sense that such governments have been forced on them, and there may well be others to come.

Lying outside the eurozone, the UK has the right to refuse to implement some of the Commission's suggestions and cannot be fined. But the Commission tells us that eventual membership of the eurozone is stipulated in the treaties. This is despite the specific right granted to the UK that we remain outside the eurozone. Denmark, too, has by common consent negotiated that right, while Sweden has also taken it, unilaterally and more controversially. Inside the eurozone, some countries are in a recession and unemployment has risen sharply, provoking a violent response from voters. Prior to this eurozone crisis developing, many people in the UK had no idea that such differences existed within the EU or that such a degree of interference from Brussels or Frankfurt in their own government was inherent in being part of the euro.

I write this not to challenge the inherent right of EU member states to be part of the eurozone or to handle economic questions in their own way and come closer together in their economic performances. Initially in the debate around the Maastricht Treaty and the euro it was argued that in joining the eurozone a country did not bind itself into being part of a single economic government. That argument has been abandoned as impossible to sustain in the midst of the eurozone crisis. The UK coalition government, outside the eurozone, has been since 2011 virtually an advocate of an economic government within the eurozone. The UK government has not sought to deny the eurozone countries the right to define new powers and new governance. That will require more harmonisation of most economic decisions and more, not less, integration. The question we ask the eurozone members, in relation to those countries, like us, outside the eurozone and determined to stay out, is: why not embrace tolerance for difference? Let us agree a framework for the single market and environmental policies, which we have already worked out together, and offer that structure to countries like Turkey, already a candidate state and those who aspire to EU membership but are not yet ready to undertake all its rules embodied in the *acquis communautaire*. We, for our part, will do everything to facilitate in treaty forms as required the restructuring of the eurozone and how it relates to those EU countries who wish at some future date to be able to join.

As recently as February 2002 the British government was preaching that 'taxation is a matter for Member States, in keeping with the principle of subsidiarity; tax reform should promote wider economic reform and not create additional barriers to trade; and the economic priority for Europe is reform to promote growth, prosperity, jobs and social inclusion'.* It went on to argue that 'the Government does not accept that tax harmonisation is an inevitable consequence of EMU. EMU does not require, either in principle or in practice, the harmonisation of direct taxation . . . or that there is an inevitable path leading from monetary, via fiscal, to political union.' Against that position a month later, in the run-up to the presidential elections in France, Jacques Chirac called for 'genuine fiscal harmonisation' and went on to say that 'in an open, competitive Europe with a common currency, it is damaging for the French

*HM Treasury, *Realising Europe's Potential: Economic Reform in Europe*, Cm 5438, February 2002, p. 33.

to always be taxed more than everyone else'. His message was clear: he preferred not to rely on France itself lowering French taxes; he wanted low-tax economies like the UK and Ireland to have to raise theirs, so levelling taxes up and not down.

President Sarkozy's 2010 plan for an EU-wide Tobin tax failed, despite being backed by the Commission. In late March 2012 Wolfgang Schäuble, the German Finance Minister, proposed a two-stage approach with the first step being a levy on company shares, widening to bonds and derivatives later. Sweden supported Germany, the British opposed any agreement at EU level and somewhat surprisingly, if one forgets that they have relatively large financial services industries, Luxembourg opposed and the Netherlands and Ireland expressed deep reservations. The Commission wanted a tax on stocks, bonds and derivatives from 2014 to raise up to €57 billion. But it only had the support of nine countries. This issue will continue with France introducing a unilateral transaction tax in the summer of 2012. and its new President, François Hollande, continuing to advocate an EU-wide Tobin tax even if not adopted globally by some of the EU's key competitors. If the OECD, for example, was ready to adopt a single Tobin transfer tax then the UK could consider doing so but not while the US and other key countries refuse. The UK already has a tax on the sale of company shares and the countries in the eurozone, and those who aspire to be, may want to adopt their own tax structures, which, provided they do not run counter to single market legislation, would be acceptable.

The implications of tax harmonisation within the eurozone are profound and go wider than just taxation. Harmonisation will not just be confined to taxes on industry in order to ensure equality for the single market. In a competitive marketplace, we in Britain believe, one can stultify competition by stressing the need for a level playing field for all costs carried by industry. Regions within the eurozone wanting to attract jobs will have to look at ways of reducing unit labour costs. That means pay and benefits and the costs of starting up a business may have to vary within and between eurozone countries. This is one of the reasons why we are so opposed to the detailed working time directives. Trying to ensure that the regulatory climate is sensible does not mean that regulations in every field of employment and environmental responsibilities need to be the same. Some eurozone regions are so poor they must be able to incentivise industry. They must also be able to offset some of their own uncompetitive aspects such as cost of travel, in the case of remoter regions in the eurozone. Ireland, for example, Britain's closest neighbour, with whom we have a common border and many special bilateral arrangements, has a corporate tax rate of 12.5 per cent – half of Britain's and much lower than that of any other country in the eurozone. It claims that shipping costs, by sea or by air, and geographical isolation militate against a single eurozone corporation tax, but inside the eurozone it will be hard to sustain that argument. These are difficult issues for the eurozone countries and there is no perfect solution but these need to be eurozone decisions. For non-eurozone countries there are problems as well if we are all not to lose the benefits of the single market, but they are of a different dimension and importance and need to be discussed with the European Economic Area (EEA), comprising the member states of the EU plus Norway, Iceland and Liechtenstein, and with countries such as Turkey and some of the Balkan states outside the EU.

The growth in the importance of financial services associated with Frankfurt, Paris, London, Rome, Madrid and no doubt eventually Warsaw and Nicosia, is relevant to the Single Market. Just as England moved out of agriculture and was first into the Industrial Revolution, so the UK has had to move out of some manufacturing industries such as shipbuilding, textiles and to some extent mass car production. It was both wrong and very difficult to continue to protect our manufacturers in these markets as the developing world began to manufacture in the same areas. British expertise in trade, finance brokerage and insurance has become highly marketable worldwide, and London has thrived and still does well despite the global crisis. It has thrived not by accident, history or even luck, but because key decision makers in the financial services industry prefer to live in London than in Frankfurt or Paris, but that preference cannot be taken for granted. Nor will London continue to be preferred unless successive governments set a competitive fiscal climate which encourages the UK financial services industry. What caught up with the industry was successive governments' attachment to regulating with a light touch, being flexible and not too intrusive. There is a hubris inherent in Keynes's animal spirits that attracts people to the financial services industry, and, as was demonstrated in the late 1920s and 1930s, those spirits have to be tempered and even controlled. We discovered this to our cost as a nation, when the UK had to underwrite Northern Rock in 2007 and later HBOS and RBS. They had operated under too light a touch. But we were not alone. In New York too the regulatory climate was allowed to relax too much, as shown in 2008 and beyond by Lehman Brothers and many others. Within a single market attitudes to regulation in London should not be allowed to become too different from attitudes in the eurozone. There is more suspicion of markets in London in 2012 than before, more anti-globalisation. But there is still rational debate about the all-important climate in which business is conducted. Making London more attractive to business is a serious concern for Britain but also, we realise, for Frankfurt and Paris, which have never accepted the permanent dominance of London and have striven to take business away from it for centuries. Again we must establish a framework within the single market which may differ between member states but not perhaps between eurozone member states. As the eurozone gradually takes on more and more of the character of an economic government, there could easily develop a framework of regulatory provisions that are designed to build up financial services in the eurozone but under the single market it could not discriminate against single market member states. In 2012, outside the eurozone, London trades worldwide in all currencies and makes money on these transactions. The eurozone makes money in having no transaction fees by lower costs. It is not unreasonable for us outside the eurozone to say to those in the eurozone that we will not accept EU treaty changes added to cope with the eurozone crisis which also remove safeguards for countries like the UK who have no intention of joining the eurozone. More integration within the eurozone cannot mean less freedom inside the single market.

France, in particular, dislikes the so-called Anglo-Saxon model for financial services. It has long wanted co-ordination of economic policies to be considerably increased so as to be better able, as France sees it, to react to external shocks. It would like corporate tax to be more harmonised or at least a minimum rate be fixed – this would be the first step towards a European tax. It does not stop there. In order to be able to harmonise taxes in Europe, fiscal decisions, which will affect the internal market, should be made by QMV, and not by unanimity. The same, France believes, should be the case for social harmonisation. Such QMV, however, cannot be expected to impact on those outside the eurozone. The eurozone can come to the single market with a single view but the structure of decision-making within it cannot allow the eurozone to carry an automatic majority. A weighting on QMV for the single market has to be negotiated. When Gerhard Schroeder said in January 2001: 'You cannot have a common currency that is not embedded in a common and appropriate fiscal and economic policy,' he believed the need for this embedding would become clear. He was right, it has done exactly that, but it has become clearer that some embedding of the single market is needed to ensure the influence and voice of those outside the eurozone.

Advocacy of the deregulated competitive approach to economic government took a hammering in Europe, and particularly in the eurozone, after 2008 and that continues to 2012. An economic government for the eurozone needs to be matched by a wider governance for a European single market than that of the European Commission, otherwise fiscal decisions will be slowly brought within that internal market of the eurozone at the expense of an outer single market. There is no room for a continuation of the 'hand-me-down' decisions from the Commission and the EU treaties. There will have to be a Secretariat with a secretary general and a weighting for QMV that would not allow, for example, Turkey, the UK and Norway and, say, one other country to be outvoted by the EU. But it might be possible to agree that whoever held the post of Trade Minister/Commissioner within the eurozone would be the worldwide negotiator for the first period of tenure of the restructured single market, the position alternating thereafter between eurozone and non-eurozone countries.

Since Maastricht there has been a determination in the Commission to make all new applicant countries sign up for eventual membership of the single currency and the eurozone in 2012 has grown to encompass seventeen countries. Yet the UK only signed up, as part of Maastricht, for a non-binding recommendation which fell well short of the more structured measures defined for members of the eurozone and linked to a

European central bank with no powers outside the eurozone. All that points to a clearer redesign being needed for the restructured single market of the eurozone and non-eurozone countries.

The original design of EMU* deliberately avoided making provision for fiscal transfers of the sort that we have seen which made the monetary union between West and East Germany work. The then political leaders feared using such a mechanism because of its unpopularity with the richer countries, which were beginning to realise around the time of Maastricht that EMU had become a very expensive adjustment mechanism. Ten years after monetary union within the Federal Republic of Germany annual fiscal transfers amounted to the entire GDP of the Czech Republic. Yet the Delors Report in 1989 warned the designers of EMU that 'the permanent fixing of exchange rates [between the countries of the eurozone] would deprive individual countries of an important instrument for the correction of economic imbalances'. The report went on to say that 'if sufficient consideration were not given to regional imbalances, the economic union would be faced with grave economic and political risks'. We have learnt from the collapse of the eurozone that this prediction was correct. To understand why this warning was not acted on, it is necessary to understand the community method as the original eurozone designers did. They knew that an imbalance would take place and they knew that it

*David Marsh, *The Euro: The Politics of the New Global Currency* (New Haven, CT: Yale University Press, 2009).

would necessitate fiscal transfers. But they also knew members of the eurozone would only transfer such money in a crisis and then only if they had political control over how the money was spent. Because the designers wanted further integration they were content to wait on a crisis. They knew that in the US 45 per cent of federal taxes are used to iron out imbalances between regions and for the first 150 years of US monetary union there were bitter disputes between regions. In 1999 an American economist, Professor Hugh Rockoff, warned Europe: 'For countries already committed to monetary union, the lesson is that providing a system of fiscal transfers for distressed regions and lender-of-last-resort facilities, or perhaps some form of deposit insurance, for those regions so that real shocks are not multiplied by banking crises, is of the utmost importance.' The Eurozone countries will have to have their own budget with their own mechanisms for the correction of imbalances and their own distribution of monies to sustain the CAP, the CFP and the Social Fund. This budget will also include those EU countries outside the eurozone but who decide under the new restructuring of Europe to continue to aim for eurozone membership.

The community method is the most important aspect of the inner workings of the European Community and perhaps the least understood. Behind it lies a body of theoretical writings, and a true bureaucracy, not very large in comparative terms, but a bureaucracy in the sense that the administrators who run the Community and now the Union feel themselves responsible to an idea of Europe. That 'idea of Europe' is championed by politicians and civil servants in the member states who feel free to promote and extend that idea with little regard for democratic answerability. The community method has none of the democratic constraints that influence elected leaders, who have to listen to the views of their people and be responsive to and ultimately governed by those views. The community method has been defined as 'the process whereby political actors in several distinct settings are persuaded to shift their loyalties, expectations and political activities toward a new centre, whose institutions possess or demand jurisdiction over the pre-existing national states'.* Behind the method is the notion of spillover – when integration takes place in one area but not in another, the resulting imbalance spills into the static area, creating a momentum for change everywhere. In this way institutions are created or existing ones adapted, sucking in new tasks and the powers to deal with them. The only proven way to stop or check this process has been the readiness of one or more states to exercise the veto system incorporated in the treaties. It is not surprising, therefore, that the Commission is always advocating the ending of all vetoes and their replacement with qualified majority voting (QMV). For those who wish to set limits to the process of integration, retaining a treaty-based veto format has an immense advantage. That is why adopting a Constitution Treaty in 2004 to replace the treaties as amended over time had great dangers. This apprehension lay at the root of why many of

*Ernst B Haas, *The Uniting of Europe: Political, Social, and Economic Forces, 1950–1957* (Stanford, CA: Stanford University Press, 1958), pp. 11–16.

us in the UK demanded that it and the Lisbon Treaty required a referendum – something which was conceded by Prime Minister Blair before the 2005 general election, but then abandoned in 2006. The Treaty of Lisbon did at least revert to amending prior treaties and member states ratifying through their own constitutional procedures and entered into force on 1 January 2007.

Over time the language of the treaties has been interpreted by the European Court of Justice (ECJ). The ECJ has done so in accordance with its longstanding politically motivated support for the community method. The ECJ, some would argue, was established and designed to buttress the pursuit of the community method. At least a treaty, by contrast to a constitution, remains the vehicle of the member state and as such can be interpreted by that state's own procedures. For instance, the Federal Republic of Germany's Constitutional Court has already made important judgements on whether ratifying the Treaty of Lisbon would be consistent with the German constitution.* This is an additional safeguard and it proved very important to German interests over the 'no bailout' clause in the arrangements over European Monetary Union (EMU) after the euro crisis of 2009. In the UK it would be open to the government to encourage appeals to the newly created Supreme Court

---

*The court in a meeting on 30 June 2009 made ratification subject to legal limits which if breached meant future EU law will be 'declared inapplicable in Germany' (Hans-Jürgen Schlamp, 'What Lisbon ruling really means for the EU', Spiegel Online International, 1 July 2009).

for any disputed interpretation over the language of the European treaties.

The European Commission is the tool for the furtherance of European integration. There was never any doubt in the mind of the most powerful President of the Commission to date, Walter Hallstein, that 'We're not in business, we're in politics' and that the Commission was under the community method going to become the government of Europe. When a later President of the Commission, Romano Prodi, talked about the Commission as the government of Europe his words were dismissed by some as unrepresentative of EU opinion. Yet in some parts of the European Union his words were accepted as being even then an accurate description. For people to whom the community method is crucial, QMV is not an optional extra but an essential part of the community dynamic. There are arguments about whether an institutional determinism* operates within the Brussels system but what cannot be scoffed at is the community method record. It has over years a history of delivering the integrationists' objectives. Many who practice and espouse the community method within the Commission recognise no limits to the process of integration nor any legitimate boundaries to the erosion of the nation state.

The UK government believed that the Lisbon European Council meeting in March 2000 'marked a recognition not only that all EU economies needed to undertake further structural

Susanne Bodenheimer, *Political Union: A Microcosm of European Politics, 1960–1966* (Leiden: A. W. Sijthoff, 1967).

reforms, but also that the traditional community method, which had served the EU well in the construction first of a Customs Union and then of a Single Market, would not always be appropriate to this challenge.'* They believed the future lay more in regular and vigorous peer reviews, the sharing of best practice, and effective communication with agreement on guidelines and quantitative and qualitative indicators leading to national reforms tailored to fit individual member states' circumstances. This has not been the Commission approach. A European research area was a key element. Yet by 2007, EU gross domestic expenditure on R&D was €228,681 million, the equivalent of 85 per cent of the figure in the USA. The number of full-time research equivalents in the business enterprise sector was only 662,000 in the EU, compared with 1,135,000 in the USA. By 2010 the Commission was warning of an 'innovation emergency'. The Lisbon strategy has failed. Take the Common Agricultural Policy (CAP), which had its own political dynamic in Franco-German agreement that stemmed from the ECSC. All these years later, despite endless criticism because of its gross distortions of agricultural markets in poor developing countries and from those appalled by its distortion of the Community Budget, the CAP still survives in 2012. It weakens the EU's negotiating hand in the World Trade Organization and damages our case against US protectionism. In all logic it should be reformed. But it remains stubbornly unreformed. Thirty years

*HM Treasury, *Realising Europe's Potential: Economic Reform in Europe*, Cm 5438, February 2002, p. 29.

ago we believed the Germans would no longer be prepared to pay for it and even now with the French close to being net payers it survives.

The way forward is to acknowledge that the Lisbon Declaration about economic performance and future growth marked a new recognition that the community method was not always appropriate for all member states in the twenty-first century, certainly not for achieving member states' much-needed economic reform and restructuring (see Chapter 1). To uphold that judgement all logic points to a restructuring of EMU and of the eurozone, to a wider European single market based, as in treaty language, on the social market with its own balance between integration and economic deregulated competition. Such a restructuring of Europe is an admission that the global market has made an unfavourable judgement on the present design, which is not capable of providing all member states with the stability and prosperity that can be achieved with a different design.

The British people have become hostile to ever greater integration and the characteristic language emanating from Brussels, or from Euro-enthusiasts at home, about how the UK is always supposed to be 'missing the boat' or 'waiting in the sidings while the train is leaving the station'. In its most developed form the advocates of more European integration often point to the UK decision not to attend the Messina Conference in 1955, discussed in Chapter 7. Scant regard is given in retrospect about Messina to the fact that there were no

UK political leaders of substance in the parties ready to advocate signing up to anything even approximately close to the Treaty of Rome. An opportunity only exists if it is feasible, if it is part of the political reality of the time.

The UK is not ready to be sucked into a form of economic government which becomes a broad-based, all-singing, all-dancing government, with fiscal transfers and greater integration. That may prove to be the case for Denmark and possibly Sweden, and also for some eurozone countries currently living very uneasily within the zone – not just Greece and Portugal but perhaps Spain, even Italy and Ireland. Restructuring the single market could provide the opportunity for an ordered generous restructuring of eurozone membership with far fewer repercussions within Europe or worldwide than if countries were to split off on their own, maximising the chance of serious contagion on other vulnerable states within the eurozone. It could strengthen Europe overall. But it does entail an open admission of what many have been fully aware of privately: that eurozone membership involves an inevitable path leading from monetary via fiscal to political union. What must also be openly admitted is that not just a full economic government but a full political union within the eurozone is a fundamental redesign of the present EU and that it is logical for some member states to decide to stay within the single market and outside the eurozone, and in effect to separate out a new European Economic Community (EEC) from a new European Union (EU).

Chapter 9

The separation of powers: good fences make good neighbours

The European Union has developed into a unique entity. There has been nothing remotely like it in modern history and we are unlikely to see its equivalent develop in other parts of the world. Its uniqueness stems from our European history, diverse, complex and itself not something which, one hopes, as the crucible for two World Wars, will be reproduced anywhere else. Europe is now seen as a formal grouping of nation states but this was not a feature of its early history. It is likely in the next few years that the EU will change again from a one-size-fits-all pattern to a more variegated pattern. Not all that has happened in EU has worked. It has moved from a Common Market, to a European Community, to a European Union.

Europe is, and has long been, multi-ethnic yet predominantly Judeo-Christian. Nevertheless, Muslims have centuries-old ties with parts of Europe. When the Arabs and Berbers conquered Spain in the eighth century, it became a majority Muslim country, which then changed back to being Christian. Today, apart from

Turkey the other European country which has a predominantly Muslim population is Bosnia & Herzegovina. But the movement of Muslim people from north Africa to France, from Pakistan and Bangladesh to the UK, and from Turkey to Germany, has altered the balance. Religious chauvinism has erupted in the past and will do so again, from time to time. But the values of the Enlightenment remain. Despite pogroms and the Holocaust, tolerance has remained in most parts an abiding feature. Racial intolerance continues to raise tensions in some of our cities. But the tolerance shown by the majority of our peoples has usually overridden that minority who still practice racism, hold to anti-Semitism and identify the Muslim faith with extremism. We need constant vigilance and positive programmes to combat prejudices that exist, and a vigorous democratic and inclusive debate about how to live more harmoniously together. Our own countries in the EU have been subjected to separatist movements: the Basques in northern Spain, the IRA in Northern Ireland, antagonisms between the Walloons and Flemings in Belgium and the problem France has in dealing with Corsica. The Roma range all over Europe and, particularly in Romania, present problems. Inward migration from north Africa by boat presents difficult challenges. Economic migration contributes to wealth overall but to tensions and suspicions in inner cities.

The challenge for Europe is to remain united with all this diversity. This will be best achieved by being more adaptive and less rigid in the structures we have developed and more imaginative in the way they are redesigned. We must learn from experience. The EU has evolved into the most integrated regional grouping of nations in the world. Already it demands much, politically and economically, of its member states. But many of our peoples feel they are being dragged along behind an almost self-perpetuating European elite, for whom ever greater European integration has become virtually a religion. The EU is based on treaties. A constitution was rejected by the Dutch and the French in their referendums in 2005. The European Community had developed pragmatically a broadly sensible mixture of intergovernmental, supranational and shared decision-making procedures. This separation of powers has, however, been under constant attack from this elite, who wanted only the supranational powers to expand and the inter-governmental powers to diminish.

The European Council developed initially without being mentioned in the treaties. It has been brought, reluctantly by some, within the institutional framework of the EU. The European Court of Justice (ECJ) always had specific com-petences over supranational decision-making but a limited role. It was meant to have no role at all in intergovernmental decision-making. There are many good reasons for insisting that the ECJ be kept tightly to the supranational aspects of the EU and not allowed to infiltrate the whole field of EU decision-making. But the European elite saw the ECJ as the enforcer of integration and has steadily built up its authority.

To describe what the EU is, vast forests of paper have been used and innumerable words spoken. The quest continues for a single or a few words to describe the EU, and no two are more frequently brought to bear to this end than 'confederal' or 'federal'. Some even describe the EU as 'confederal federalism'.* Passions are exercised on behalf of such words and concepts, so far producing more heat than light in the process. It would be simpler and clearer if instead of trying to encompass the EU within a short description we settled for it being unique and then defined very carefully the differing elements that make up its uniqueness. Which elements must be retained across the whole? Which elements can be chosen freely for a section of the whole and not apply to all?

The word 'federal' has too many diverse interpretations to act as a catch-all term for this unique Union.† The distinction between integral federal theory, which has hitherto dominated in Europe, and what is called covenantal federal theory, now emerging on both sides of the Atlantic, which does not view federalism explicitly or exclusively in territorial or spatial terms, is a fascinating development, potentially of great significance. Integral federalism in Europe was founded in France in 1930 by Robert Aron amongst others, with a journal, *Ordre Nouveau*, calling for anti-nationalism, decentralisation and mutualism to counter Franco-German confrontation. They drew on corporatism and subsidiarity as put forward by Althusius and

*John Kincaid, 'Confederal Federalism and Citizen Representation in the European Union', *West European Politics* (1999), vol. 22, no. 2, pp. 34–58.
†M. B. Stein, 'Changing Concepts of Federalism since World War II: Anglo-American and Continental European Traditions', paper presented at the XVI Congress of the International Political Science Association, Berlin, August 1994.

Proudhon and modern social Catholic thinkers. Dissolved in 1939, the movement re-emerged in 1944 championing a post-war European Union. The Christian Democratic and Social Democratic political parties then took over implementation and began to promote a European federal union. The extent of the union envisaged is often unclear but some continue to advocate transferring powers to European supranational institutions in areas such as defence, foreign policy and economic and monetary matters as well as a European social system, a structure of Union law and protection for ethnic groups and minorities under European rules and regulations.

The covenantal approach by contrast conceives of federalism not in corporatist terms. It stresses regional, ethnic and linguistic pluralism. Covenantal federalism is an organisation in which there are 'several species', including confederation, federalism, associated state arrangements, common markets, consociational politics, unions, condominiums and other types of functional arrangements. The covenantal approach also has deep European origins and was carried to America by Protestant reformers of both English Puritan and Dutch or German Calvinist faith. The covenantal conceptual framework to some is more modern and better fitted to help the European peoples adapt to our new decentralised internet world, and it may offer a way of meeting some of the concerns of the demonstrators against globalisation seen in Seattle, Prague, Genoa and more recently London. The two approaches are, however, so different that using the word 'federal' as a link is both confusing and misleading.

Historically, we know how confederations, through a number of steps, have acquired more executive authority and then evolved through federation into a national state as a federal union. The Federal Republic of Germany arose out of the nineteenth-century German Confederation and of course the United States of America emerged out of the Articles of Confederation (1781–9) that preceded the Constitution of the United States. This process is what concerns many people, particularly in the UK and Denmark, to name two identifiably worried countries about the EU's future development in these terms. That concern is also becoming more apparent in the Netherlands, a hitherto federalist-leaning country. It is the responsibility of those of us who believe our unique Union cannot be modelled on what has happened elsewhere not to just reject federal models but to come up with a restructuring of Europe in the second half of the twenty-first century that takes account of experience, particularly that of the eurozone, created initially in the Treaty of Maastricht.

The underlying concept of a single European federal state* would allow for so-called national governments in the existing named member states. It would even allow those so-called states to retain their monarchies but alongside, a single federal state would build up its competences in all fields of EU activity, in particular what has broadly remained intergovernmental: foreign policy, defence and fiscal policy. That process would

*Pier Virgilio Dastoli, 'An EU Constitution and Federalism after Nice: A New Chance or Requiem for a Myth?', *International Spectator* (2001), vol. 36, no. 1, pp. 51–9.

deliberately destroy the self-governing nature of the nation states we are familiar with inside the EU. Its form could vary, but some suggest a chamber of states could be established to represent national governments either as delegates of the national parliaments or directly elected, as in the case of the US Senate. A chamber of representatives is suggested to represent the peoples of Europe, which would be directly elected on the basis of Europe-wide political parties and one electoral system. A European federal budget would be introduced, initially allocating, say, 7–10 per cent of European GDP to ease problems in the eurozone, which for transfer payments has at present an EU budget ceiling, although this is due to be renegotiated by the end of 2013. A European federal budget would be bound to increase with its competences into a budget appropriate for that of the more mature federal states in Europe of around 40 per cent of GDP or more. Such a single federal European state is, to some people in Europe, a legitimate political objective; to others it is a dangerous and destabilising objective. It is clear that in the UK public opinion is firmly against a single federal European state.

Another argument used by some in favour of a single federal European state or, as I believe is a better description, a country called Europe, is that it is a natural pooling of sovereignty which has become necessary in the twenty-first century. We saw in the last century many examples of specific sovereignty, hitherto thought to be sacrosanct, being voluntarily given up without abandoning a nation's self-governing status. The Bretton Woods Agreements in 1944 on monetary matters were followed by the creation of the United Nations, the International Monetary Fund and the World Bank. The creation of NATO followed when the Soviet Union had emerged as a major threat. In all these international bodies the essentials of democratic self government were, however, preserved. A nation that signed up to membership of these global institutions retained the right to secede and in the last analysis there was a provision for a nation state to distance itself from the consensus or ultimately to assert the power of veto.

There were many reasons, historical, emotional and practical, why the self-governing nature of the member states was retained. One constant factor was, and remains to this day, how the United States of America sees itself and the demands of the US Congress to ensure no US President diminishes its constitution, which is based on self-governing principles. European countries have governments that in large part control the votes in their parliaments. Europe does not practise a separation of powers as the US does. The US Senate and the House of Representatives zealously guard their rights as legislatures separate from the executive, to an extent that is often difficult for us to understand. Take the example of the Kyoto Treaty. Europe blamed President George W. Bush soon after his administration came into office for refusing to support Kyoto. The treaty, however, had to be ratified by Congress, which had already decisively rejected it under President Clinton with Democratic and Republican Senators voting for a wrecking amendment by ninety-five votes to nil. The Kyoto Treaty lost all chance of ratification long before Bush took office. Similarly, at present Congress will not ratify the treaty creating the International Criminal Court, which has nevertheless, and in my view wisely, been ratified individually by all EU member states. One of the reasons the US Congress objects so strongly is that the US military could, theoretically, be tried by the International Court in some rare circumstances and this degree of international authority is not something Congress is ready to live with.

At present in the EU a self-governing member state, having made every reasonable attempt to agree within the EU on defence, foreign policy and security decisions, can just about make its own governmental decisions. This tortuous EU procedure is much clearer within NATO, which acts by consensus, albeit with the US being the strongest influence. A number of member states in both organisations do not want this to change in the EU. If there is to be a further slide towards a single federal state in Europe the UK Referendum Act of 2011 should ensure a referendum in the UK and it would likely be lost.

On 15 December 2001 the heads of government, meeting at Laeken, in Belgium, issued a joint declaration called 'The Future of the European Union'. It announced what had been long anticipated, a convention composed of the main parties involved in the debate on the future of the EU prior to the inter-governmental conference (IGC) envisaged for 2004. The former French President Valéry Giscard d'Estaing was to be chairman, with two former Prime Ministers, Giuliano Amato of Italy and Jean Luc Dehaene of Belgium, as vice-chairmen. The secretary of the convention was to be Sir John Kerr, formerly head of the

British diplomatic service. There was a twelve-person presidium, which met ten times a month, and a 105-member plenary, which met once a month. Giscard d'Estaing was quick to liken the Convention to the famous meeting in Philadelphia which drew up the constitution of the United States.

The Laeken Declaration used assertions and questions as the technique for raising controversial issues on the future design of Europe on which member states disagreed. In declaring 'no taboos', the Belgian presidency cleverly widened the scope of the convention to include all the integrationists' key demands for the Union's future development and a myriad of other lesser decisions included because they represented the summation of member states' wish lists. An extract of the declaration was published in newspapers all over the EU under the subtitle 'This Union Is Yours'. However, assertions such as this do not create feeling and we know that a majority of Europeans had then, and still very likely have today, no clear idea of what the EU is, let alone where it purports to be heading.

The scope and sweep of the declaration were breathtaking. Nothing in the wording of the declaration, however, on the face of it precluded taking as the leitmotif of the convention the separation of powers between the supranational and the inter-governmental. There was something for everyone; for instance it asked: 'Can we thus make a clearer distinction between three types of competence: the exclusive competence of the Union, the competence of the Member States and the shared competence of the Union and the Member States?' It also asked: 'How [can we] ensure that a redefined division of competence does not lead to a creeping expansion of the competence of the Union or to the encroachment upon the exclusive areas of competence of the Member States?' It reiterated a decision taken and annexed to the Treaty of Nice on the need to examine the role of national parliaments in European integration and whether they should be represented in a new institution alongside the Council and the European Parliament. Laeken also questioned whether the President of the Commission should be appointed by the European Council, appointed by the European Parliament or directly elected by the citizens. Among its other questions were: 'How can a more coherent common foreign policy and defence policy be developed?' 'How is the synergy between the High Representative and the competent Commissioner to be reinforced?' 'Should the distinction between the Union and the Communities be reviewed? What of the division into three pillars?'

The declaration went on to state: 'What [EU citizens] expect is more results, better responses to practical issues and not a European super-state or European institutions inveigling their way into every nook and cranny of life,' and asked: 'Does Europe not, now that it is finally unified, have a leading role to play in a new world order, that of a power able both to play a stabilising role worldwide and to point the way ahead for many countries and peoples?'

One of the features of the politics surrounding the declaration was that the British Prime Minister, Tony Blair, used the occasion to dilute his previous publicly stated opposition to a new constitution for the EU, saying that the EU's present four treaties could 'in the long run' form a constitution. This was a typical shift of position taken on the hoof: whereas Britain had earlier maintained that what was being discussed was just a simplification and updating of the Treaties, now it could apparently live with a constitution or a treaty.

Simplification of the treaties was not a new development. The European University Institute in Florence had previously been asked by the European Commission to study the possibility of drafting a basic treaty in a way which would restructure the primacy law of the EU without altering its substance and also to look at the procedure for amending the treaties. They produced two reports in May and July 2000. The first report managed to suggest wording which reduced the 350 articles of the Treaty on European Union and the EU Treaty to 95 clauses. The second report drew a distinction between amendments which covered fundamental principles which would require an IGC or, as they suggested, a convention, followed by what the report called a super-qualified majority in the Council by member states. This was not the situation that had hitherto applied, where a prior IGC and unanimity of member states were required for all treaty amendments. The other amendments would be more detailed and would not be thought to affect the balance of power between the member states and the institutions; it was suggested they could be agreed by a super-qualified majority in the Council on the basis a proposal by the Commission, without the need for an IGC. A super-qualified majority would be something like four-fifths of the member states and be designed to stop any single member state blocking treaty amendments.

When the Constitutional Treaty was rejected by the French people on Sunday 29 May 2005 and the Dutch on Wednesday 1 June, Tony Blair disregarded advice from officials and his Foreign Secretary, Jack Straw, that the issues were now 'dead in the water'. With two founder members voting against, this was the moment to end ever greater integration and stop the dreams of Europe's 'Imperial Presidency'. Instead, following eight years of gestation, in December 2009 the Lisbon Treaty entered into force, without the promised referendum. The greatest responsibility for this lies with both British Prime Ministers, Blair and Gordon Brown, for there is little doubt that had there been a UK referendum the treaty would have been rejected.

Where a few EU nations did not wish competence to be exercised by the European Commission while others did want a European position, provision had been made in 1999 under the Amsterdam Treaty for such countries who wanted to engage in 'enhanced co-operation'. A big area where enhanced co-operation was thought to be suitable was the various projects based upon a wish of some continental countries to integrate legal systems. This is the range of questions raised by *corpus juris*.* The purpose of this flexible alternative for developing the

---

*'A comprehensive collection of the laws of a jurisdiction.' Aaron X. Fellmeth and Maurice Horwitz, *Guide to Latin in International Law* (Oxford: Oxford University Press, 2009).

EU was to avoid the endless blocking of particular initiatives in a politically sensitive area by a number of countries, foremost among them the UK. There are, however, real differences between the British legal system and that of the main continental European countries. This became manifest in the discussions over extradition in the aftermath of the 11 September 2001 terrorist attacks in the United States and has continued into 2012. Yet an agreed European extradition order for major crimes such as terrorism emerged fairly easily; lesser crimes proved more difficult and for a number of countries the breaking point was reached with a long list of far less serious crimes which were proposed should be covered by extradition orders. Lurking in the background was a deep reluctance to diminish the pre-eminence of the jury system in favour of judges and a wish to maintain the onus of proof lying on the prosecution with the assumption of innocence until proved guilty.

It is rational for those who wish to embrace Corpus Juris to take the Charter of Fundamental Rights within this structure rather than try to obtain the endorsement of all member states. The charter was the product of the first convention, established at the Cologne summit in 1999 and initially chaired by Roman Herzog, a former President of the Federal Republic of Germany. For the British, who have still to absorb the full implications of making the European Convention on Human Rights, which was signed up to in the late 1940s, justiciable in the British courts, this charter is an odd mixture of wishful thinking, good sense, vague protestations and aspirational language. It would be unacceptable in Britain for it to be given legal weight and to be applied by the European Court of Justice. It endorses or guarantees existing rights under national laws without giving any reason as to why it is either necessary or helpful for the EU to take a position on the right to 'marry and found a family', to conscientious objection, to health care and to 'access to services of general economic interest', whatever that means. The charter is not innocuous, and it should not be endorsed by citing the usual Foreign Office rider that the words are meaningless. Within almost every sentence there is scope for an integrationist Court of Justice to widen competences and to poke its nose into the judicial system that most people in Britain believe is the natural preserve of a member state. The charter endorses the absurd position of affirmative action on gender but not on race. It also prohibits the extradition to the United States of people who have fled to Europe after committing multiple murders; one is left to assume this is because they would be eligible for the death penalty, but it does not solve the more delicate questions surrounding genuine concerns about existing extradition legislation from the UK to the USA. As has been pointed out, under Article 54 of the Charter there is an inhibition placed on any individual or political party that might wish to campaign against such a provision, which we know is deeply resented by many Americans.*

The other core question that has been hotly bargained for

*Brian Hindley, *Nice and After: The EU Treaty and Associated Issues* (London: Centre for Policy Studies, 2001).

over the years in the development of the EU is QMV, its validity and its weighting. Of course, over time in the discussions on QMV, there has to be a recognition of changes in population. After reunification Germany constituted 17.05 per cent of the EU's population, while the next largest country, the UK, had 12.30 per cent. Germany's proportion was so much larger that it was felt it had to have more weight in EU decision-making. Eventually when there was no agreement to give it more votes than the twenty-nine already allocated to each of the four largest countries, there was support for a procedure that reflected Germany's size by making it necessary under QMV for a decision to have the support of 62 per cent of the total EU population. That can be delivered, when a decision has been adopted by QMV in the Council, by a member state requesting verification that the member states constituting a qualified majority on the voting formula also represent 62 per cent of the total population. If they constitute less than 62 per cent, then the decision in question shall not be adopted. This means that a proposal can be blocked by three of the 'big four' (Britain, France, Germany and Italy) if Germany is one of the three but not by Britain, France and Italy without Germany. That formulation is an additional reason why the UK should never accept in some crucial areas of decision-making QMV without a right of veto.

For the UK there are definite limits to the extension of QMV. Yet when further extensions were raised during the time of the 1997–2010 Labour administration, the British government's position all too often simply shifted from protest to acquiescence. The UK should have argued that the alternative to the greater use of QMV in sensitive areas would be the introduction of the veto for the six largest member states – Germany, France, the UK, Italy, Spain and Poland* – as it operates in the Security Council for the Permanent Five of China, France, Russia, the UK and the US. In the UN the veto nations by unwritten convention do not hold the office of secretary general and it would be sensible for veto nations in any European construction to be ineligible to hold the positions of President of the Commission or High Representative for Foreign and Security Policy. However, for many member states in the EU to introduce a veto is an anathema and there is no sign of it being seriously considered. The UK has exercised its veto with care and consideration in the Security Council since 1973, when it entered the European Community, and it has taken into special consideration the views of its EU partners. But, initially alongside France, we have refused to accept wording which fetters our ultimate right to form our own judgement. The language introduced in the Lisbon Treaty, however, has gone too far in pressurising both France and the UK to conform to an EU CFSP.

If the UK had not had the unfettered right to exercise its judgement in the Security Council events would have been different and in some cases more damaging to world stability. In

*UN population estimates for 1 July 2012 (millions): Germany 82.0, France 63.5, UK 62.8, Italy 61.0, Spain 46.8, Poland 38.3.

some cases the mere existence of the veto is sufficient to make important differences to the decision-making in the Security Council. In all the twists and turns of policy in the Middle East, perhaps because of the Balfour Declaration of 1917, the creation of Israel became inevitable. The UK has positioned itself differently to the US but even under Ernest Bevin, it was on the side of Israel's right to exist. The anti-Semitism that found its most horrific form in the Holocaust in Europe hastened the creation of Israel but the Palestinians can reasonably question why they should bear the brunt of this European responsibility. Many Arab–Israeli wars later there is no agreement on whether the demarcation of a Palestinian state's territory should reflect the boundaries existing before defeat on the battlefield or after. The UN Charter points to the former, realpolitik the latter. A compromise that accommodates the realities of war over the return of territory, with the need for territorial compensation, is probably the best hope. Walls and barbed wire now deface Jerusalem as they did, and in some parts still do, in Belfast. The EU has been far more generous and far sighted about the need to put money into helping the Palestinians than has the US. But it has not always been as thoughtful about Israel's security fears, about the practical difficulties of controlling suicide bombers and the facts that particularly ethnic wars create, whether we like it or not, new realities. For the EU to hold a position of influence in the diplomacy of the Middle East I have no doubt there will be important occasions in the future when that is best done by the UK and France holding to their veto powers in the Security

Council and hopefully being joined soon by Germany as a permanent member without a veto.

There was a time, as this book demonstrates, when the UK could rely on France at least to defend the nature of the EU as a union of self-governing nation states. But that reliance has begun to fray and it is no longer certain that France will not accept its place being subsumed by the EU. While hitherto Britain could rely on Germany, Holland and even Belgium accepting the case for free trade and not seek a solution to our economic difficulties through protection, that too is no longer so certain. Sweden, Denmark, Poland and the Czech Republic are more likely allies. Acceptance that the US nuclear shield saved western Europe from the massive nuclear bullying power of the Soviet Union from 1946 used to be common ground in Germany and Italy, but that assumption can no longer be relied on. So in many areas the old certainties, boundaries, limits, are not as fixed, nor as certain, and there is a developing culture in the EU elite that wishes to have no limits, no ultimate point beyond a member state can claim its right to assert that there must be unanimity.

Turning now to Britain's recent relationship with France, British governments have on issues of war and peace had different viewpoints from their French counterparts. France only just came on board for the Gulf War in 1991 and was not ready to stay and enforce the humanitarian no-flight zones over Iraq. Regarding the 2003 invasion of Iraq, France was a critic, the UK a participant. Over Libya there was agreement despite German opposition and non-involvement in NATO's implementation of the no-fly zone. Co-operation between France and Britain has often been of a very high order and such co-operation in the Balkans continues in many different spheres. Yet all the Presidents of the Fifth Republic – Charles de Gaulle, Georges Pompidou, the more liberal Valéry Giscard d'Estaing, Jacques Chirac and Nicolas Sarkozy on the right; François Mitterrand and most recently François Hollande on the left – while at various times feeling it necessary to pay some regard to the Gaullists whom they relied on or whose votes they wanted, have nevertheless moved inexorably towards a more integrationist stance in Europe. This is despite the results of two referendums, the first only narrowly won over the Maastricht Treaty in 1992 and the second lost over the Constitution Treaty in 2005. Two voting days separated by a fortnight to elect a President have held off the far right in France, typified by Le Pen *père* and *fille*. But the fact that Jean-Marie Le Pen came second in the first round of the presidential election in 2002, and that Marine Le Pen took 18 per cent of the vote in the first round of the 2012 elections, coming third, may be a sign that the French elite are dangerously out of touch on ever greater integration and France may not remain on its present course, particularly if within the eurozone austerity continues and its crisis remains longer than the French people currently anticipate.

In 2012 we have reached a position where the UK cannot expect a French government to support establishing limits to progressive integration within the EU. In Germany all three of the main political parties are integrationists, with no provision for referendums. In other EU countries public opinion is more reluctant than the governing elites to go down the path of European integration. In Denmark in June 1992 a referendum rejected Maastricht but the Danes were forced to vote again in May 1993, when they accepted. Sweden is outside the eurozone by government decision without a formal opt-out. The Netherlands voted against the Constitutional Treaty in 2005. Public concerns over greater integration are masked under parliamentary voting and come to the surface in referendums. In Ireland in 2001 a referendum was held to ratify the Nice Treaty, which the government lost but subsequently won in a repeat performance fifteen months later.

Yet public opinion is very rarely fixed. It evolves, but that process on some issues can take a very long time. At some point the British people might identify with Europe, to the extent of feeling they are truly European citizens, content that decisions on foreign, defence and economic policy should be taken at the European level in a federal United States of Europe. But until that point is reached – which I believe is far off, if it is reached at all – then the people of this country must be free to make some important choices at the UK level. We now have devolved governments in Scotland, Northern Ireland and Wales, which I welcome. Scotland will vote in 2014 in a referendum on becoming an independent sovereign nation. That is their choice – I hope they will choose that the power of decision-making covering defence, foreign and macroeconomic policy should remain with the UK.

Those British citizens who believe in greater integration within Europe are sufficient in number, however, to be able to expect to have their say in referendums on these issues. On issues that go to the heart of British democracy, people want to feel they count, that they can influence their own destiny. Why ever-increasing European decision-making evokes so many doubts and questions in people's minds is that they cannot identify with so much of what it encompasses. People still want to be able to influence the nature of the society in which they live and spend their lifetime, the levels of taxation, benefits and pensions, the level of unemployment, the amount of redistribution or the amount of their earnings that they can keep to spend as they wish. These choices are the bedrock of a democracy. In the UK after the polls close in most elections, the new government takes office within hours, usually representing one party but very rarely with a majority of the votes cast. We normally have a vigorous opposition whose duty is to oppose, delay and block legislation, slowing the pace of reform and bridling the wish of any government to use its parliamentary majority to impose its will at its speed. We live with swings of the electoral pendulum and are not surprised if they produce clear variations in govern-ment policy. We wish to preserve that political ethos, not in aspic, but in a recognisable form, until something emerges which is convincingly better. We adapted to a hung parliament and coalition government in 2010, which legislated for five-year fixed-term parliaments. The alternative vote, however, received short shrift in the 2011 referendum. The British people expect their government to fight for their parliamentary democracy, their unwritten constitution and their constitutional monarchy, stripped of formal powers but vested with the mantle of continuity. They do not want their Prime Minister to appear presidential. Just as Cromwell was disowned when he became the Lord Protector, so the people want the ultimate privilege of a democracy to kick out those who govern them and to sense that Parliament can remove Prime Ministers who get above themselves. People know the reality of Lord Acton's famous dictum, 'All power tends to corrupt and absolute power corrupts absolutely', because they have witnessed it happening to four British Prime Ministers: David Lloyd George, Neville Chamberlain, Margaret Thatcher and Tony Blair.*

The UK is not, and will not be, permanently in a minority of one on this issue of maintaining identifiable self-government for the nations of Europe. Public opinion in other countries is starting to express somewhat similar sentiments. The UK is voicing a more widespread concern than is yet acknowledged. We may not find the same countries with us on all the same issues, but drawing on a varied combination there is a potential in 2012 for allies in restructuring the existing EU if for no other reason than the failures of the eurozone. What is now needed is for the UK to have a worked-out position over EU reform. If at all possible that position should cross the party political divide in the UK and marry up with public opinion. We must have the

*David Owen, *In Sickness and In Power: Illness in Heads of Government During the Last 100 Years*, rev. ed. (London: Methuen, 2011).

courage, if need be, to stand out for a while on our own. Nothing makes the smaller member states more nervous about standing up to the Commission or the Franco-German alliance than if they doubt whether, for all the tough talk, the UK will in the last analysis hold firm. The occasion for restructuring the EU now is that the eurozone is demonstrably facing a deep-seated crisis. The G8 meeting at Camp David on 19 May 2012 analysed the problem but could not solve it. The UK has lectured to the eurozone on what it should do. Now is the time to propose a comprehensive European restructuring.

The key to any new definition of Europe and of the EU lies in the separation of powers, an acceptance of a supranational Europe around the eurozone to be called the European Union, alongside a larger, predominantly intergovernmental, Europe outside the eurozone returning to being called the European Community. This, for Europe today, holds the key to remaining united. This is a different separation of powers to that of the executive from the legislature, created by the founding fathers of America at the Philadelphia Convention of 1787. At that convention America was claiming for the first time the right to have its own foreign and defence policy, which had not been formally handed over by the British following the Declaration of Independence in 1776. What we in Europe need to do is to go back to the simple values that have guided us over centuries past in our human relationships in villages, towns and cities, something which may jar with some who believe that in our globalised world there should be no limits, no boundaries and not even any nations. It is summarised by the words of the Massachusetts-born poet Robert Frost, in his poem 'Mending Wall': 'Good fences make good neighbours.' The skill is to place those fences in an ordered way, taking account of geographical, cultural and historic differences between nations.

Those in the EU who want to tear down all border controls, as with Schengen, must be free to do so. Normally a nation state takes responsibility for its frontiers by having border controls and customs controls. In 1985, after many years of relaxing controls and waving people and vehicles through in ever greater numbers, Belgium, the Netherlands, Luxembourg, France and Germany lifted virtually all controls as part of the Schengen Agreement. First outside the EU treaties, then absorbed into EU law by the Amsterdam Treaty in 1999, the Schengen area now comprises twenty-six European countries in this passport free zone, which includes four non-EU countries. All but two EU member states, Ireland and the UK, are required to implement Schengen. Some 400 million travellers a year now use this freedom to move freely across state boundaries. But this undoubtedly convenient mechanism began to come under increasing criticism as criminals, drug traffickers and terrorists abused its freedoms. Despite common rules that govern the standards that must be maintained on border checks, only recently has there been harmonisation of the detailed information necessary for visas. Schengen members are reviewed by their peers every five years on their compliance and their technical provisions. For example, Greece which joined in 2000, has had two reviews and numerous detailed suggestions for improving its performance across their long land and sea frontier with Turkey. The EU's own border agency, Frontex, reported in 2012 that illegal entries across this frontier will remain, at least into 2013, at levels as high as 50,000. During the 2012 presidential election, the Sarkozy government put the annual number of illegal immigrants currently entering the Schengen area at 400,000. The French people are becoming ever more exasperated. Britain is virtually certain to remain outside the Schengen *acquis* in perpetuity, marking a clear separation of powers over border controls. It is France and French public opinion which is likely to determine the future of Schengen.

Under the Lisbon Treaty, the UK and Ireland have the right to opt in to future EU justice and home affairs (JHA) legislation. This whole area is fiendishly complicated. Denmark has an opt-out arrangement from Title V. Before Lisbon came into force, EU member states had the option of allowing their national courts to refer cases falling under EU crime and policing law to the European Court of Justice. Most did so; the UK, Ireland and Denmark did not. The ECJ could not, however, rule on infringement cases brought by the European Commission. The transitional arrangements apply to all member states that have yet to accept the European Court's jurisdiction in this area.

Denmark has had a long-standing opt-out from JHA matters since 1993. Under the Lisbon Treaty, Denmark cannot opt into any new EU JHA measure or into a measure that would amend a pre-Lisbon law. Its opt-out is less flexible than the UK's opt-in, because Denmark cannot opt into new JHA legislation, even if the government of the day wants to. However, in Lisbon, Denmark secured changes to its JHA protocol, ensuring that it can keep existing pre-Lisbon EU crime and policing measures 'unchanged' and outside the jurisprudence of the European Court or the powers of the Commission, irrespective of any subsequent amendments to legislation.

One example of the EU crime and policing legislation, the European Arrest Warrant (EAW), will become subject to the UK's bloc opt-in/opt-out decision in 2014, i.e. before the next general election. It has been adopted by all member states, including the UK and Ireland. However, the 2014 decision, specified in Article 10 of the Protocol on Transitional Provisions, applies only to the UK. EAWs were introduced in the UK following Royal Assent of the Extradition Act 2003. The history of their implementation remains controversial. The Serious Organised Crime Agency and, in Scotland, the Crown Office and Procurator Fiscal Service are the designated authorities in the UK responsible for processing EAWs, and compile figures on how many requests for surrender have been issued and received by the UK under the EAW regime. With regard to individuals wanted in connection with terrorist attacks in the UK, the process was employed with regard to a suspect not involved in the successful attack of 7 July 2005, but rather the failed repeat attack on 21 July in the same year. That suspect, Hussain Osman, was arrested in Italy in August 2005 under a EAW, and was extradited to the UK.

To date, there appears to have been no official discussion or consideration of extending the application of EAWs to non-EU member states. A similar scheme operates, however, among the Nordic countries, crucially covering three EU members (Denmark, Finland and Sweden) and two non-members (Iceland and Norway), and there are links between the two. A recent report by Open Europe has examined the possible consequences of an opt-out by the UK in 2014, and how a future arrest warrant scheme might evolve from that. Were there to be a restructuring of the EU treaties and the EEA Treaty, it might be possible to arrive at a mutually agreed solution for dealing with the practicalities of extradition and arrest between all the suggested wider European Community members which would be compatible with the inner, more integrated, EU.

Meanwhile those who want to retain fences or rebuild ones that need to be erected as a result of experience must be free to do so. We can all remain good Europeans but the extent to which we identify with Europe or with our own nation state will vary. We will live easier alongside each other if the structures of our governance accept our differences as well as our similarities, as, by and large, good neighbours do.

Chapter 10

A restructured Europe

'If proof were needed of the maxim that the road to hell is paved with good intentions, the economic crisis in Europe provides it. The worthy but narrow intentions of the European Union's policy makers have been inadequate for a sound European economy and have produced a world of misery, chaos and confusion.'

Amartya Sen, 'The crisis of European democracy', *International Herald Tribune*, May 24 2012.

In all the controversy about sharing a common currency within the eurozone since 2009, involving Greece, Portugal, Ireland, Spain and Italy – the countries that have found themselves with the deepest problems – it is easy to ignore one simple fact: maintaining a eurozone, whatever the size, which remains the most likely outcome, will involve much greater integration for those countries that manage to stay in it. The very thing is happening which Hugh Gaitskell warned, fifty years ago, could come about if the UK joined the Common Market. The countries of the eurozone will start to look more like states in the USA. Gaitskell, Attlee's Chancellor of the Exchequer and by 1963, when he died, an extremely popular leader of the Labour Party, has been proven right.

On 7 February 2012 the German Chancellor, Angela Merkel, indicated very clearly the direction of travel that she intends to follow if the CDU party, which she leads, remains in government after the federal elections in Germany in the autumn of 2013. The eurozone crisis for her is to be the springboard to a replacement for the Lisbon Treaty. She said: 'Step by step, European politics is merging with domestic politics.' She called for 'comprehensive structural reform' of the EU with closer integration to overcome what she called 'major shortcomings'.

She had, some months earlier, in a move barely noticed in the UK, signed up to campaigning with fellow Christian Democrats across Europe for direct elections for the posts of President of the Commission and, much more surprisingly and far-reachingly, President of the European Council. The European Council came into operation after the Paris meeting of heads of government in December 1974, when it was decided to meet together three times a year as the main political driving force. The Treaty of Lisbon provided for the European Council to meet twice every six months and to elect a President by a qualified majority to chair and drive forward its work. The post of President had hitherto been filled by rotation: one member state took the chair of the EU every six months. The Council President even under the Lisbon Treaty was specifically designed to be an inter-governmental co-ordinator of the meetings of heads of government, not a politician elected with their own agenda. Now the post is filled permanently by a person chosen by the other heads of government for a thirty-month term, renewable once for a maximum total period of five years. The President at this level and in that capacity ensures the external representation of the Union on issues concerning its common foreign and security policy, without prejudice to the powers of the High Representative of the Union for Foreign Affairs and Security Policy, who chairs meetings of EU foreign ministers. It runs diametrically against any intergovernmentalist pillar in a European construction for the President of the European Council to be elected in any other way than by its heads of government.

Chancellor Merkel now clearly intends to use her position to persuade member states to cede further powers to the EU and she believes the European Commission ought to function more as a European government, with the Council of Ministers acting as a 'second chamber' alongside a strengthened European Parliament. These changes are more far-reaching than any adjustments contained in the 2012 Fiscal Pact Treaty, which falls outside the European treaties and has had difficulty already in winning public acceptance in France, Ireland and the Netherlands.

Yet, intriguingly, the German Chancellor went on to stress:

'We want to have Great Britain in the European Union. We need Britain, by the way. I want to say this emphatically, because Britain has always given us a strong orientation in matters of competitiveness and freedom and in the development of the single European market.' But she divulged no details as to how this could be done. She is well aware of the UK legislation whereby a referendum has to take place before any more powers are ceded to the EU. She knows too that many member states are against substantial changes to the treaties. Hopefully she will look seriously at these proposals for European restructuring.

Gerhard Schroeder, the Social Democrat German Chancellor from 1998 to 2005 and the person who, with the agreement of the trade unions, helped restore German competitiveness within the eurozone, argues for the same constitutional changes as Chancellor Merkel while advocating a rerouting 'away from pure austerity towards growth'. He is explicit: 'The European Council must give up powers and should be transformed into an upper chamber with similar functions to the Bundesrat in Germany.' His advocacy shows how broad is the consensus amongst the German political parties, as he argues that 'the current situation makes it clear that you cannot have a common currency area without a common financial, economic and social policy'.*

One way to meet Chancellor Merkel's aspirations was given support by Viviane Reding, the EU Commissioner for Justice,

*Gerhard Schroeder, 'Austerity is strangling Europe', *International Herald Tribune*, 4 May 2012.

Fundamental Rights and Citizenship and previously a Luxembourg Christian Democrat MP. She argued for another convention, the normal EU mechanism for creating a new treaty, seemingly unaware of the depth of feeling in many countries heartily fed up with ever more treaty amendments. Some countries fear that public opinion in their own countries will not easily endorse a long complicated process of treaty amendment, with or without referendums, coming so soon after the rigmarole of ratifying the Lisbon Treaty after the Constitutional Treaty had run into the ground.

Commissioner Reding's five-point plan, apart from a convention, includes giving the European Parliament full legislative powers with the right to initiate legislation and the right to elect the Commission. The aim would be to have a treaty ready by 2016, which would be ratified by 2019. The treaty would enter into force in 2020 provided two-thirds of the member states had ratified. Those states which did not want to be party to such a treaty or which failed to ratify it would become associates and, in an effort to accommodate Britain, could remain – how, she did not specify – a member of the single market. This could either be as a mere appendage, signing up for the European Economic Area (EEA) Treaty, or it could involve restructuring that treaty in ways to include more countries in a wider and larger single market.

The EEA already brings together the twenty-seven EU member states, soon to be joined by Croatia, plus Norway, Iceland and Liechtenstein; were Turkey to be asked to join, that would make a total of thirty-two states. The Agreement on the European Economic Area, which entered into force on 1 January 1994, covers a single market, referred to as the 'Internal Market', and when a country becomes a member of the European Union, it also applies to become party to the EEA Agreement (Article 128), thus leading to an enlargement of the EEA.

The EEA Agreement provides for the inclusion of EU legislation covering the 'four freedoms' – the free movement of goods, services, persons and capital. In addition, the agreement covers co-operation in other important areas such as research and development, education, social policy and the environment, consumer protection, tourism and culture, collectively known as 'flanking and horizontal' policies. It guarantees equal rights and obligations within the Internal Market for citizens and economic operators in the EEA.

The EEA Agreement does not cover the following EU policies: the Common Agricultural and Common Fisheries policies (although it contains provisions on various aspects of trade in agricultural and fish products); the customs union; the Common Trade Policy; the Common Foreign and Security Policy; justice and home affairs (even though the EFTA countries are part of the Schengen area); or monetary union (EMU).

A book called *The Future of Europe* by Jean-Claude Piris, who served as legal counsel of the EU and director of its legal service from 1988 until 2010, gives an informed insider view of a path to greater integration accompanied by a denial that it involves the EU becoming a federation. He considers four options for reform. The first option, substantially revising the EU treaties, he rejects because it looks unrealistic and unobtainable. The second option would be to continue to operate on the current path but he expresses little enthusiasm for it. The third and fourth options are based on the eurozone, one softer and one bolder, but both involving more differentiation between its member states and an *avant-garde* grouping. The 'softer' option would involve the interested member states choosing all the options offered by the current treaties. The 'bolder' option involves the adoption of an additional treaty that the author believes offers many advantages, is legally feasible and not as complex, as he explains in some detail, as it appears at first sight.*

What Piris's book does not address is Merkel and Reding's acceptance of a single market that continues with the UK actively involved while not being ready to support an ever-closer union for all member states. The UK may not be the only member state that will decide not to join this additional treaty for an integrated eurozone. Hence, perhaps, the suggestion that the changes can be triggered by two-thirds of the member states.

A restructuring of Europe which grapples with the advantages of continuing to build on the existing single market and not relying on simply enlarging the EEA handed down on tablets of stone by the countries of the EU is negotiable, but almost

*Jean-Claude Piris, *The Future of Europe. Towards a Two-Speed EU?* (Cambridge: Cambridge University Press, 2012).

certainly not without an initial argument and a testing of the UK's resolve. The design I outline for Europe would be inclusive in its concept. To bring it about would involve using different parts of existing treaties. It could even come into effect by dint of using the unanimity provision for treaty amendment in the European Council, leaving those member states to hold referendums that wish to. Nothing would be agreed until all was agreed. The negotiating process would, it would be hoped, include Turkey and other non-EU countries. The legitimate safeguard of treaty change by unanimity, which has been built in from the start of the Common Market, would continue with the aim of broadly presenting two reworked treaties: one for a continuing European Union, the other for a European Community-wide single market. It recognises that the eurozone's flawed design has to be corrected, and that that needs treaty amendment going much further than the Fiscal Compact.

The skill will be to keep the restructuring of existing European treaties to the minimum, using their present wording as far as possible and mainly providing for opt-outs and opt-ins within national decision-making. The integrationists can claim to have achieved much that they have long dreamt of. Also they are irrepressible, constantly coming back to ask for more. They have history behind them, knowing that federal structures come about not just through brick-by-brick building but through transformation driven by crisis.

Any timescale for restructuring the EU will be determined by what happens in the eurozone. The timescale set in the Fiscal

Compact Treaty, negotiated by twenty-five member states in 2012, is a leisurely one. It states that within five years that treaty should be part of the EU Treaties. This is something which apparently Nick Clegg, the UK Deputy Prime Minister and Liberal Democrat leader, takes credit for suggesting, implying that by 2017 at the latest all EU member states will be ready to ratify such an arrangement. Whether this was discussed within the UK coalition is unclear. But all the signs are that the coalition has felt inhibited by deep division on many European questions and is way behind the pace of events in the eurozone.

Prime Minister David Cameron's mistake was not to opt out of signing the Fiscal Compact Draft Treaty but to opt out of negotiating a far more comprehensive design. He had to shift his ground to becoming involved as part of the twenty-seven arguing within an inclusive process about a treaty outside the EU treaties. He implied that acting in this way was illegal but took no action. During that negotiation the Czech Republic joined the UK in not signing up and since then France under President Hollande and other countries have developed serious doubts about the Fiscal Compact. The importance of these constitutional issues facing the UK means that Cameron should from now on wherever possible in the European Council speak on behalf of the UK as a whole, having previously discussed Britain's negotiating position with the leader of the opposition, Ed Miliband.

The Fiscal Compact Treaty is more limited in scope than Chancellor Merkel wants in the medium term. However, it appeared negotiable and a lot of it reiterates provisions that already exist. Merkel's skill throughout the early years of the eurozone crisis has been to play for time. She knew that Greece would have to be given very substantial help but she wanted Greece to carry much of its debt, and for private bondholders to carry part of the cost, not just eurozone governments. Bail-outs have always presented Germany with great problems, for the German Constitutional Court is ready at any time to rule on a breach of the 'bail-out clause' within the existing treaties. The court procedure is always lengthy, traditionally gives the German government time to adjust, and can be cumbersome. The court is very keen to accommodate on controversial issues if the Bundestag takes additional responsibilities to deal with difficulties or inconsistencies thrown up by the EU treaties. Prior to June 2012 Chancellor Merkel protected with considerable determination both German interests and her own vision of what needs to be achieved in the medium term. She knew that the Fiscal Compact would prove to be insufficient and that there would need to be further treaty amendment and greater integration for the euro to survive after the German federal elections in 2013. But that timescale looks likely to be overtaken by events in Greece and Spain. There is a growing urgency, clearly expressed at the May G8 meeting, about the global consequences if Greece were unable to stay within the disciplines of the new eurozone. No one can be sure whether the fear of contagion is justified. But we can be sure of one thing: the more that is done by agreement and without prescription, the less likely the global economy is to be damaged.

The German–French civil service elite who have, from the start, driven the euro project have had difficulty, after the French Assembly elections, in resolving differences between Chancellor Merkel and President Hollande. Hollande may well come to regret conniving with the technocratic President of Italy, Mario Monti, and the People's Party Prime Minister of Spain, Mariano Rajoy, in putting Merkel against the ropes at the end of June in the Heads of Government summit meeting. She was very careful in what she conceded but it may be some time before she consents to restoring the German-French duopoly. Hollande has some sympathies with that part of the French socialists who are not federalists and have over the years striven to check ever greater integration, particularly over the EU Constitutional Treaty in 2005. Any French Government has difficulty in espousing integration which comes close to a country called Europe. The French elite will try and subsume more integration into the EU and the eurozone while pretending little has fundamentally changed. This sleight of hand, using the procedures of the community method, will not, however, hide the significant steps towards greater integration involved in a banking union. Merkel has already agreed in June to some new initiatives over economic growth but she will not endorse indiscipline and will not agree to use German funds until she is assured that a new disciplined framework has been agreed.

Will such Franco-German initiatives for the eurozone be any more successful than the previous ones? The hope will be that even if the pretence continues that what is emerging is not a single eurozone nation, the money markets will see that what is emerging is, in their jargon, 'joint and several liability for sovereign debt' within the eurozone and the 'fiscal union' that monetary union has always carried within its wake. It will not just be in the UK, however, that the peoples of Europe, as distinct from their elites, will question, becoming citizens of a United States of Europe (USE) with the euro as their currency, as in the USA with the dollar. It demands a huge leap of the imagination and public opinion will question whether the leaders are just trying to save the euro, or to save the face of three generations of political leaders who have got the construction of Europe, particularly the eurozone, wrong and much else besides. But there will also be an idealism about integration in those Europeans who find the concept attractive as part of European solidarity. In the UK the consequences for our economy are such that it is strongly in our interests that the eurozone settles its problems and survives in a coherent manner. Nevertheless it is possible, but unlikely, that the further integration demanded by the European elite for the eurozone will lead to some individual member states rejecting eurozone membership, whether they are already inside the zone or waiting to join.

President Hollande is a fully committed European integrationist. His role models in French politics are three French socialists: Jacques Delors, Lionel Jospin and François Mitterrand. On the issue of further integration within the eurozone he is likely to go with the Franco-German consensus, whether Angela Merkel remains Chancellor after the 2013

German federal elections or is replaced by a Chancellor from the SDP. Nevertheless, Hollande knows that the French people only voted by the narrowest of margins for the euro in the referendum on the Maastricht Treaty in 1992, and he no doubt also knows that in the final television debate only a superb performance by Mitterrand tilted the balance in favour of the 'Yes' vote. European Prime Ministers in Denmark, the Netherlands and Sweden will also know they will probably have huge difficulty in persuading their own citizens to follow the path of ever-greater integration. All these countries have lost or feared that they would lose referendums if conceded on greater integration. Other newer members, Finland and Slovenia and even Austria, have endured criticism within their borders when their citizens have been asked to pick up the costs of weaker eurozone countries. Of course it is possible that out of the chaos of the eurozone crisis will come an inner core of political unity. But it is all happening when there is a deep division of opinion emerging between Social Democrats in Europe, who believe that demand management and economic growth in Europe have been neglected, and Christian Democrats, for whom austerity is the way of restoring competitiveness. It is true that irrespective of party there is a German attitude more favourable than most to austerity, but that does not appear likely to be the Spanish way or the Italian way. We are seeing under President Hollande how France is trying to balance austerity with economic growth. But Europe is not strong enough economically to be the master of its own fate. World financial markets keep intruding on the

European debate with their own market assessment, and retaining international confidence is not something the European leaders can ignore.

If the German people are persuaded by their politicians to fund a continuing eurozone after 2013, based on much greater integration, and the UK facilitates this as part of an overall restructuring, then many existing EU member states will be only too ready to continue in or to aim for eurozone entry, despite an accompanying German bias towards austerity. That should be a choice for individual member states. Those countries who do not want to participate will have the right to help in the design of what best suits them. Eurozone reform is not a one-way street and its restructuring raises fundamental issues that will force a restructuring elsewhere. It cannot be pushed through in isolation.

Britain must not remain passive any longer, reacting only to the proposals of others. This is our EU by treaty. It is not pedantic to insist it can only legally be changed by unanimity and the UK must now start to champion a credible but different design to set alongside German–French reforms of the eurozone. The UK must have the determination to stay at the negotiating table until there is unanimity. No walk-outs, just quiet persistence. Where the UK can act with others so much the better, but Britain must have the confidence to set out its design for Europe – a wider Europe and a deeper Europe, living alongside and in harmony with each other. Turkey deserves to be involved in restructuring of the existing EU treaties rather than left outside. Including the EEA countries, Iceland, Norway and Liechtenstein, makes sense. (The EEA was to have Switzerland as a member, but a referendum on joining returned a 'No' vote; however, that has been largely circumvented and Switzerland is in fact closely associated.)

The setting up of the EEA on 1 January 1994, as the then President of the European Commission, Jacques Delors, claimed, marked a further step in the long-standing process of rapprochement between the European Union and the EFTA countries. In a foreword to a book called *The Agreement on the European Economic Area*,* he wrote: 'There is no doubt that the implementation of the Agreement will have positive effects on the economy of the continent as a whole. This is likely to produce new economies of scale and to boost competitiveness, as did the completion of the Single Market amongst the 12 Member States of the European Union.' This book provides a valuable description of the Area. It explains that the EEA did not entail a customs union because, within a free trade area as then existed, the countries belonging to it had their own customs tariffs for goods imported from outside the area, and rules of origin were needed in this context to lay down the conditions a product had to fulfil in order to gain the so-called originating status. Now that so many of the EFTA countries are member states of the EU (see Chapter 2), it is possible to envisage that a

*Thérèse Blanchot, Risto Piipponen and Maria Westman-Clément, *The Agreement on the European Economic Area (EEA): A Guide to the Free Movement of Goods and Competition Rules* (Oxford: Clarendon Press, 1994).

restructured EEA as part of a single market would also be a customs union. One of the main differences between the then EEC and the EEA in 1994, the exclusion of agricultural products, would remain, though in modified form.

A wider Europe should aim to have Turkey fully involved. Turkey is an associate member of the EU and since 31 December 1995 has been in a customs union with the EU, whereby goods may travel between the two entities without restriction. At one time Turkey had every prospect of becoming a full member. Sadly, that has receded to such an extent that French and German public opinion is against full EU entry. A lot of that hostility stems from a popular fear of Turkish workers flooding in and creating more unemployment. But the provision of the free movement of labour is not a prerequisite of a single market. The EU accepts that today, and a number of member states are holding back the date for this aspect of the Treaty of Rome to come into effect, thus buying time. Many Turkish people live in Germany and a new mechanism, without involving the totally free movement of labour but within any restructuring, brings Turkey in, in an honourable way, allowing it to identify itself with and join in a single market, and would settle the long-standing problem of Turkey being an associate member but as yet without any hope of being admitted to full membership.

Turkey is in a unique position as a long-standing member of NATO and being actively involved in the 57-member Organisation of the Islamic Conference. The Turkish

Parliament voted against allowing the US and UK to use Turkish territory to invade Iraq from the north in 2003. They also made it clear to Iraq that they would invade rather than see a Kurdish state emerge in the south. Turkey is forging substantial trade and economic links with the post-Saddam Hussein Iraq, and is again becoming a regional power with greatly improved relations with Russia, Greece and even Armenia. Relations with Israel, once good and strategic, are at present strained. Turkey would add to the strength of Europe and its economy and could fit comfortably within a single market. Delay much longer and the EU will force Turkey to withdraw its existing application and settle for being a regional power outside the Union. For that to happen would be a tragic lost opportunity. It would mark a considerable achievement for any European restructuring if it could attract Turkey to membership of the wider grouping that can and should emerge around the single market. It would not, however, be fatal to such a new grouping if Turkey refused.

The ruling Turkish Justice and Development Party, AKP, was first elected in 2002 and was re-elected for a third time in June 2011. It appears in EU terms as a Muslim equivalent of a Christian Democrat party. What has been achieved by its Prime Minister, Recep Tayyip Erdoğan, is quite remarkable, different but comparable to that of Mustafa Kemal Atatürk, who laid the secular foundations of modern Turkey. Under his charismatic but authoritative direction Erdoğan reforms of civil and minority rights, then challenged the military, who had an embedded position within the constitution; now Turkey has a Defence Minister, for the first time, who is a wholly political appointment, not encumbered by undue military influence. The AKP still has room to develop more tolerance of dissent and more sensitivity to personal liberty, and to be less hostile to democratic constraints on governmental power. But it is a recognisable European political party. They need to continue the reform process but there are no longer grounds for questioning Turkey's political credentials to being a European nation.

In matters of economic and industrial performance, Turkey has become a mainstream European country. While the EU was bailing out its banks and some of its countries in the eurozone, Turkey, which made significant changes after its 2001 economic crisis, had a stable banking system which respected traditional deposit taking and lending. After a recession in 2009 it has bounced back in a most impressive way, growing at rates closer to China than any European counterpart. Roads, schools, health and education have visibly improved throughout the country. Unemployment and inflation look set to fall to within the range of existing EU members. GDP is forecast to continue to grow. Illiteracy rates amongst women in a country granted suffrage in 1934 stayed far too high initially, but have come down from 40 per cent to 20 per cent over the last twenty years. Turkey's Ninth Development Plan, running between 2007 and 2013, aims to increase female labour force participation to 29 per cent, resulting in a 15 per cent reduction in poverty levels. Efforts are under way to reduce the unregistered parts of the economy.

Turkey has seen the problems of just focusing politically on becoming a regional power. It took an initiative with Brazil over Iran when the United Nations 5+1 negotiators were making little progress. It was important for Turkey to show that it had diplomatic clout with Iran but unfortunately that clout was not felt everywhere. During the Arab Spring it was the Arab League, rather than Turkey, that made the political running regionally on Libya and to a lesser extent, Tunisia and Egypt. Nevertheless, the Arab League failed over Syria, and Turkey, which at one time had been close to the Assad regime, has toughened its stance. Expectations remain that it will be needed to help deliver a settlement in that country.

Eurozone membership, however, and deeper integration are not something that Turkey needs or wants. It has handled its own currency well. It does not wish to have its new-found influence in regional foreign affairs and security policies curtailed. The European Community Political Co-operation would suit it better than an EU CFSP. Where Turkey would fit naturally into Europe is within a single market structure which includes all EU countries and all the countries currently involved in the EEA. It is highly desirable that Turkey should contribute from the start to such a restructuring.

Like the UK, Turkey is too large a country to fit into the single market as a mere appendage, which is the relationship of the existing EEA countries to the EU. The EEA incorporates the prior legislation adopted by the EU and it is simply passed down. There is no need to dismantle the existing single market legislation. But some adjustment and a newly structured shared administration of a single market of some thirty-two nations or more would be necessary. This would not be an insuperable task. It would mean living with the EU procedures involving co-decision between the European Council and the European Parliament and recognising that the EU would continue to be the major influence shaping legislation but it would not be the only decision maker. A new single market would probably need its own court to rule on trade disputes, but this might be done by adapting the ECJ for single market questions in a way that reflected the wider membership of the single market. It must not lead to the loss of the single negotiator on international trade forums, which has been one of the most successful aspects of the present EU single market. It could mean, initially, starting with the EU Trade Commissioner holding that post double-hatted and working under a secretary general, rather than president, of the single market, as well as the President of the EU Commission. The UK, Turkey, Norway and Poland with the European Commission could be asked to take the lead on single market redesign in much the same way as Germany and France have been in discussions with the Commission and have led the way with the ECB in the redesign of the eurozone.

Of course, all existing EU member states must have their say in designing the economic and political contours of this larger single market. It would adopt as its core the existing EU single market legislation but with less prescription on the free movement of labour; that would stay in the EU and the eurozone.

There could be a readiness to incorporate more EU environmental legislation than in the current EEA, for the larger the number of European nations involved, the more likely Europe will carry influence in the global environmental debate.

Some will argue that the boundaries between the EU and the EEA should be more substantially changed but that is not likely to be easily agreed, for the integrationists will want to retain all the features of a single government in the integrated eurozone, hoping eventually that it will emerge in effect as a single state. Some will argue that the UK and some other member states can achieve its objectives by remaining in the existing EU and negotiating substantial opt-out provisions, such as the one for social policy that Britain negotiated at Maastricht. It was no accident that that opt-out did not last and the Labour government of 1997 decided to opt in, because many Social Democrats believe in tying together social and economic policy. The EU will also argue, not unreasonably, that it cannot have constant switching around within the eurozone and that the European economic government they aspire to introduce will only be supported by other member states if it is accompanied by a European social policy. These arguments have substance and I do not see EU countries that aspire to eurozone entry supporting opt-outs from EU policies which are thought to be central to eurozone survival and, longer term, a single government. For much the same reason, many smaller countries will not want to weaken the CFSP as they almost all see greater integration in this area as being of benefit to them, finding it difficult as they do to sustain a global presence relying only on their own resources. For the UK, and some other existing EU states with a restructured single market, it will be a question of accepting or rejecting what's on offer within an EU that's more and more based on the eurozone.

Any restructuring of Europe will only appeal to all EU member states if there is clarity about its objectives. Separating out a wider and larger single market deals essentially with a British problem: namely the reluctance of the British people to contemplate further integration. The quid pro quo, not unreasonably, is that the UK should not seek to prevent that degree of integration within the eurozone that its existing and aspiring members believe to be essential. In the internal UK debate, there is a tendency to want to have it all ways. That is not going to be an option.

It will, however, be open to the UK to choose to stay within the *acquis communautaire* of the existing EU, even if the British people have no intention of joining the eurozone. But we have to accept that the *acquis communautaire* will change to fit the new disciplines that will face aspiring eurozone members and that the UK cannot expect to obstruct such changes. There will therefore be a choice as I envisage in my suggested formulation of two questions for any UK referendum: the single market and the EU with a more integrated eurozone, or the single market alone. The single market countries, if there was any wish to do so, could choose to reactivate the consensual Political Co-operation arrangement that operated in the 1970s and 1980s.

The EU and eurozone countries could come to such a co-operative framework with their own common but increasingly single policy on foreign affairs and security, reached eventually through QMV. But there would be no QMV in Political Co-operation; it would function like NATO, of which almost all the members of the single market would already be part.

Some of those countries currently candidate members of the EU and those aspiring to that status would be eligible to join such a restructured single market and wider European Community rather earlier than the EU is likely to offer member-ship. This would help countries such as Macedonia, Serbia, Montenegro, Bosnia & Herzegovina, Albania, Moldova and even eventually Ukraine. It would also be good for the unity of Europe. By virtue of overlapping membership, such a European Community ought to have close and good relations with the inner core of the eurozone and non-eurozone EU countries.

As for the inner eurozone it would function at its own pace ever more as a European government with its own currency, the euro, at its core. Slowly and inevitably its economic government would most likely gravitate into one government. The present structures surrounding EMU, the CAP, the CFP and the CFSDP, as well as the EU institutions – the Commission, the ECJ and the ECB – would become more like government departments with similar functions as in other nation states. The old terminology might remain for some time in accordance with the wish of those who want to stress continuity and also want to continue to hold to the unique structures of the EU and claim that it is not a federation or a country. Maybe it could remain a unique union which would, as in the past, go on adding new elements of statehood, including common defence and common legal systems. All that would be for the participating countries to choose, no longer encumbered or held back by those reluctant to take such steps for fear of creating a momentum towards a federal union.

The constitutional arrangements for the inner eurozone need not concern overmuch those in Britain who would never consider joining such an arrangement. In addition to being in the wider single market, in a referendum the UK would offer the option to remain in the EU with the possibility of joining the inner eurozone. Such an eventual move would be on offer for all existing EU members not yet ready to join, but believing they might eventually do so. The UK referendum voters would need to accept the more disciplined path towards eurozone entry already envisaged in the Fiscal Compact Treaty as well as the further steps towards integration being championed by those who advocate a single economic government.

Although logically the inner eurozone should be called the United States of Europe (USE), as I have argued in this book in all probability its members would wish it to be seen as the EU so as to present it as a continuous development and help ensure minimal changes in the treaties. In which case, as I have already suggested, the wider Europe should stress its continuity by reverting to calling itself the European Community, which some have already been members of and in the case of Turkey initially applied to join. These aspects of continuity from the European Common Market, the European Community and the European Union could be very important in quickly forging an overall agreement and doing so within the existing wording of the EU treaties.

Of course there may well be referendums in countries where they are part of the national constitution, but the degree of consent across the EU may be such that all could be done under the unanimity rules for treaty amendment. It would make sense to try to have the inevitable UK referendum on the principles of the changes early to give greater certainty for other countries in the detailed negotiations. Any formal ratification of the eventually agreed position could then follow in Parliament. The leaders of the Conservative and Labour parties should try very hard to agree the principles of such a restructuring first amongst themselves. Smuggling through the restructuring suggested here without a referendum under the 2011 Referendum Act on the grounds that there was no new transfer of power to the EU would rightly arouse deep suspicion. It would help other EU member states if both of the UK's large parties had a simple and similar mandate for such a position well before the 2015 general election. Restructuring Europe is an issue of such vital national interest that I cannot stress enough the advantage to other EU member states of a joint approach.

The Liberal Democrats and UKIP might prefer two different options, a commitment respectively to eventually joining the eurozone or a withdrawal from all European structures. The reality is these preferences would be covered in the two formulations for referendum questions I proposed in the Introduction and which are repeated again here:

Do you want the UK to be part of the single
market in a wider European Community?   Yes/No
Do you want the UK to remain in the
European Union, keeping open the option
of joining the more integrated eurozone?   Yes/No

Whatever happens in the negotiations in Europe in 2012 and beyond, a lot of inter-party consultation will be needed in the UK. Already this sort of consultation and hopefully co-operation looks as if it will happen over the referendum on Scottish independence. It is every bit as important that it should happen over Europe. Liberal Democrats may wish to leave the present coalition to prepare a distinctive stance on any European referendum and that is their decision to make. They are free under the Fixed-Term Parliament Act to support the continuation of a minority Conservative or the introduction of a minority Labour government at any time. They do not have to wait until the 2015 general election. Liberal Democrats may, for example, focus their attention on voting 'Yes' to the second proposed question. In many ways it would be a good thing for the inner core eurozone concept to have a party champion in the UK for there is a body of opinion in the Labour and Conservative parties, not just in the Liberal Democrats, that genuinely wants ever greater integration and has wished for some time to be in a European federal union.

Europe has become an inescapable choice. The pace has been forced by the urgent needs of a collapsing eurozone. The big challenge is to involve Turkey for this holds the potential for Europe to come out of the whole restructuring process enriched, having solved two problems, the design of a eurozone and the continued exclusion of a large and significant EU associate member. It might be possible to make a decision in principle in the period between the German federal elections in autumn 2013 and the UK general election in May 2015. But that timetable may slip or even need to be advanced before autumn 2013 if pressure builds up internationally on the eurozone in late 2012. If the past is anything to go by, there will be the usual British reluctance to face up to the reality, and indeed immediacy, of Angela Merkel's eurozone plans. She will fight for her formulation and politicians in the UK must fight for theirs, hopefully based on a constructive proposal similar, if not exactly identical, to the one proposed here. Much may depend on whether Greece, Portugal, Italy, Spain and Ireland are successful in their eurozone survival strategies.

This suggested restructuring might also prove to be a way of bringing Conservative and Labour divisions over Europe, stemming from as far back as 1971, to an end. For there has never been any disagreement in either party about the need for a European free trade area, nor after 1987 for the European Community. For Labour, given Tony Blair's support in government for the eurozone and much EU integration, it may be harder. This was brought home by Lord Mandelson's speech in Oxford on 4 May 2012, when he argued for Britain eventually joining the eurozone. He said: 'The decision to move into currency union is now demanding a version of the EU based on collective fiscal governance. Something much more akin to political union than we have openly debated in the past.' He went on, interestingly, to say: 'Assuming that this major advance in the eurozone does take place, then we will have something more akin to a European Union inside a European Community.' He believed that in a decade, Britain would be the only state in the EU, certainly the only large state, outside the eurozone. 'Effectively the EU will have been rebooted with the UK on the outside.' This would be a very plausible prediction if it were not for the referendum in the UK which he now believes is inevitable and will happen before the decade is out. In fact such a referendum, I believe, will come much earlier than that.

Unless the UK declares soon its wish to change the structure of Europe the question for any referendum commitment at the 2015 general election will be a simple 'Yes' or 'No' to withdrawing from the EU. Such a question involving the UK leaving the single market is, I believe, dangerous to the economic strength and prosperity of the United Kingdom, and not good for Europe. It would nevertheless very likely result in a 'No' vote and a complete withdrawal.

The relatively young but experienced leaders in the Labour shadow Cabinet would be wise to start out now on an in-depth discussion within their party to align it more closely with British public opinion on Europe. Labour's grassroots membership may find the restructuring of Europe which I am suggesting, more attractive than older former Labour ministers who, in the main, embraced the integrationist views of Jacques Delors when he addressed the TUC conference in 1988. There are strong political arguments for Labour not delaying otherwise they will risk trailing behind public opinion close to the 2015 general election and might be forced to make a desperate bid to prevent the Conservatives from attracting votes with an offer to the electorate of an early referendum.

There are few better guiding speeches for Ed Miliband on the instincts of the British people, which have not much changed, than that of Hugh Gaitskell at the Labour Party conference on 3 October 1962. A federal Europe, Gaitskell said, referring to the continent, 'may well be the answer to their problems. It is not necessarily the answer to ours.' In an earlier TV broadcast on 21 September, referred to in Chapter 2, Gaitskell crystallised the issue of a federation as a nation becoming 'no more than Texas or California'. The challenge to Britain that Gaitskell foresaw as a possible outcome emerging from the then Common Market has, because of the eurozone, now become a reality fifty years later. His was a prescient speech. It came from a leader who understood where the European project could lead. He had lived for a year in Vienna in 1933–4 and was a true internationalist, albeit a sentimentalist about the Commonwealth. Still, better that way than a cynic. Even today the Commonwealth connection is underestimated by the UK political elite. It is an important and continuing part of Britain's legacy and still provides one of several good arguments for the UK, on its merits, retaining permanent membership of the UN Security Council.

Any UK political party that from 2012 on ignores the rapidly emerging political, not just economic, challenge over eurozone reform is putting its head in the sand. Only the complete collapse of the eurozone will stop a redesign and that now looks unlikely; even if Greece, Portugal, Italy, Spain and Ireland cannot live with the German austerity model, the euro will survive. The US and the rest of the world see a eurozone collapse as threatening their economies. For this reason the present eurozone members may manage to stay within it; certainly a substantial core will survive. Yet the continued dominance of austerity as a European discipline may put off some countries which had previously expected an easy pathway to eurozone membership. A few countries may, even in the eurozone, find the undemocratic nature of some of what has already emerged in the zone's handling of Greece and Italy as making for second thoughts about the desirability of eventual or continued membership. There is little doubt that the fiscal and economic discipline for some to remain in the eurozone will be difficult to live with, in which case more EU countries may choose only the wider single market European Community. These and many other eurozone questions will play out during the design period from now until 2013 or 2016. One side effect of such a restructuring will be that the traumas of the 2013 five-year EU budget negotiations may largely be avoided. Temporary arrangements are now much more likely to be adopted for this period. The British rebate question will also probably stay on ice during this period of transition.

In the last analysis, setting the limits to European integration and insisting that the UK remains a self-governing nation all depends on British foreign and security policy. It is by far the most important criterion. Put simply, it is no longer possible to envisage the UK continuing self-government on defence within NATO while also being in a substantially integrated eurozone. Eventually in such a set-up, no country will retain unfettered control over defence. The UK today should not move an inch further over the present design of foreign and security policy, but if we can achieve Political Co-operation in a single market we will need none of the present elaborate EU mechanisms and we would be better to opt out of the EU and the eurozone and remain a self-governing nation.

It is being argued, given the present crisis, that Britain must remain outside any eurozone for only a decade. Yet we need two decades or more to be absolutely certain that all its design flaws will have been solved. Some have believed all along that the eurozone is in itself such a fundamental governance issue that they have been prepared to say we should *never* join. On balance I have wanted hitherto to keep my options open. But experience over the last few years has convinced me that eurozone membership is not open to the UK as an issue of principled governance. There always has been a need in Europe for boundary lines and limits defined with the utmost care to safeguard the positions of those who wish to remain sovereign nations. There is no reason for the UK to accept being pushed or pulled across the lines that preserve our self-government. There is another option, restructuring Europe. It is not a case for the UK of federalism or bust. On this issue, Britain must be ready to fight and fight again. We are best at doing this internationally when Labour and the Conservative parties agree on what constitutes the national interest. Over the last hundred years that bipartisanship over our security has been vital for our survival and we must rediscover the key to its return. I suspect that at its core is patriotism, love of one's country. Not in the sense 'My country right or wrong', nor in the old-fashioned sense of the word whereby the Union Jack is a symbol of a long-lost Empire. It may be that the Scottish people will decide to leave the United Kingdom. That is their choice, as it has been for some time a choice for the people of Northern Ireland to unite with the South. But the fundamental decision is for the British people, the English, the Scots, the Welsh and the Irish, who want to stay citizens of one country. They already live in a multi-racial country, a multi-cultural country. Many would say they are Europeans. But they do not instinctively want to fly the European flag or play the *Ode to Joy* on ceremonial occasions. If they change and become identifiably European citizens, it will take many decades, even centuries. The pace of any such transition cannot be forced by the political elite. It will grow gradually. It would be far better for the peace, harmony and prosperity of those who wish in 2012 to live in the United Kingdom if we were to do so within the consensual framework of the European Community we voted to remain in during the referendum of 1975.

The EU belongs to Britain as much as to any other member state. The British public do not like to feel they are being pushed around. We are loyal members of clubs, but not afraid to restructure a club or an institution to better suit different circumstances. There is, I believe, a majority view of what being involved in Europe means and we expect our politicians to uphold that view. When things are clearly going wrong we expect them to come up with solutions. But we want a referendum on that solution when it has been agreed, at least in outline. We are not satisfied with the present structures. We are not looking for our politicians to take Britain out of the single market and we understand why we need a larger grouping of nations to enhance world trade. We recognise too that environmental hazards cannot be dealt with within the framework of a single nation, or even a small number of nations. We do not want to do damage to the interest of those EU member states who are in the Eurozone or who wish to join it. We just want our politicians to stand their ground for us. The British do not like defeatism or triumphalism. We just want our politicians to uphold our right to democratic self-government in this country. That is what we identify with and what if need be we are ready to fight to defend. These are attitudes which we believe in, attitudes that go back to Magna Carta. We are not afraid of change, We have no deep-rooted dislike of foreigners; we are content to live in a multi-racial Britain. We are neither jingoistic or chauvinistic. We are ready to be convinced that in the twenty-first century we may need different forms of economic self government, but the emphasis is on being convinced. We want no more spin doctors' tricks, no further sleights of hand with the wording or timing of any referendum. A referendum has become inevitable in the UK. As long as the British people know that the safeguard of a referendum has been unequivocally conceded then any British government can offer a substantial prize to the other EU Member States. Namely to offer to use the simplest and quickest procedure available for making Treaty amend-ments by acting within the European Council under the unanimity procedure. This could be particularly useful if the eurozone came under sudden pressure from a global withdrawal of investment and needed to respond within days. Who knows whether that might come within months but even on the more leisurely timetable starting negotiations on eurozone political union in 2013 a referendum would have to come in the UK before 2016 at the latest. There is an urgent need for the UK to negotiate with clarity and determination over the two different but interrelated issues of restructuring a new single market and a new eurozone.

Index